Cape Coast Corner

Makah, Chimakum, Quinault

Jay Miller, PhD, ed

© 2020

context
Marine Fringe & Mountain Background

Living along the shores rimming the sharply rugged Olympic Mountains, upthrust from the ocean floor 35 million years ago by plate techtonics, are tribes of distinctive ancestral languges sharing a similar culture and society based on rank and riches. Oldest, by far, are the Quileute and Hoh of the Chimakuan language isolate once spread from Pacific shores through the southern Straits, where Chimakums around Port Townsend battled on until a devastating attack on their fort at Hadlock led by Seattle, who lost a son, and his warriors. Those Chimakum not enslaved eventually found refuge at Port Gamble among Klallam sawmill workers.

At the tip of the cape are Makahs, whose Nootkan language links them to the Nuchalnulth tribes along the west coast of Vancouver Island, with the Nitinat, actually Ditidat, directly across from the cape since the island slants southeast like a wedge into the Straits of Juan de Fuca, named for a Greek sailor who told fantastical tales about a passage into the interior. It is due to his background that Mt Olympus and the Olympic Mountains, and even the state capitol of Olympia owe their fanciful names. Though sharply peaked and up to eight thousand feet high, river valleys down the sides provide trails through the Olympics used by hunters and harvesters of plants and shed mountain goat wool for weaving.

Klallams are the most distinctive of the Straits Salish branch, relying on reef nets because their island and shore homes had no major streams or rivers and huge salmon runs, especially Fraser River sockeye, crowded through their waters. Proud of being known as 'fierce' or 'strong' people, they aggressively occupied the north shore of the peninsula, dividing the Chimakuans, especially the further away Chimakums.

From the south, probably through the Chehalis Valley, came the Tsamosan branch of Coast Salish, including the Quinault, who benefited from the huge lake upriver where blueback sockey salmon thronged. Bluebacks are the largest of the sockeyes, averaging over five pounds.

A fascinating linguistic aspect of these interactions was a shift from nasals /m, n/ to dentals /d, b/ as noted for the name of the Ditidat above. Quileute and Hoh made this change, but Chimakums did not, as shown by the Boas grammar herein (p.111). Makah made the change, as did Nitinat, but not the other Nootkans up island. Suspicion thus falls on the contentious Klallams, who use three nasals /m, n/ and /ŋ ~ ng/, as the impetus for this shift to dentals as a way of obviously distinguishing the sounds of friend from foe, or so it seems from these distributions. Yet further afield, Lushootseed and Twana made the shift, while Nooksack on the slopes of Mt Baker did not. Still, Klallam raided widely, with constant local tensions against Makahs.

Assembled here are the classic 1870 account of Makahs by their former school teacher, artist, and goad, James Swan, who worked gathering collections for the Smithson both locally and among Haidas. His personal collection of fine examples remains in Port Townsend. Franz Boas so respected his work and knowledge that he visited him in Port Townsend. Of note, George Gibbs, who spent a decade in the Northwest putting his Harvard legal and linguistics education to work, approved and annotated the Swan manuscript in footnotes for the Smithsonian when he himself was later based in DC.

Following Swan is an early systematic report of the Chemakum language by Franz Boas, founder of academic anthropology in the US, based on work with Louise, a washerwoman traumatized by the fate of her people and given to binge drinking with her male companion.

With funding from the Morris Jesup North Pacific Expedition at the American Museum of Natural History in New York City, Boas sent Livingston Farrand to Taholah to collect stories,

context
especially from the very traditional Bob Pope ~ Tōshin, who worked with a series of ethnographers in succeeding years, especially Ronald Olson. He lived in the last longhouse in the village, on the banks of the Quinault River, which his son burned to the ground at his father's death. Pope's autobiography ends this collection.

Across the Olympicas to the east is Hood Canal, dotted by villages of the Twana, who suffered severely from epidemics. Since more survived along the Skokomish River, which enters at the elbow or bend of the canal, the reservation for Twana and its residents became known as Skokomish.

Klallams moved from Lower Elwah to the top of Hood Canal to work at the Port Gamble Mill just before 1855 treaty making at Point No Point. They were supposed to move to the Skokomish Reservation, and Rev Eells, both the minister and agent there, had their houses burned to force them to do so, but they refused, again based on past intertribal hostilities. Elwahs stayed in their homeland, while Jamestown Klallams bought Dungeness homesteads and thus escaped from federal and state control until they were eventually regranted federal recognition 10 February 1981. Ron Allen, long their chair, went on to national prominence in native issues, and currently head of the native gambling commission in Washington state.

Contents

4 Makah of Cape Flattery by James Swan

117 Chemakum Language by Franz Boas

124 Quinault Tales by Livingston Farrand

173 APS Farrand archive

189 Misp^h 197

199 James Gilchrist Swan 1818-1900

205 Bob Pope (1830?-1930?) 207

208 index 212

Makah

SMITHSONIAN CONTRIBUTIONS TO KNOWLEDGE

THE INDIANS OF CAPE FLATTERY,
AT THE ENTRANCE TO THE STRAIT OF FUCA,
WASHINGTON TERRITORY

BY
JAMES GILCHRIST SWAN

Commission
To Which This Paper Has Been Referred
    George Gibbs
    Jeffries Wyman

Accepted For Publication, June 1868

Joseph Henry,
Secretary S.I

Collins, Printer
Philadelphia

Advertisement

THE following memoir on the Makah Indians was prepared at the request of the Smithsonian Institution by Mr. James G. Swan, who, for several years, resided among them in the capacity of teacher and dispenser of medicines under the Government of the United States. Mr. Swan had previously become well acquainted with the Indian tribes of the Pacific, and had published a small work detailing his adventures among them. In 1855 he accompanied the late Maj. Gen. Stevens, then Governor of Washington Territory, while making treaties with the Makahs and other tribes, and was subsequently appointed to the position above mentioned.

For the information of those not acquainted with the relation of the United States to the Indian tribes it may be remarked that where lands occupied by them are required for settlement, or where their proximity to the whites is found inexpedient, it has been the practice to extinguish their possessory rights by treaty, paying them generally in annuities of money or goods, and setting apart a portion of land, sometimes within their original territory, in other cases at a distance, for their exclusive occupation, upon which no white settlers are allowed to intrude. These tracts are known as reservations, and are under charge of government "agents," often assisted by teachers, mechanics, &c.

In the absence of Mr. Swan, the editorial supervision of the work was committed to Mr. George Gibbs, who has added a few notes.

Joseph Henry,
Secretary S.I

Smithsonian Institution, 1869

Makah

Prefatory Note

THE philological family, to which the Makahs belong, is that known on old maps as the "Wakash Nation," a name given by Captain Cook from the word of greeting used by the Indians of King George's, or Nootka Sound, where he first met them. For the purpose of classification it may be convenient to preserve the name of Nootka, which has been usually recognized, as that of the language in general, although it originally sprung from an equally trivial source. It is to be observed that there are no nations in our sense of the word among these Indians, but those speaking even the same dialect of a common language are often broken up into separate bands under different chiefs, and their various appellations belong only to localities. Occasionally a chief, more powerful and sagacious than the rest, will bring several of these under his control, but his power is after all limited, and dies with him.

The territory occupied by this NOOTKA family is not as yet clearly defined on the north. Generally speaking, it embraces, besides that of the Makahs, on the south side of the Strait of Fuca, described by Mr. Swan in the following paper, Vancouver Island, with the exception of a small part of its northeastern border, occupied by intrusive bands of the Ilailtsa, and the southwestern portion extending from Sooke Harbor to above Komooks in the Gulf of Georgia, which is held by tribes of the Shehwapmukh or Selish family. It also covers part of the adjacent continent on the Gulf of Georgia and Johnston's Straits, being thus enclosed by Selish tribes on the south and east and by those of the Hailtsa {Heiltsuk} on the north. The Kwilleyutes on the coast of Washington Territory, south of the Makahs, are a remote branch of the Selish {no!}, and the Clallams, lying east along the southern shore of Fuca Strait are another tribe of that family, closely connected with the Sooke and Songhus {Songhees, Lkungen} Indians of the southeastern end of Vancouver Island.

George Gibbs.

Washington, January, 1870. (v)

Makah

Table of Contents

Name of the Tribe	1
Geographical Position	1
Character of the Reservation	2
Census of the Tribe	2
Physical Characteristics	3
Dwellings	4
Picture Writing	7
Social Life	10
Festivals	13
Sports of Children	14
Dress	15
Personal Ornaments	17
Care of Children	18
Food, and Method of obtaining it	19
Fishing and Sealing	27
Trade	30
Tools	33
Canoes	35
Whaling and Fishing Gear	39
Boxes, Baskets, Mats, &c.	42
Feather and Dog's-Hair Blankets	43
Gambling Implements	44
Mats, Baskets, Ornaments, &c	45
Weapons, Bows, Arrows, Fish and Bird Spears	47
Songs	49
Method of Warfare	50
Government	52
History, Traditions, &c.	55
Mythology	61
Winter Ceremonies	62
Legends	64
Masks and Masquerading	69
Shamanistic Ceremonies	73
Shamanism, or Magic and Medicine	76
Diseases	79
Remedies	80
Funeral Ceremonies	85
Superstitions	86
Computation of Time	91
Legend of the South Wind	92
Vocabulary of the Makah Dialect	93/ 86
Local Nomenclature of the Makah (vii)	105

Makah

List of Illustrations

Figure 1. Thunderbird of the Makahs.	9
Figure 2. Makah Indian in Wet Weather Dress.	16
Figure 3. Headdress and Pendant of Dentalium.	16
Figure 4. Harpoon Point and Line.	20
Figure 5. Sealskin Buoy.	20
Figure 6. Whaling Canoe.	21
Figure 7. Whaling Paddle.	21
Figure 8. Saddle of Whale's Blubber.	22
Figure 9. Halibut Hook	23
Figure 10. Halibut Chopper	23
Figure 11. Ladle of "Big-horn"	26
Figure 12. Spoon of *Aploceras* Horn	26
Figure 13. Wooden Ladle {No Fig 14}	27
Figure 15. Stone Adze	34
Figure 16. Chisel	34
Figure 17. Stone Hammer	34
Figure 18. Canoe, showing Method of Scarphing	37
Figure 19. Clyoquot Paddle	37
Figure 20. Canoe under Sail	38
Figure 21. Codfish Hook	41
Figure 22. Fish Club	42
Figure 23. Fish Club	42
Figure 24. Kak-te-wahd-de	42
Figure 25. Wooden Bowl	42
Figure 26. Wooden Bowl	42
Figure 27. Wooden Trencher	43
Figure 28. Wooden Dish	43
Figure 29. Wooden Bowl of Maple or Fir Knot	43
Figure 30. Wooden Bowl of Maple or Fir Knot	43
Figure 31. Conical Hat	45
Figure 32. Bark Basket	46
Figure 33. Bow and Arrows	47
Figure 34. Bird Spear	48
Figure 35. Mask	69
Figure 36. Mask	69
Figure 37. Mask	69
Figure 38. Mask	69
Figure 39. Mask	70
Figure 40. Mask	70
Figure 41. Mask	70
Figure 42. Dress of Female Performer in the Tsiahk	74
Figure 43. Dress of Male Performer in the Tsiahk	74
Figure 44. Rattle used by Medicine Men (ix)	77

Makah

The Indians of Cape Flattery
At the Entrance to the Strait of Fuca
Washington Territory

THE tribe of Indians who inhabit the region about Cape Flattery is known among the whites and the Indians who reside further eastward, on the Straits of Fuca, as the Makah, or more properly speaking, Mak-kah, the word being strongly accented on both syllables. They are also called by the tribes on the western coast of Vancouver Island, "Klas-set" {Kla-iz-zarts, Classets} and by those tribes residing between the Columbia river and Cape Flattery, "Kwe-net-sat'h." The tribal name among themselves is "Kwe-net-che-chat" {q^{w}idičč'a•t$\underline{x}$}. All these different names have the same meaning, and signify "the people who live on a point of land projecting into the sea," or, as we term it, the "Cape People." There are other tribes who reside on promontories, but the Makahs appear to be the only one who are particularly called "Cape Indians."

Geographical Position. – At the time of making the treaty between the United States and the Makah Indians in 1855, known as the treaty of Neeah Bay, which was effected by Governor Isaac I. Stevens, of Washington Territory, who was also Superintendent of Indian Affairs, the tribe claimed as their land, all that portion of the extreme northwest part of Washington Territory lying between Flattery Rocks on the Pacific coast, fifteen miles south from Cape Flattery, and the Hoko river, about the same distance eastward from the cape on the Strait of Fuca. They also claimed Tatooche Island, which lies at the southern side of the entrance to the Strait, and separated from the main land of the cape by a channel half a mile wide.

This tract of country was ceded to the United States, except a portion of the extreme point of the cape, from Neeah Bay to the Wäatch creek on the Pacific, both points being nearly equally distant from Tatooche Island, say six miles each way. The reserved portion, as can be readily seen, by reference to the maps of the United States Coast Survey, is separated from the main body of the peninsula by a tract of swamp and meadow land, partially covered with a dense forest, and partially open marsh, extending from Neeah Bay to the Pacific, a distance of about four miles. The general appearance of this low land, and the abrupt and almost precipitous hills which border it on both sides through its entire length, [2] show almost conclusively, that at a not very remote period, the waters of the Pacific joined those of Neeah Bay, leaving that portion of the cape which is included within the boundaries named by the treaty, an island. This hypothesis is supported by a tradition of the natives to that effect, which will be noticed in another portion of this paper. Even at the present time, the waters of Wäatch creek at very high tides, flow, by one of its branches, within a few rods of the waters of Neeah Bay. The whole of this region is of a mountainous character, and is the termi nation of the Olympic range, which has its highest peak far in the interior, near Hood's canal. From the snow-covered mountains in the rear of Dungeness, the range gradually becomes depressed, till at Cape Flattery it assumes the character of hills, five or six hundred feet in height. These hills are composed of conglomerate, clay-stone, tertiary sandstones, and occasional boulders of granite. Small veins of bituminous coal have been found on the cape, but as yet nothing of practical value. With but very few intervals, the whole of this portion of Washington Territory is covered with an almost impenetrable forest, which at Cape Flattery is composed of spruce and hemlock, and a dense undergrowth of crab

Makah

apple, alder, elder, gualtheria, raspberry, wild currant, and rose bushes. The only land belonging to the Makahs, suitable for cultivation, is at Tsuess, where an open prairie of sandy loam affords material for farming; another open spot is on a hill at Flattery rocks, where the Indians cultivate some potatoes; and several acres at Neeah Bay have been cleared from the forest at great expense and labor, for the use of the Reservation officers and employes, who are stationed at that point. The Wäatch marsh is fit for a stock range only during the summer, and its best portions could not be cultivated save by extensively draining the land, and preparing it for the plough. The soil at Neeah Bay consists of a stiff clay loam and ridges of rich black earth, formed by the decomposition of the animal and vegetable matter thrown out by the Indians, and accumulated for centuries. The humidity of the climate is extreme, consequently the cereals do not ripen, nor has it been found possible to cure hay. Very excellent potatoes, however, are raised, and the soil and climate are well adapted to the growth, in perfection, of root vegetables of various kinds. The animals most common are elk, deer, black bears, wolves, beaver, otter, raccoons, skunks, minks, squirrels, etc. But these are found in limited numbers, although they abound in the interior. They are not much sought after by the Indians, who devote their attention more particularly to marine animals, such as fur and hair seal, porpoises, whales, and fish of various kinds, which are plentiful and form the principal part of their food.

Census of the Tribe

During the month of October, 1861, I took a census of the Makah tribe, under the direction of the United States Indian Agent. This service was performed by visiting every lodge in the different villages, at a time when the whole tribe were in winter quarters. The villages at that time were Bäada and Neeah, at Neeah Bay; and Wäatch, Tsuess and Hosett, on the Pacific coast. There were six hundred and fifty-four souls, all told; viz, men, 205; women, 224; boys, 93; girls, 93; infants, 39. Again, in October, 1863, I took another census of the tribe for the Indian Department. The village of Bäada [3] had then been removed within the limits of the Reserve, and joined with Neeah village. This census showed a table of 202 men, 232 women, 111 boys, 95 girls, and 23 infants, a total of six hundred and sixty-three. It appears from the above, that from 1861 to 1863, there had been but little change in the whole number, the births and deaths being nearly equal. While other tribes have been decreasing since 1852 (at which time the smallpox swept off a large number of them), this one seems to have been spared. The fact may be accounted for, in great measure, by their distance from the white settlements, and the small quantity of alcoholic poison which finds its way among them. But morally they are not at all in advance of their neighbors, and if the means of procuring whiskey were as readily at hand, they would soon become as degraded, and their numbers be as rapidly reduced, as the Chinook, Chihalis, Cowlitz, Clallam, Chemakum and other tribes of Washington Territory.

Physical Constitution. – The Makahs are of medium stature, averaging about five feet four inches; a few men of the tribe may be found who measure six feet, but only three or four of that height were noticed. Their limbs are commonly well proportioned, with a good development of muscle. Some are symmetrically formed, and of unusual strength. Although to a superficial observer they present much similarity of appearance, yet a further acquaintance, and closer examination, show that there is in reality a marked diversity. Some have black hair; very dark brown eyes, almost black; high cheek-bones, and dark copper-colored skin; others have reddish hair, and a few, particularly among the children, light flaxen locks, light brown eyes, and fair skin, many of them almost white – a fact perhaps attributable to an admixture of white blood of Spanish and Russian stock.[1]

The custom of flattening the forehead, as observed among the Chinook, Chihalis, and other tribes south of Cape Flattery, does not appear to be in general use among the Makahs. This practice is not common among the Clyoquot and Nootkans (*Tokwaht*) to the north, and as the Makahs have intermarried with the tribes both north and south, we find it confined principally to those families who are related to the Kwinaiults, Chihalis, and Clallams. It is not uncommon to see children, belonging to the same parents, some of whom have their heads as nature made them, while others are deformed by compressing them in infancy. I am not prepared to state positively what mental effect is produced by this compression of the skull, but from my own experience among the children there seems to be but little difference in their capacity for acquiring information, or in their desire for instruction; the most proficient, however, appear to be those with naturally formed heads. It would require an extended and close observation for a series of years, marking the growth of these children to mature age, and noting the various peculiarities of a number selected for the purpose, before any reliable results could be had on which to found a correct judgment. [4]

These Indians are not remarkable for the special perfection of any of their organs, as that of sight, or hearing, or smelling; or for any corporeal faculties, as speed in running, agility in climbing, or of diving and remaining long under water. I have seen them occasionally run foot-races on the beach, climb poles set up for the purpose, and swim and dive in the bay, but they do not excel in any of these athletic exercises. They do excel, however, in the management of canoes, and are more venturesome, hardy, and ardent in their pursuit of whales, and in going long distances from the land for fish, than any of the neighboring tribes. They are, in fact, to the Indian population what the inhabitants of Nantucket are to the people of the Atlantic coast, being the most expert and successful in the whale fishery of all the coast tribes.

They do not appear to be a very long-lived people. At the present time (1864) there is but one old man who was alive at the time the Spaniards attempted to make a settlement at Neeah Bay in 1792. He could remember the circumstance well a few years since, but is now in his dotage. He was then a small boy, and if we assume that he was but five years old, it would make him now seventy-seven years of age. I have inquired of a number of men whose appearance indicated advanced age, and with the exception above named, have found no one who personally recollected the visit of the Spaniards, although all remembered hearing their fathers mention it. Threescore years may be safely set down as the limit of life among those who escape the casualties incident to their savage condition; and, I think, from my observations among them, that an Indian at sixty years is as old as a white man at eighty. The average longevity is of course far below this standard, but I have no data that would warrant a positive statement of what that actually is; it could only be ascertained by an accurate record of births and deaths during a series of years.

---

[1] In Holmberg's Work will be found an account of the wreck of a Russian ship, the survivors of whose crew lived several years among the Makahs. As late as 1854, I saw their descendants, who bore in their features unmistakable evidence of their origin. GG

Makah

Dwellings. – The houses of the Makahs are built of boards and planks, split from the cedar. These are principally made by the Indians of Vancouver Island, and procured by barter with them. There is very little cedar about Cape Flattery, and such as is found is small and of inferior quality. Drift logs, however, are frequently thrown on the shores by the high tides of winter, and whenever any such are saved they are either split into boards or made into canoes. The process of making the boards is very primitive. A number of long narrow wedges are cut from the yew, which is selected for its hardness; little rings of withes, made like a sail-maker's "grummet," are fastened on the head of the wedge to keep it from splitting under the blows of the stone hammer. These hammers are shaped like a pestle, and made from the hardest stone that can be found. They are very neatly formed, but the process is tedious and laborious. A description will be found under Arts and Manufactures. The Indian first strips the bark from the log, and cuts off the end as squarely as he can; he next cuts transversely through the top of the log, as far from the end as the required length of the plank, and as deep as the required thickness. A horizontal cut is then made across the end of the log with the axe, and into this are inserted the wedges, about three inches apart. These are struck successively with the stone hammer till the split is effected; more wedges are then inserted in the longitudinal split on each side of the board, and all being [5] regularly driven in, the board comes off very straight. The first piece being rounded on the top, is a mere slab. The process is repeated until the log is entirely split up. The widest and best boards are from the centre, and are highly prized. I have measured some of them which were over five feet in width. The choicest are reserved for use in the interior of the lodge, or to paint their rude devices upon.

When a sufficient number of boards is procured, they next proceed to the erection of the house. The roofs of all these houses are nearly flat, the least possible inclination being given them that will allow the water to pass off freely. They are intended to accommodate several families, and are of various dimensions; some of them being sixty feet long by thirty wide, and from ten to fifteen feet high. To support the weight of these flat roofs it is necessary to have large timbers. These are usually hewn down evenly, and are set up, either parallel with the length of the house (in which case only one great timber extends along it), or else across the width, when three or four are used. A space of the required size having been cleared of stones and rubbish, and properly levelled, stout posts, notched on the top, are securely inserted perpendicularly into the ground. The friends and neighbors join to assist. Then all unite at one end of the beam and raise it as high as they can at one lift, when it is blocked up. Stout poles, with their ends lashed together crosswise, are now inserted under the beam, and while some hoist it, others are lifting at the poles, till finally, after excessive labor and waste of strength, the end of the timber is raised and placed on the top of the notched post; the other end of the beam is then raised, supporting posts are placed under the centre, and the first portion of the building is finished. Whenever one of these large beams is to be lifted, or when any work requiring the united exertions of several is to be done, it is usual for some one, generally an old man, to give the word. He may be seen at such times seated a little distance off, with a stick in his hand, with which to strike a blow on a board as a signal. When all is ready, he calls out "Shaugh shogh," which they all repeat, and at the word "Shogh" he gives a blow with his stick and all lift together. The expression is equivalent to "Now then, hoist!" or if to move a canoe, "Now then, haul!"

Makah

Other posts are next set in the ground, which serve to form the frame for the sides and ends. Smaller timbers are fixed on these posts parallel with the large one, then poles are placed at right angles across the whole, and on these are lastly laid the roof boards, which are made slightly concave on one side and convex on the other, and are set alternately, overlapping like tiles. The sides and ends are now to be built up with boards. First, double rows of poles are set up perpendicularly all around the house, at distances of four or five feet from each other, the rows themselves being about four inches apart. A board is then placed between these rows of poles, with one of its edges resting on the ground. Withes made from twisted cedar twigs are passed round the poles, and on these withes another board is laid, with its lower edge overlapping the one beneath; this process is repeated till the sides and ends are complete. Moss and dry sea-weed are then stuffed into all the scams, and the house is considered habitable.

The bed places are next to the walls of the house, and raised about eighteen inches from the ground; on them are laid Clallam mats, which, being made of bulrushes [6] and flags, are better adapted for sleeping upon than the cedar bark mats of their own manufacture. These mats are rolled up at one end of the bed so as to form a pillow, and on them the Indian lies down, with generally no other covering than the blanket he has worn through the day. Sometimes a thickness of eight or ten mats is used, but commonly from three to five. They make a very healthy and easy couch by themselves, but some of the more luxurious add a sack full of feathers. These bed places are arranged all around the sides and ends of the lodges, and are separated from each other by the boxes containing the family wealth, consisting of blankets, beads, and clothing, which are piled up at the head and feet. Directly in front of them is a lower platform, usually three inches from the ground. On this, other mats are laid, and here the family and visitors sit and eat or talk as the case may be. The fire is in front of it, and a chain depending from a beam overhead, serves to hang the pots or kettles on, while cooking. Over the beds are stowed the provisions belonging to the family, packed away in baskets, while above the fire are hung such fish or other food as they may be desirous of drying in the smoke.

The dwellings of the Makahs are not removed except for some emergency. They are collected in villages, each containing from eight to fifteen houses. The principal one is situated at Necah, to which locality that formerly at Bäada, on the eastern point of the bay, has been removed, and the two thus combined comprise fifteen dwellings and two hundred and forty-one inhabitants. The other villages are Wäatch, on the Pacific coast, at the mouth of Wäatch creek, four miles from Neeah, consisting of nine dwellings and one hundred and twenty-six residents; Tsuess, four miles south from Wäatch, containing eight houses and ninety-nine residents, and Hosett, at Flattery Rocks, consisting of fifteen houses and one hundred and eighty-eight persons. The above constitute the winter residences of the tribe. Early in the spring they remove to their summer quarters, which are the villages of Kiddekubbut, three miles from Neeah; Tatooche Island, and Ahchawat, between Tatooche Island and Wäatch. At these three spots are houses, similar to those in the other villages, which are left standing when the tribe goes into winter quarters. Occasionally, when an Indian has not sufficient boards for both, he will remove the roof-boards to whichever house he is occupying. To do so, they place two canoes abreast and lay the boards across the top. Each house is generally owned by one individual, and the families who occupy it with him are his relatives or friends, who are accommodated free of rent. They usually, how ever, make presents of food, or render assistance in various ways when required; but they are not obliged to do either unless they wish. The houses are all placed fronting the beach, and usually have but one door. Some, however, have a small opening in the rear, through which wood and water are brought in. They have no buildings set apart for public purposes, but when an unusually large gathering takes place, they proceed to the largest lodge, which is always thrown open for the accommodation of the tribe.

The reason why the roofs of the houses are so different from those of the Chihalis and Chinooks, at the Columbia river, is that they are used to dry fish upon. Now, the Chinooks and Chihalis, as well as all the tribes on the sound and [7] coast, store great quantities of fish for their winter's use; but the fish they dry are salmon, which require to be cured in the smoke and protected from the sun and rain. Consequently, the tribes above mentioned use pitched roofs, or roofs much more elevated than those of the Makahs. But the staple of the Makahs is halibut, which, to be properly cured, is cut into thin slices and dried, if possible, in the open air without smoke; the best portions being those that have kept white and free from any color. As the climate is very humid, it is rare that a season is propitious for the curing their fish; so they have their roofs as flat as possible, and during fair weather, in the fishing season, not only are these covered with the slices of fish, but quantities are hung on horizontal poles fastened across the ends of the uprights that form the side fastenings to the houses. The appearance of one of the lodges on a fine day in summer when plenty of fish are drying is that of a laundry with clothes out bleaching. When the weather threatens to be rainy, the occupants proceed to the roof, and by removing several boards, they can stow away their provender in a very few minutes, and again replace it in the open air on the return of fair weather.

The interior of a lodge often presents a curious domestic scene. In one corner may be seen a mother rocking her child to sleep, securely lashed in its cradle, which is suspended by strings to the top of a pliant pole, that moves with every motion of her hand. If the mother is engaged in making baskets or mats, she transfers the string from her hand to her great toe, and moving her foot, produces the required motion, not unlike that of a modern baby jumper. In the centre a chain hangs from the roof, supporting over the fire the kettle in which is the food for her husband, while a boy, having cooked his own meal, is taking it alone. In another part of the house, separated from this apartment by a board set up on edge to serve as a partition, is another family, the father holding an infant in his arms, while another child is playing with kittens; the child's mother seated on the bed, wrapped in her blanket, and a group of friends in the centre cooking their supper.

Picture Writing. – In almost every lodge may be seen large boards or planks of cedar carefully smoothed and painted with rude designs of various kinds. With one exception, however, I have found nothing of a legendary or historic character, their drawings being mostly representations of the private totem or *tamanous* of individuals, and consisting of devices rarely understood by their owners and never by any one else. The exception referred to is a representation of the thunder-bird (*Thlu-kluts*), the whale (*chet-up-uk*), and the fabulous animal supposed by the natives to cause lightning (*Ha-hek-to-ak*). This painting, is on a large board in the lodge of one of the chiefs of Neeah Bay, and was executed by a Clyoquot Indian named "Cha-tik," a word signifying painter or artist. A painting is termed *Cha-tai-uks*, and writing *Chu-tatl*.

The coast Indians, as well as those I have conversed with, living on Puget Sound, believe that thunder is caused by an immense bird whose size darkens the heavens, and the rushing of whose wings produces peals of thunder. The Makahs, however, have a superstition which invests the thunder-bird with a twofold character. This mythological being is supposed by them to be a gigantic Indian, named, in [8] the various dialects of the coast tribes, *Ka-kaitch*, *Thlu-kluts*, and *Tu-tutsh*, the latter being the Nootkan name. This giant lives on the highest mountains, and his food consists of whales. When he is in want of food, he puts on a garment consisting of a bird's head, a pair of immense wings, and a feather covering for his body; around his waist he ties the *Ha-hek-to-ak*, or lightning fish, which bears some faint resemblance to the sea horse (hippocampus). This animal has a head as sharp as a knife, and a red tongue which makes the fire. The Thlu-kluts having arrayed himself, spreads his wings and sails over the ocean till he sees a whale. This he kills by darting the *Ha-hek-to-ak* down into its body, which he then seizes in his powerful claws and carries away into the mountains to eat at his leisure. Sometimes the *Ha-hek-to-ak* strikes a tree with his sharp head, splitting and tearing it in pieces, or again, but very rarely, strikes a man and kills him. Whenever lightning strikes the land or a tree, the Indians hunt very diligently with the hope of finding some portion of the *Ha-hek-to-ak*, for the possession of any part of this marvellous animal endows its owner with great powers, and even a piece of its bone, which is supposed by the Indians to be bright red, will make a man expert in killing whales, or excel in any kind of work. Those Indians, however, who pretend to possess these fabulous relics carefully conceal them from sight, for they are considered as great "medicines," and not to be seen except by the possessor. A tale was related to me, and religiously believed by them, respecting the possession of a quill of the thunder bird by a Kwinaiult Indian, now living, named Neshwats. He was hunting on a mountain near Kwinaiult, and saw a thunder bird light on a rock. Creeping up softly, he succeeded in securing a buckskin thong to one of its wing feathers, fastening the other end at the same time to a stump. When the *T'hlu-kluts* flew off, the feather was drawn from the wing and kept by the Indian. The length of this enormous feather is forty fathoms. Neshwats is very careful that no person shall see this rare specimen, but his tale is believed, particularly as he is very expert in killing sea otter, which abound on that part of the coast.

    I saw an instance of their credulity on an occasion of a display of fireworks at Port Townsend a few summers since. A number of the rockets on bursting displayed fiery serpents. The Indians believed they were *Ha-hek-to-ak*, and for a long time made application to the gentlemen who gave the display, for pieces of the animal, for which they offered fabulous prices. So firm is their belief in this imaginary animal, that one chief assured me if I could procure him a backbone he would give two hundred dollars for it. One of the principal residences of the T'hlu-kluts is on a mountain back of Clyoquot, on Vancouver Island. There is a lake situated in the vicinity, and argund its borders the Indians say are quantities of old bones of whales. These, they think, were carried there by the *T'hlu-kluts*, but they are very old, and it must have been many years ago. I have not seen these bones, but have heard of them from various Indians who allege that they have seen them. If they really do exist as stated, they are undoubtedly the fossil remains that have been deposited there at a time when that portion of the continent was submerged, and respecting which there is a tradition still among them. The painting above described, although done by an Indian, does not fully represent the idea of the Makahs respecting the *T'hlu-kluts*. But, having by me a copy of Kitto's Cyclopaedia [9] of Biblical Literature, I showed some of the chiefs the cut of the Babylonian cherubim, which came very near their idea of its real form. It was perfect, they said, with the exception of not having the *Ha-hek-to-ak* around its waist, and of having feet instead of bird's claws, which they think are necessary to grasp whales. But when I informed them that there were no whales in Babylon, they were fully persuaded that the identity was the same, claws being given to the *T'hlu-kluts* who live near water, and feet to those living in the interior. Of their religious belief in this thunder-bird, I shall make further mention in their *ta-ma-na-was* ceremonies. In the design the *T'hlu-kluts* is represented as holding a whale in its talons, and the accompanying figures are the *Ha-hek-to-ak*. These animals the bird is supposed to collect from the ocean, and keep concealed in its feathers.

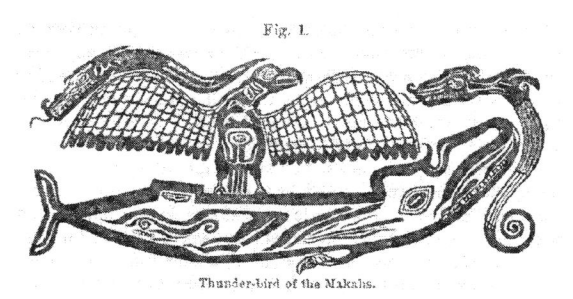

Among the most remarkable specimens of their painting which I have seen, was a design on the conical hats worn during rain, and another on a board in a chiefs lodge, afterwards placed at the base of a monument erected over his body. The circular design for the hat was said to represent a pair of eyes, a nose, and mouth. The other was a rude one, in which eyes are very conspicuous. The form of these designs is a distinctive feature in Indian painting, but I never could learn that they attached any more meaning to them than we do to the designs on a shawl border, or the combinations of a calico pattern artist.[2]

Fig. 1. Thunder-bird of the Makahs.

I have painted various devices for these Indians, and have decorated their *ta-ma-na-was* masks; and in every instance I was simply required to paint something the Indians had never seen before. One Indian selected from a pictorial newspaper a cut of a Chinese dragon, and another chose a double-headed eagle, from a picture of an Austrian coat-of-arms. Both these I grouped with drawings of crabs, faces of men, and various devices, endeavoring to make the whole look like Indian work; and I was very successful in giving the most entire satisfaction, so much so that they bestowed upon me the name of *Cha-tic*, intimating that I was as great an [10] [2 June 1869] artist as the *Cha-tik* of Clyoquot.[3] In the masks I painted, I simply endeavored to form as hideous a mixture of colors as I could conceive, and in this I again gave satisfaction.

I have noticed in Indian paintings executed by the northern tribes, particularly the Chimsyan, Haida, and others north of Vancouver Island, a very great resemblance in style to that adopted by the coast Indians. Whether or not these tribes have any legend connected with their pictures I have no means of ascertaining. There are, however, but very few persons among the coast Indians who are recognized as painters, and those that I have met with, either could not or would not give me any explanation. My object in painting for them was to find out if they really had any historical or mythological ideas which they wished to have represented, and I have invariably inquired on every occasion; but I never could get any other information than that they wished me to paint something the other Indians could not understand. I am satisfied, so far as

---

[2] The constant recurrence of certain conventional figures in the ornamentation of all the tribes from Cape Flattery to Sitka would seem to indicate a symbolical meaning, now lost. Examples may be found in the Clyoquot paddle; in the trencher and dish; aud two of the masks, *post*. GG

[3] {George Miles *James Swan, Chā-tic of the Northwest Coast*, Drawings and Watercolors from the Franz and Kathryn Stenzel Collection of Western Art, Beinecke Rare Books and Manuscript Library, Yale, 2003}

this tribe is concerned, that, with the exception of the thunder-bird drawing, all their pictures and drawings are nothing more than fancy work, or an attempt to copy some of the designs of the more northern tribes; and as they have always evinced a readiness to explain to me whatever had significance, I have no alternative but to believe them when they say that they attach no particular meaning to their paintings.

Social Life. – The Makahs, in common with all the coast tribes, hold slaves. These were formerly procured by making captives of the children or adults of any other tribes with whom they might be at variance. But latterly, since the advent of the whites, they have obtained their slaves mostly by purchase from their neighbors on Vancouver Island, or those further xip the Strait of Fuca. Children seem in all cases to be preferred, because they are cheaper, and are less likely to escape than adults. The price varies, according to age, from fifty to one hundred blankets. These slaves are for the most part well treated, and, but for the fact that they can be bought and sold, appear to be on terms of equality with their owners, although there are instances where they have received rather harsh usage. In case one is killed by his master, which occasionally happens, no notice is taken of the occurrence by the rest of the tribe. Many of the men who were born of slave parents, and have resided all their lives with the tribe, have purchased their freedom; while others, who were bought, when children, from other tribes, have regained their liberty as soon as they have grown up, by making their escape. In fact the only slaves who are sure to remain are those who are born in the tribe; all others will run away whenever a safe opportunity presents to enable them to get back to their relatives. In former times, it is said, the slaves were treated very harshly, and their lives were of no more value than those of dogs. On the death of a chief, his favorite slaves were killed and buried with him, but latterly, this custom seems to have been abandoned, and their present condition is a mild kind of servitude. The treaty between the United States and the Makahs makes it obligatory on this tribe to free their slaves, and although this provision has not thus far been enforced, it has had the effect of securing to the latter better treatment than they formerly had. Instances are not rare where a master has married his slave woman, and a mistress has taken her slave man as her husband. The children [11] of such connections are considered half slave, and although some of the more Intelligent have acquired wealth and influence among the tribe, yet the fact that the father or mother was a slave is considered as a stigma, which is not removed for several generations. Their status, as compared with the African slavery of the Southern States, is rather that of bond servants; they are the hewers of wood and drawers of water. They appear to have no task-work assigned them, but pursue the same avocations as their owners; the men assisting in the fisheries, and the women in manufacturing mats and baskets, and other indoor work, or in preparing and curing fish. Formerly, it was considered degrading for a chief, or the owner of slaves, to perform any labor except hunting, fishing, or killing whales; proficiency in any of these exercises was a consideration that enabled the most expert to aspire to the honor of being a chief or head man; but since the tribe has been under the charge of an agent of the Government, and it is seen that no distinction is made between bond or free, but that both are treated alike, the old prejudice against labor is wearing away, and men and women, with the exception of a few among the old chiefs, are willing to engage side by side in such work as requires to be done for the agency. And it is to be hoped that, in a few years, under the judicious plan of the treaty, slavery will be gradually abolished, or exist only in a still milder form. The division of labor* between husband and wife, or between the males and females, is, that the men do all the hunting and fishing, and cut the firewood. The women dress and cure the fish or game, bring wood and water, and carry all burdens of whatever nature that require transportation. They also attend to the household duties of preparing and cooking food; but the men wash and mend their own clothes, and in many instances make them. This custom is not confined to the slaves, but is practised by all. The women also provide a portion of the food, such as berries and various edible roots, and, to a limited extent, cultivate potatoes. The fact that they assist in procuring food, appears to secure for them better treatment by the men, than is usual among the buffalo-hunting tribes east of the Rocky Mountains. The husband, however, claims the privilege of correcting the wife, and some of them receive very severe beatings; but, on the other hand, they have the privilege of leaving their husbands, which they do for a slight cause. The marriage tie is but a slender bond, which is easily sundered, although it requires much negotiation when first contracted. Among the common people it is simply a purchase, payment being made in blankets, canoes, and guns, or such other commodities as may be agreed upon; but where the girl is the daughter or relative of a chief, a variety of ceremonies takes place. One of these, which I have witnessed, displayed a canoe borne on the shoulders of eight men, and containing three persons, one in the bow of the craft in the act of throwing a whaling harpoon at the door of a lodge; one in the centre about to cast a seal-skin buoy, which was attached to the harpoon; and one in the stern with a paddle as if steering. The ceremonies in this instance represented the manner of taking a whale.

The procession formed on the beach a short distance from the lodge, and in front of it an Indian, dressed in a blanket which concealed his head, crept on all fours, occasionally raising his body to imitate a whale when blowing. At intervals the Indian in the canoe would throw the harpoon as if to strike, taking studious [12] care, however, not to hit him; then the same evolutions were performed as is customary in the whale fishery. A party of friends followed the canoe, who sang to the accompaniment of drums and rattles. The burthen of their song was, that they had come to purchase a wife for one of their number, and recounted his merits and the number of blankets he would pay. When they reached the lodge the representative of the whale moved to one side, while the man in the canoe threw his harpoon with such force as to split the door, which was a single plank, in halves. The door, however, was kept barred, and the party, after piling a great number of blankets and a couple of guns against it, rested awhile, hoping to be admitted. After another chant, and the adding of a few more blankets to the heap, another harpoon was thrown against the door; but to no purpose, the damsel was obdurate, and the price not sufficient to satisfy her parents. This operation may be said to be symbolical of Cupid's dart on a large scale. The party effected no thing, and returned home. A few weeks later another lover, who was acceptable to the girl, came from Nittinat on Vancouver Island, with a great number of friends in five large canoes. These approached the shore, side by side, very slowly, the Indians in them standing up, singing and brandishing their paddles; they stopped just outside the surf, and one of the men delivered a speech, stating what they had come for and what they would pay. Then they all landed, and, having hauled their canoes on the beach, formed a blanket procession. First came a *ta-ma-na-was* or medicine man, dressed up with a gaudy display of finery, with his face painted red, and a bunch of eagle's feathers in his hair, a large wooden rattle in one hand and a bunch of scallop shells in the other, with which he kept time to a song. Next him was a man with a blanket over one shoulder, and holding one corner of another blanket, which was stretched out by an Indian who walked behind him holding the other corner, and also the corner of a third blanket, which was in like manner held by a third Indian behind. In this manner eighty-four blankets were brought by the procession, single file, and deposited one after the other at the door of the lodge, which in this instance was open, showing that the suitor was favorably received; but the eighty-four blankets were not enough, so the procession returned to the canoes and brought eighty-four more blankets in the same manner. These were all piled up outside the lodge; but the parents were in no haste, their daughter was too valuable, and the lover must wait. This he did for a week with all his friends. Every day a speech was made, and every night songs and dances were performed. At length the parents yielded, and the maiden was carried off in triumph, very much to her own satisfaction as well as that of her lover. The blankets, guns, and other articles used in the purchase, are not usually retained by the parents or relatives of the bride, but are returned to the bride groom, who takes them home with his new wife and distributes them to the friends of both. In short, what is said to be paid for a wife, is simply the amount which the bridegroom will give away to the assembled friends.

 A girl is considered marriageable as soon as she arrives at puberty. On the appearance of the menstrual discharge she is immediately secluded, by being placed behind a screen of mats or boards in a corner of the lodge. A number of little girls are in attendance day and night for a week or ten days, who keep up a constant [13] singing. They relieve each other as they get tired; but the girl is never left alone, nor do the songs cease except at slight intervals. At the expiration of this first period, the girl is taken out to be washed. The little girls form a procession, at the head of which she walks, with her face concealed in her blanket, the children singing as loud as they can scream. Arrived at the brook she is required to sit naked in the cold water half an hour, and is then taken back to the lodge. She is bathed in this manner three times a day for a fortnight, and her hair tied up in two bunches, one on each side of her head, which are wound round with cloth, strips of leather, beads, brass buttons, and other trinkets. The only dress worn is a cincture of fringed bark about the waist, reaching to the knee, and a blanket. At the expiration of a month the ordinary dress is resumed, and a head dress of the shells of the dentalium put on. This is the distinctive mark of all young girls until they are married. After this first period they are not compelled to live apart on the monthly return, nor are they required to be secluded after giving birth to a child. Love matches are frequently made, and whenever the parents are opposed the young couple will hide themselves in the woods for a day or two, and on their return the matter is amicably arranged.

 Marriages usually take place at an early period. The men take for wives either the women of their own or the neighboring tribes; but they are prohibited from marrying any of their own connections, unless the consanguinity is very remote. I do not know of an instance nearer than a fourth cousin. I knew of one young man who was in love with his own cousin, and the Indians spoke of it to me in terms of contempt; they said he wanted to marry his sister, and it was not permitted. Polygamy is practised among the Makahs, but is not general. None of them, however, have more than two wives, and these are on terms of perfect equality. If one thinks herself ill treated, she will leave and get another husband, in which event she will take her children with her. If the wife dies, the father takes the children; but while the mother lives and they need her care, she invariably takes them with her to her new abode. The facility with which the wives can leave their husbands and take others, gives rise to great confusion, particularly to the mind of a stranger seeking information relative to their domestic affairs. Chastity among the females is a thing much talked of, but it appears to be more honored in the breach than the observance, and, although they are not so grossly licentious as the Clallams and other tribes on the Sound, yet the men have great occasion for jealousy.

The festivals are but few, and are confined to the *ta-ma-na-was* ceremonies, which usually take place during the winter months; to certain "medicine" performances, which will be alluded to hereafter, both of these closing with feasting and dancing, and the *pot-lat-ches*, or distributions of presents, which are made at all seasons of the year. The *ta-ma-na-was* is allied to a religious ceremony, and will be treated of under that head. The pot-lat-ches occur whenever an Indian has acquired enough property in blankets, beads, guns, brass kettles, tin pans, and other objects of Indian wealth, to make a present to a large number of the tribe; for the more an Indian can give away, the greater his standing with the others, and the better his chance of attaining to the dignity of a chief among his people. [14]

Whenever it is the intention of an individual to make such a distribution of his property, a number of his friends are called in solemn council; an inventory of the articles is made, and the amount each one is to receive is decided upon. The names of the persons who are to be thus favored are then announced in the following manner: One of the party, seated on the ground with a board before him and a stick in his hand, acts as a herald. The person about to give the presents then announces a name, which, if satisfactory to the assembled friends, is repeated, whereupon the herald strikes a blow on the board with his stick, and calls the name in a loud voice; this is repeated until all the names are called to whom presents are to be given, and the articles each is to receive decided upon. Messengers are then sent to invite the guests. If the party is to be a large one, there will be from fifteen to twenty messengers who go in a body, with painted faces, and sprigs of evergreen in their hair. They enter the lodges with songs, and one of their number announces the intended feast and calls aloud the names of all who are invited. On the set day these assemble at the lodge of the Indian who gives the entertainment, and, after much feasting, singing, dancing, and masquerade performance, which sometimes lasts several days, the articles are distributed. The blankets are displayed on poles, or cords stretched across the lodge for the purpose, and all the other articles are placed so as to be seen by the assembled guests, who are seated at one end of the lodge opposite the goods. The herald, after making a speech, extolling the great liberality of the donor, strikes the board with his stick, and calls a name; thereupon an attendant takes the intended present and deposits it in front of the person who is to receive it, where it remains till all are served. Then a song is sung, a dance performed, and the party retire.

Sometimes these parties are composed of children. The parents of a boy or girl who are ambitious for the child, give presents to the children of the tribe. Invitations are sent to the parents, and the names of those children who are to receive the offerings are given. The entertainments are similar to those in the case of adults, except that the performers are children, who dance and sing and go through a variety of plays. The dancing is certainly not graceful; it consists in a clumsy sort of jump, with about as much ease and agility as a person would display while attempting to dance in a sack. The children have a variety of plays, some of which resemble those of white children, and were undoubtedly learned by observation of the customs of those they have seen at Victoria and other places on the Strait and Sound. For instance, peg-tops, which they call *ba-bet hl-ka-di*, and battledore and shuttlecock, which is termed *kla-ha-tla* (*kla-hak*, shuttlecock; *ko-ko-wi*, battledore). They also make little wagons, using for wheels sections of kelp stems, cut transversely and about an inch thick. These stems are cylindrical and hollow, and the little wheels answer exceedingly well for their miniature carts. They are quite as expert as most white children in the manufacture of miniature ships and schooners; some of which are very creditable pieces of work. But their chief pleasure is to get into a little canoe, just large enough to float them, and paddle about in the surf. It is this early and constant practice in the management of a canoe and the use of the paddle, that makes them so exceedingly expert when they become of maturer years. Another pastime of the boys is to imitate the killing of a whale. One will [15] select a kelp stem of the largest size, and trail it along the beach. The other boys, armed with miniature harpoons with wooden buoys attached, follow after, and dart their harpoons into the kelp, until it is full or split, when they get another, and keep up the game with eagerness for hours. Another sport is to set a pole upright in the sand and climb to the top, which they do readily by tying a piece of rope so as to form a loop, which is passed once around the pole, forming stirrups for the feet. As they climb, the rope is slipped up by the feet, but becomes fast on pressing the weight upon it; this affords a foothold, till the hands are raised for a fresh grasp of the pole, when the feet are again lifted, and thus alternately by hands and feet, they rapidly ascend to the top. The use of the bow and arrow is early learned by the boys, and is a favorite source of amusement. A description of them will be found under Arts and Manufactures. The amusements of the girls consist in dressing up clam shells with strips of rags, and setting them in rows in the sand to resemble children. They are also very fond of dolls, and appear much pleased with any toys such as white children use. They are early taught to make little baskets and mats, and their simple sports are varied by excursions into the woods after berries, or among the rocks, at low tide, in search of shell fish. Like the boys, they are accustomed from infancy to the use of canoes, and may be seen on any pleasant day throughout the summer, paddling in any pool of water left by the receding tide, or in the little bays formed at the mouths of the brooks by the sand which may have been washed in during high water. During the spring, when the flowers are in bloom and the humming birds are plenty, the boys take a stick smeared with the slime from snails, and place it among a cluster of flowers. This slime is an excellent bird lime, and if a humming bird applies his tongue to it he is glued fast. They will then tie a piece of thread to its feet and holding the other end let the birds fly, their humming being considered quite an amusement. They however are cruel to all animals, and particularly birds, which they torture in every conceivable manner. Among their sports is wrestling, which is common not only with the boys but the men also. The parties are entirely naked, and at a signal advance and seize each other by the hair. Each then strives to throw his antagonist, and the victor is rewarded by the shouts of his friends.

Formerly, deadly combats or duels were often fought. Each fighter being armed with a dagger held in the right hand, grasps firmly with the left the long hair of his antagonist; then holding each other fast, they inflict wounds with their knives till one or both are mortally wounded, or else both are exhausted, when friends interfere and the parties are separated. Some fighting is done with big stones instead of knives, when each tries to beat the other's brains out; but these gladiatorial scenes are of very rare occurrence of late years. The most common practice in vogue at present is shooting each other with guns or pistols.

Makah

Dress. – The usual dress of the men consists of a shirt and blanket; but some, especially the old men, are content with a blanket only. Nearly all of them how ever have suits of clothes of various kinds, which they have procured from the whites; but these are only worn on occasions of visits to the settlements up the Strait, on the arrival of strangers, or when at work for the white people, and are usually taken off when they return to their lodges. It is not an unusual sight to [16] see an Indian who has been well dressed, even to stockings and shoes or boots, perhaps for several days while with white people, or who may have, been at work all day come out of his lodge at night, or as soon as he leaves work, with nothing on but a blanket. This change from warm clothing to nearly none at all causes colds and coughs to be prevalent among them. During rainy weather they wear, in addition to the blanket, a conical hat woven from spruce roots, so compact as to exclude water, and a bear skin thrown over the shoulders. They are not particular in the arrangement of their dress, even when they have clothes to put on, and may occasionally be seen parading with a cap on the head, boots on the feet, and the body only covered with a blanket.

Before blankets of wool were procured from the whites, their dress was composed of robes made of skins or blankets woven from dogs hair or from the prepared bark of the pine which is found on Vancouver Island. Very comfortable blankets were also made from the down of birds woven on strings to form the warp. These garments are still occasionally worn, and a description of their manufacture may be found under the proper head.

Fig. 2. Makah Indian with his wet-weather fishing dress, blanket, bear skin, and hat.

The dress of the women usually consists of a shirt or long chemise reaching from the neck to the feet; some have in addition, a skirt of calico like a petticoat tied around the waist, or petticoats made of blankets or coarse baize. Formerly their entire dress was merely a blanket and a cincture of fringed bark, reaching from the waist to the knees. This is called wad-dish, a name they apply to their petticoats of all kinds. Some of the women, particularly the younger ones, have of late years dressed themselves in calico gowns, which are always of an antique pattern and open in front instead of the back. Occasionally a ~~squaw~~ who has been to Victoria and seen the fashions of white women will array herself in hoops, but these articles, so [17] necessary to the dress of civilized females, together with bonnets, are not at all becoming to a ~~squaw~~, and it is doubtful whether the fashion will ever obtain among these natives. A Makah belle is considered in full dress with a clean chemise; a calico or woollen skirt; a plaid shawl of bright colors thrown over her shoulders; six or seven pounds of glass beads of various colors and sizes on strings about her neck; several yards of beads wound around her ankles; a dozen or more bracelets of brass wire around each wrist; a piece of shell pendent from her nose; ear ornaments composed of the shells of the dentalium, beads and strips of leather, forming a plait three or four inches wide and two feet long; and her face and the parting of the hair painted with grease and vermilion. The effect of this combination of colors and materials is quite picturesque, which is perhaps the only praise that it merits.

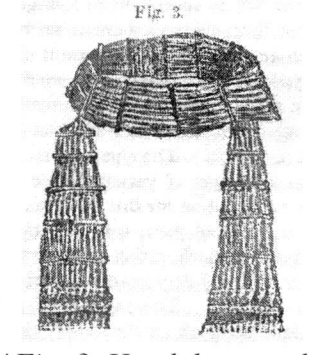

Fig. 3. Head dress and a pendant of dentalium.

Makah

Both sexes have their noses pierced, and usually, although not constantly, suspended from them a small piece of the haliotis shell (the "abalone" of the Californians), obtained from Vancouver Island, particularly on the eastern side in the Cowitchin district, where specimens of a large size are found. Some wear pieces of this shell two or three inches square as ear ornaments. The men wear their hair long, but on whaling excursions they tie it up in a club knot behind the head. They frequently decorate themselves by winding wreaths of evergreens around the knob, or stick in a sprig of spruce with a feather. At times they vary this head-dress by substituting a wreath of sea-weed, or a bunch of cedar bark bound around the head like a turban. They paint their faces either black or red, as fancy may suggest, or in stripes of various colors. I have never been able to discover any particular signification for this practice, although I have frequently inquired. Some have told me the red paint was to keep the sun from burning their faces; others paint themselves black, either to show that they have stout and courageous hearts, or because they feel depressed; and others again because they happen to be in the humor of so doing. The method of painting is first to rub the face well with deer's tallow, upon which they apply the dry vermilion or red ochre if these colors are desired. If they wish to produce black, pulverized charcoal is first mixed with bear's grease or deer's fat, and rubbed between the hands, and then applied to the face. The other colors are put on dry. The mode of coloring the face in stripes is to dip a thin slip of wood in the dry paint and lay it carefully on the face, producing a red mark the width of the stick; narrow marks or lines are made with the edge of the stick. The lines thus drawn are more uniform and more clearly defined than if laid on with a brush, and are done quite rapidly. During the berry season the children paint or stain their faces with the juice. A coarse quality of red ochre is often used for painting their faces, and also the inside of canoes. This pigment is made by the Kwilleyute Indians, who reside thirty miles south from Cape Flattery. It is found in the form of a yellowish clay or ochre, which oozes in a semi fluid state from the banks of the river at certain places. This is collected, squeezed into balls the size of a hen's egg, and then wrapped in rags and baked in the hot ashes till it acquires the desired hue. If heated too much the color becomes a dark brown, and is not so highly prized. When used it is pulverized and mixed with oil, for painting canoes, or applied dry to the face like vermilion, although some blend [18] it first with grease and rub it between the palms of the hands before applying it. Another paint is made from hemlock bark found on decayed roots, or in the forks of old roots that have been long under ground. This is dried at the fire, and, to be used, is rubbed on a stone with spittle and then applied to the face. They all prefer vermilion, however, when they can get it, nor are they averse to using blue or yellow when they can procure those colors dry, which they occasionally do from the whites. During the grand *ta-ma-na-was* or *duk-wal-ly* performances the face is painted black, and a wreath of cedar bark dyed red is worn around the head. During the *tsi-ak* or *medicine ta-ma-na-was* the face is painted red, and the wreath is of undyed bark. This bark, which is prepared by beating it fine, is termed *he-se-yu*. The name of the bark which has been dried but not broken is *pit-sop*. The war paint is generally black, although some use red; but the braves use black invariably. The hair is twisted in a knot behind, and green twigs tied up with it. The tattooing consists of marks on the arms or legs, and does not seem to amount to much. It is done by drawing a threaded needle under the skin, the thread having previously been colored with charcoal and water. Some prick in the color with a number of needles tied together, as sailors tattoo themselves. Many of these marks are merely straight lines, others show a rude attempt to represent an animal, and letters of the alphabet are sometimes seen tattooed on the

Makah

arms, the characters being copied from any old newspaper they may get hold of. They seem to attach no definite meaning to this tattooing, and most of it is done while they are children. Many have no marks at all on their persons, while others have a few on the wrists and hands, and some on the ankles; but there is nothing in their tattooing which is in any way distinctive of tribe.

Some of the tribes on the northwest part of Vancouver Island have the custom of wearing disks of wood or ivory in the under lip, and I have seen it asserted that it is the custom of all the tribes from the Columbia River north. This however is not the fact with any of the coast tribes as far as I have seen, which is from the Columbia River to Nootka. The practice of flattening the heads of infants, although, as I have said, not universal among the Makahs, is performed in a manner similar to that of the Chinooks and other tribes in the vicinity of the Columbia River. As soon as a child is born it is washed with warm urine, and then smeared with whale oil and placed in a cradle made of bark, woven basket fashion; or of wood, either cedar or alder, hollowed out for the purpose. Into the cradle a quantity of finely separated cedar bark of the softest texture is first thrown. At the foot is a board raised at an angle of about 25°, which serves to keep the child's feet elevated; or, when the cradle is raised to allow the child to nurse, to form a support for the body, or a sort of seat. This is also covered with bark, *he-se-yu*. A pillow is formed of the same material, just high enough to keep the head in its natural position, with the spinal column neither elevated nor depressed. First the child is laid on its back, its legs properly extended, its arms put close to its sides, and a covering either of bark or cloth laid over it; and then, commencing at the feet, the whole body is firmly laced up so that it has no chance to move in the least. When the body is well secured a padding of *he-se-yu* is placed on the child's forehead, over which is laid bark of a somewhat stiffer texture, and the head is firmly lashed down to the [19] sides of the cradle; thus the infant remains, seldom taken out more than once a day while it is very young, and then only to wash it and dry its bedding. The male children have a small opening left in the covering, through which the penis protrudes to enable them to void their urine. The same style of cradle appears to be used whether it is intended to compress the skull or not, and that deformity is accomplished by simply drawing the strings of the head-pad tightly and keeping up the pressure for a long time. Children are usually kept in these cradles till they are a year old, but as their growth advances they are not tied up quite so long as for the first few months. The mother, in washing her child, seldom takes the trouble to heat water; she simply fills her mouth with the water, and when she thinks it warm enough spirts it on the child and rubs it with her hand. If the child is very dirty, and they generally get thoroughly grimed up with soot and grease, a wash of stale urine is used, which effectually removes the oil and dirt, but does not impart a fragrant odor. This species of alkali as a substitute for soap is the general accompaniment of the morning toilet of both males and females. They wash as soon as they get up, and may be seen any morning proceeding to the brook with their urinals in their hands. In the winter months, in stormy weather, when they have been confined to the house, or after they have been curing fish or trying out oil, they get exceedingly dirty, and then they go through a process of scouring themselves with a wisp of grass or cedar leaves and sand and urine; after which they give themselves a rinse in fresh water and come out as red as boiled lobsters. Although, in respect of bathing, they may be said to be comparatively cleanly, yet they are not so particular about washing their clothes, which they wear till they are positively filthy before they will take the trouble to cleanse them; and as their washing is done in cold water, with but little if any soap, their clothes have always a dingy appearance. There are exceptions, however, to this, both among the males and females, particularly the younger ones, who, since the advent of the whites, seem more desirous of having clean apparel than their elders, who retain all their old savage customs.

Food, and Method of Procuring It. – The principal subsistence of the Makahs is drawn from the ocean, and is formed of nearly all its products, the most important of which are the whale and halibut. Of the former there are several varieties which are taken at different seasons of the year. Some are killed by the Indians; others, including the right whale, drift ashore, having been killed either by whalemen, sword fish, or other casualties. The various species of whales are: The sperm whale, *kots-ke*, which is very rarely seen; right whale, *yakh-yo-bad-di*; black fish, *klas-ko-kop-ph*; fin-back, *kau-wid*; sulphur bottom, *kwa-kwau-yak-thle*; California gray, *che-che-wid*, or *chet-a-puk*; killer, *se-hwau*. The generic name of whales is *chet-a-puk*. The California gray is the kind usually taken by the Indians, the others being but rarely attacked.

Their method of whaling, being both novel and interesting, will require a minute description not only the implements used, but the mode of attack, and the final disposition of the whale, being entirely different from the practice of our own whalemen. The harpoon consists of a barbed head, to which is attached a rope or lanyard, always of the same length, about five fathoms or thirty feet. [20] This lanyard is made of whale's sinews twisted into a rope about an inch and a half in circumference, and covered with twine wound around it very tightly, called by sailors "serving". The rope is exceedingly strong and very pliable.

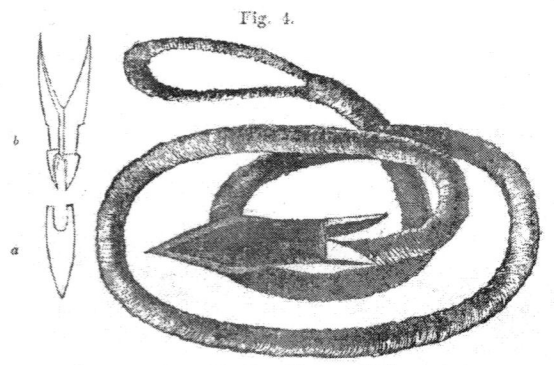

*FIG. 4. Harpoon point (kwe-kāhptl) and line: a. Blade, b. Barbs.

The harpoon-head is a flat piece of iron or copper, usually a saw-blade or a piece of sheet copper, to which a couple of barbs made of elk's or deer's horn are secured, and the whole covered with a coating of spruce gum. The staff is made of yew in two pieces, which are joined in the middle by a very neat scarph, firmly secured by a narrow strip of bark wound around it very tightly. I do not know why these staves or handles are not made of one piece; it may be that the yew does not grow sufficiently straight to afford the required length; but I have never seen a staff that was not constructed as here described. The length is eighteen feet; thickest in the centre, where it is joined together, and tapering thence to both ends. To be used, the staff is inserted into the barbed head, and the end of the lanyard made fast to a buoy, which is simply a seal-skin taken from the animal whole, the hair being left inwards.

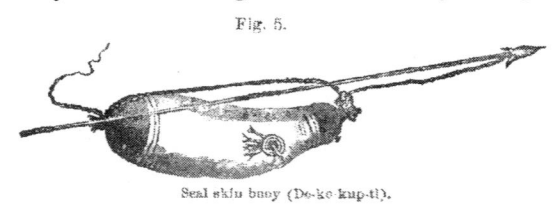

*Fig. 5. Seal skin buoy (Do-ko kup-tl).

The apertures of the head, feet, and tail are tied up air tight, and the skin inflated like a bladder.

When the harpoon is driven into a whale the barb and buoy remain fastened to him, but the staff comes out, and is taken into the canoe. The harpoon which is thrown into the head of the whale has but one buoy attached; but those thrown into the body have as many as can be conveniently tied on; and, when a number of [21] canoes join in the attack, it is not unusual for from thirty to forty of these buoys to be made fast to the whale, which, of course, cannot sink, and is easily despatched by their spears and lances. The buoys are fastened together by means of a stout line made of spruce roots, first slightly roasted in hot ashes, then split with knives into fine fibres, and finally twisted into ropes, which are very strong and durable. These ropes are also used for towing the dead whale to the shore. The harpoon-head is called *kwe-kaptl*; the barbs, *tsa-kwat*; the blade, *kut-so-wit*; the lanyard attached to the head, *kluks-ko*; the loop at the end of the lanyard, *kle-tait-lish*; the staff of the harpoon, *du-pui-ak*; the buoy, *dopt-ko-kuptl*, and the buoy-rope, *tsis-ka-pub*.

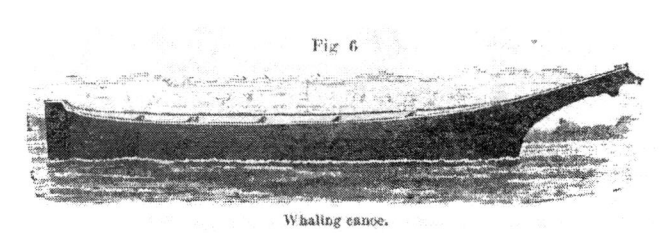

A whaling canoe invariably carries eight men: one in the bow, who is the harpooner, one in the stern to steer, and six to paddle. The canoe is divided by sticks, which serve as stretchers or thwarts, into six spaces, named as follows: the bow, *he-tuk-wad*; the space immediately behind, *ka-kai-woks*; centre of canoe, *cha-thluk-dōs*; next space, *he-stuk-stas*; stern, *kli-cha*. This canoe is called *pa-dau-t'hl*. A canoe that carries six persons, or one of and medium size, is called *bo-kwis-tat*; a smaller size, *a-tlis-tat*; very small ones for fishing, *tc-ka-au-da*.

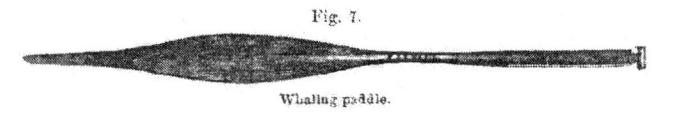

*Fig. 6. Whaling canoe.

*Fig. 7. Whaling paddle.

*Fig 8. Saddle of whale's blubber.

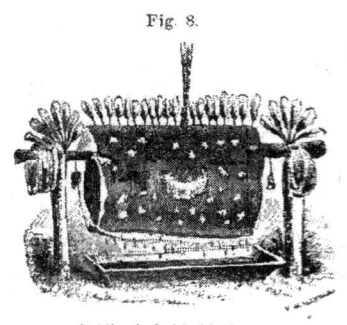

When whales are in sight, and one or more canoes have put off in pursuit, it is usual for some one to be on the look-out from a high position, so that in case a whale is struck, a signal can be given and other canoes go to assist. "When the whale is dead, it is towed ashore to the most convenient spot, if possible to one of the villages, and hauled as high on the beach as it can be floated. As soon as the tide recedes, all hands swarm around the carcass with their knives, and in a very short time the blubber is stripped off in blocks about two feet square. The portion of blubber forming a saddle, taken from between the head and dorsal fin, is esteemed the most choice, and is always the property of the person who first strikes the whale. The other portions are distributed according to rule, each man knowing what he is to receive. The saddle is termed *u-butsk*. {Waterman: *yu'b-△tsk* = taboo-piece} It is placed across a pole supported by two stout posts. At each end of the pole are hung the harpoons and lines with which the whale was killed. Next to the blubber at each end are the whale's eyes; eagle's feathers are stuck in a row along the top, a bunch of [22] feathers at each end, and the whole covered over with spots and patches of down. Underneath the blubber is a trough to catch the oil which drips out. The *u-butsk* remains in a conspicuous part of the lodge until it is considered ripe enough to eat, when a feast is held, and the whole devoured or carried off by the guests, who are at liberty to carry away what they cannot eat. After the blubber is removed into the lodge the black skin is first taken off, and either eaten raw or else boiled. It looks like India rubber; but though very repulsive to the eye it is by no means unpalatable, and is usually given to the children, who are very fond of it, and manage to besmear their faces with the grease till they are in a filthy condition. The blubber, after being skinned, is cut into strips and boiled, to get out the oil that can be extracted by that process; this oil is carefully skimmed from the pots with clam shells. The blubber is then hung in the smoke to dry, and when cured, looks very much like citron. It is somewhat tougher than pork, but sweet (if the whale has been recently killed), and has none of that nauseous taste which the whites attribute to it. When cooked, it is common to boil the strips about twenty minutes; but it is often eaten cold and as an accompaniment to dried halibut.

From information I obtained, I infer that formerly the Indians were more successful in killing whales than they have been of late years. Whether the whales were more numerous, or that the Indians, being now able to procure other food from the whites, have become indifferent to the pursuit, I cannot say; but I have not noticed any marked activity among them, and when they do go out they rarely take a prize. They are more successful in their whaling in some seasons than in others, and whenever a surplus of oil or blubber is on hand, it is exchanged or traded with Indians of other tribes, who appear quite as fond of the luxury as the Makahs. The oil sold by these whalers to the white traders is dogfish oil, which is not eaten by this tribe, although the Clyoquot and Nootkan Indians use it with their food. There is no portion of a whale, except the vertebrae and offal, which is useless to the Indians. The blubber and flesh serve for food; the sinews are prepared and made into ropes, cords, and bowstrings; and the stomach and intestines are carefully sorted and inflated, and when dried are used to hold oil. Whale oil serves the same purpose with these Indians that butter does with civilized people; they dip their dried halibut into it while eating, and use it with bread, potatoes, and various kinds of berries. When fresh, it is by no means unpalatable; and it is only after being badly boiled, or by long exposure, that it becomes rancid, and as offensive to a white man's palate as the common lamp oil of the shops.

The product of the ocean next in importance for food is the halibut. These are taken in the waters of the strait in certain localities, but as the depth of water at the mouth of the strait is very great, the Indians prefer to fish on a bank or shoal [23] some fifteen or twenty miles west from Tatooche light. The depth on the banks varies from twenty to thirty fathoms. The lines used in the halibut fishing are usually made of the stems of the (*fucus gigantea*) *Fig. 9. Halibut hook.* gigantic kelp, and the hooks of splints of hemlock. A line attached to one of the arms of the hook holds it in a vertical position, as shown in Fig. 9. The bait used is the cuttlefish or squid (octopus tuberculatus), which is plentiful and is taken by the natives by means of barbed sticks, which they thrust under the rocks at low. water, to draw the animal out and kill it by transfixing it with the stick. A portion of the squid is firmly attached to the hook, which is sunk by means of a stone to the bottom, the sinker keeping the hook nearly in a stationary position. To the upper portion of the line it is usual to attach bladders, which serve as buoys, and several are set at one time. When the fish is hooked, it pulls the bladder, but cannot draw it under water. The Indian, seeing the signal, paddles out; hauls up the line; knocks the fish on the head with a club; readjusts his bait; casts it overboard; and proceeds to the next bladder he sees giving token of a fish. When a number of Indians are together in a large canoe, and the fish bite readily, it is usual to fish from the canoe without using the buoy. This hook is called *che-bud*, and the club, sometimes fancifully carved, is called *ti-ne-t'hl*.

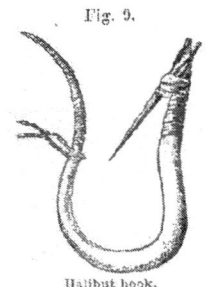

When the fish are brought home, they are first landed on the beach, where the women wash and wipe them with a wisp of grass or fern. The entrails are taken out and thrown away, and the rest of the fish carried into the houses. The heads are taken off first to be dried separately, and the body of the fish is sliced by means of a knife of peculiar construction, somewhat resembling a common chopping knife, called *ko-che-tin* (Fig. 10). The skin is first carefully removed, and the flesh then sliced as thin as possible to facilitate the drying; and when perfectly cured, the pieces are wrapped in the skin, carefully packed in baskets, and placed in a dry place. The heads, the back bones, to which some flesh adheres, and the tails, are all dried

Fig. 10. Halibut chopper. and packed away separately from the body pieces. When eaten, the skin, to which the principal portion of the fat or oil of the fish adheres, is simply warmed, or toasted over the coals, till it acquires crispncss. The heads, tails, and back bones are boiled. The dried strips from the body are eaten without further cooking, being simply broken into small pieces, dipped in whale oil, and so chewed and swallowed. It requires a peculiar twist of the fingers and some practice to dip a piece of dry halibut into a bowl of oil and convey it to the mouth without letting the oil drop off, but the Indians, old and young, are very expert, and scarcely ever drop any between the mouth and the bowl. In former times, dried halibut was to these Indians in lieu of bread; oil in place of butter, and blubber instead of beef or pork. When potatoes were introduced, they formed a valuable addition to their food, and since the white men have become more numerous, the Indians [24] have accustomed themselves to other articles of diet; flour, hard bread, rice, and beans are always acceptable to them; they are also very fond of molasses and sugar, and are willing at all times to barter their furs, oil, or fish for these commodities.

Next to the halibut are the salmon and codfish, and a species of fish called the "cultus" or bastard cod. These, however, are usually eaten fresh, except in seasons of great plenty, when the salmon is dried in the smoke. They are all taken with the hook, and the salmon fishing is most excellent sport. The bait used is herring, and unless these are plenty, they will not try to catch salmon, although the waters may be alive with them. A more extended notice of these fish and of several other varieties used for food, will be found in another portion of this paper.

The squid, which is used for bait in the halibut fishery, is also eaten. When first taken from the water it is a slimy jelly-like substance, of rather disgusting appearance, but when boiled it becomes firm and as white as the flesh of a lobster, which it somewhat resembles in taste, but is much tougher to masticate. I have found it, chopped with lettuce, an excellent ingredient in salad. The onychotcuthis {hooked squid} is also found, but it is never eaten. Skates are abundant, but as they usually make their appearance during the halibut season, they are seldom used, although the Indians like them very well; but they seem to prefer halibut. Three varieties of echinus {sea urchin} are found here, and are eaten in great quantities; they are either caught by spearing them at low tide, or are taken in a very simple manner by means of a piece of kelp. To effect this a stem of the kelp is sunk to the bottom, having a line and buoy attached. The echini go on it to feed, and after the kelp has remained several hours, it is gently drawn into a canoe and the creature picked off. The Indians collect them in this manner in great numbers during the spring months. Although a variety of bivalves is found, they do not abound as they do in the bays further up the Strait, and do not form a common article of nutriment, except that mussels of the finest description cover the rocks about Cape Flattery and Tatooche Island, and are eaten whenever the Indian appetite craves them, or when the breakers of the Pacific are sufficiently quiet to permit a search. These are either boiled or roasted in the ashes, and are very delicious cooked by either method. Barnacles, crabs, sea slugs, periwinkles, limpets, &c. furnish occasional repasts. Scallops, which are found in the bays of Fuca Strait, are excluded from their list ot food. They are considered as having some peculiar powers belonging to them, and in consequence their shells are made use of as rattles to be used in their ceremonials. Oysters were formerly found in Neeah Bay, but have been destroyed by some cause of late years; the only evidence of their former exist ence being the shells which are thrown ashore by the waves. They are found in the various bays and inlets of Vancouver Island, but the Indians do not eat them. In fact there are but few of the animal products of the ocean but are considered edible, and serve to diversify the food. Of land animals they eat the flesh of the elk, deer, and bear; but, although these abound a short distance in the interior, the Indians very seldom hunt for them, and when they kill any, as they occasionally do, they are always ready to sell the flesh to the white residents in the bay, seeming to care more for the skin than the carcass. Smaller animals, such as raccoons, [25] squirrels, and rabbits, are seldom if ever eaten by them, and are killed only for the sake of the skin. Of birds, however, they are very fond, particularly the sea fowl, which are most plentiful at times, and are taken in great numbers on foggy nights, by means of spears. A fire of pitch-wood is built on a platform at one end of the canoe, and by the glare of its light, which seems to blind or attract the birds, the Indian is enabled to get into the midst of a flock, and spear them at his leisure. On the return of a canoe from one of these nocturnal excursions, particularly in the fall, it is not unusnal to find in it a collection of pelicans, loons, cormorants, ducks of various kinds, grebes, and divers of various sorts. These, after being picked, and very superficially cleaned, are thrown promiscuously into a kettle, boiled and served up as a feast.

The roots used for food are potatoes, which are raised in limited quantities; Kammas (*Scilla Fraseri*), which is procured from the tribes south (Kwilleyute and Kwinaullts), and some from the Vancouver Island Indians; tubers of the equisetum; fern roots, and those of some species of meadow grass and water plants; the roots of several kinds of sea-weed, particularly eel grass, are also used. These and the equisetum root are eaten raw; the others are all cooked. In the spring the young sprouts of the salmon berry (*Rubuis spectabilis*) and thumb berry (*Rubus odor*atus) are consumed in great quantities. They are very tender, have a slightly acid and astringent taste, and appear to serve as alteratives to the system, which has become loaded with humors from the winter's diet of dried fish and oil. The sprouts are sometimes cooked by being tied in bundles and steamed over hot stones. After the season of sprouts is over the berries commence. The salmon berry comes first and is ripe in June; it is followed by the other summer berries till autumn, when the sallal and cranberry appear and continue till November. It is customary, when an Indian has a surplus of food of any kind, to invite a number of friends and neighbors to share it, and as they seem very fond of these social gatherings, scarcely a day passes but some one will give a feast, sometimes to a few, or it may be to a great number of persons. It is this fondness for feasts which makes them so improvident, for when they have anything they never seem satisfied until it is all eaten up. If one man is more fortunate than his neighbors in procuring a supply, instead of preserving it for his own wants and those of his family, he must give a feast, and while his supplies last the others are content to live on his hospitality; when that is exhausted they will seek food for themselves.

The articles used for culinary purposes are, for the most part, pots, kettles, and pans, principally procured from the whites, at the trading post of the Hudson's Bay Company at Victoria. The ancient method of steaming or boiling is occasionally resorted to, particularly in

Makah

cooking quantities of meat, fish, or roots, for a feast. Large bowls shaped like troughs, cut from alder logs, are partially filled with red hot stones, on which a few fern leaves or sea-weed are laid; then the food, whether fish or potatoes, or kammas, is placed on this, a bucket of water is thrown into the trough, and the whole quickly covered with mats and blankets and left to steam till the contents are cooked. "When larger quantities of food are to be prepared, the same process is employed, with the exception that, instead of using wooden troughs, a shallow pit is made in the ground. Potatoes and fish take only half an hour's [26] [4 June, 1860] cooking; but some of the roots, particularly the kammas, require a constant heat for nearly two days.

Their method of serving up food is very primitive, and the same forms are observed by all. When a feast is to consist of a variety of dishes, such for instance as hard bread, potatoes, blubber, fish, &c, they proceed in this manner: after the guests are assembled, the women begin to knead flour, and prepare it in cakes to bake in the ashes, the men meanwhile heating stones red hot. When these are ready, they are transferred by means of tongs made of a split stick, to large wooden troughs, and potatoes laid on top of them. Some water is then thrown on the heap, and the whole quickly covered with mats and old blankets to retain the steam. The potatoes having been covered up, the cakes are next placed in the hot ashes to bake. The guests meanwhile are served with dried halibut and oil; each has his allowance set before him, and what he cannot eat he is expected to carry away. Dry fish and oil constitute the first course, and by the time that is finished the potatoes are steamed, and the bread is baked. The potatoes are served first, and are eaten with oil, the custom being to peel off the skins Avith the fingers, dip the potato in oil and bite off a piece, repeating the dipping at each mouthful. The potatoes disposed of, the bread is next served; or, if they have hard bread, that is offered instead of fresh. Molasses is preferred with the bread, but if they have none, oil is used instead. If any more provision is to be served, it is brought in courses, and at the end of each course each guest wipes his mouth and fingers with a wisp of bark, puts whatever may be left into his basket, and looks out for the next course. The host is offended if his guests do not partake of everything that is set before them, and if strangers are among the visitors, it is not uncommon for four or five such feasts to be given in the course of a single day or evening, each arranged and conducted as described. I have attended several entertainments in visiting the different villages of the tribes.

*Fig 12. Spoon of aploceras horn

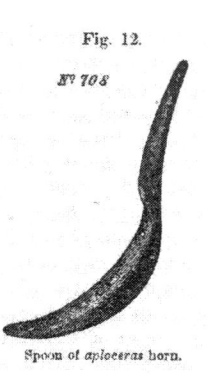

Fig 11. Ladle of "big horn. On one occasion, when an unusual display of hospitality was expected, one of the Indians who accompanied me remarked that I had better not eat too much at any one lodge, lest I should be sick, and not be able to feast at all of them, as I was expected to do. I asked him how [27] he managed to eat such enormous quantities, for his appetite appeared insatiable. He replied, that when he had eaten too much he made it a practice, before going into the next lodge, to thrust his fingers down his throat, which enabled him to throw off the load from his stomach, and prepare to do justice to the coming feast. An Indian who can perform this feat dexterously, so as to eat heartily at every house, is looked upon as a most welcome guest, who does justice to the hospitality of his host. Sometimes the feast is confined to boiled rice and

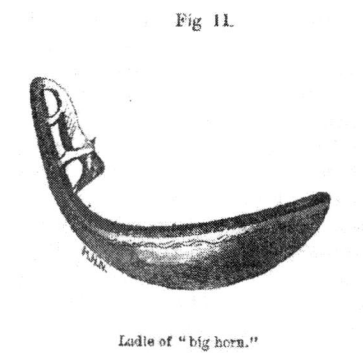

29

Makah

molasses, of which they are very fond. This is served out in tin pans or wooden platters, and eaten with spoons made of horn, procured from the northern tribes, and said to be the horn of the mountain sheep.[4] If horn spoons are not at hand, they improvise an excellent substitute which is simply a clam shell, and with one of large size an Indian will swallow quite as much rice and molasses as by any other known method.

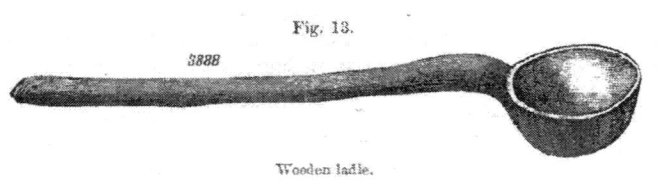

Fig. 13.
3888
Wooden ladle.

*13. Wooden ladle. #3888

After eating, they sometimes, but not always, indulge in a whiff of tobacco; but smoking is not a universal practice among them, and is rather as a stimulant than a mere luxury; the pipe is more Fig. agreeable to them in thf ir canoes, when tired with fishing or paddling; then the Indian likes to take out his little pouch of smok ing materials, and draw a few whiffs. The article generally used is the dried leaves of the *Arctost uva-ursi* mixed with a little tobacco; they also use, when they have no uva-ursi, either the dried leaves of the sallal *Gaultheria shallon*, or dried alder bark. Smoking, however, is practised even less than among some of the tribes east of the Rocky Mountains, and there are no ceremonials connected with its use. Occasionally an Indian will swallow a quantity of the smoke, which, being retained a few seconds in the lungs or stomach, produces a species of stupefaction, lasting from five to ten minutes and then passing off. The calumet, or pipe of peace, with its gayly decorated stem, is quite unknown among these Indians. They are content with anything in the shape of a pipe, and seem to prefer a clay bowl, to which they affix a stem made of a dried branch of the *Rubus spectabilis*. They simply scrape off the bark and take out the pith, and the stem is finished. The smoking occupies but a few minutes of the time devoted to a meal; when they have finished, each guest gathers what provision he may have left, and all proceed to the next lodge, where another feast has been prepared; and when all is over, they return home with their gleanings.

Otter, Fish, Seals, &c, Taken By The Makahs. – Besides those already named, other varieties are taken, some of which are not used for food. As several have [28] not been described in any work of reference I have seen, I shall have to describe them simply by their common and Indian names. The cottoids are very plenty and of several varieties, all of which are eaten. The largest, which is called *tsa-daitch*, measures twenty-seven inches in length. It is an uncouth, repulsive-looking fish, dark greenish-brown, the body larger in proportion to the head than other sculpins; but it is of good flavor, either boiled or fried. One specimen weighed ten pounds. The buffalo sculpin, *kiib-bis* and other small varieties, are quite common, and are usually taken with spears. The *kla-hap-pak* resembles the "grouper" of San Francisco. Its color is red; the scales large and coarse; the meat white, and in large flakes. It is excellent, either fried, boiled, or baked. The whites call it "rock cod," but it is not of the cod species, although the flavor and appearance of the flesh, when cooked, resemble that. The *tsa-ba-hwa* is much like the rock-cod of Massachusetts. It is variously marked, but the general color is olive-green on the back, shaded down to a yellow belly, and covered with reddish or brown spots or freckles; some are of a sepia-brown, with blue spots. It is a nice pan fish when fresh, but soon gets soft. Its flesh varies in

---

[4] The ladles are made of wood, or of the horns of the "big-horn," (*Ovis montana*; the spoons of those of the mountain goat, *Aploceras americana*. – GG.

color with the locality where it is taken, and the difference of food, and may be found with shades ranging from a pure white to a greenish-blue the latter color being very disagreeable to most of the white men, who regard it as produced by a poisonous agency. I have eaten freely of this fish, and found that the color of the flesh made no difference either in flavor or quality it can be taken by the hook while trolling for salmon, but is usually caught near the rocks with small hooks and lines. The cultus or "bastard cod," as it is termed by the whites, which abounds, and is taken at all seasons of the year, forms an important article for fresh consumption. This fish, in general appearance, somewhat resembles the true cod, but differs from it in many material respects. The dorsal fins are double, and extend from the head to the tail. These, as well as all the other fins, are thick, gelatinous, and palatable. This also differs from the common cod, in wanting the barbel under the lower jaw, which is longer than the upper, and in having both upper and lower jaws armed with strong teeth. The liver contains no oil, but the flesh has a portion of fat mixed through it. It is most excellent food, and especially when cooked, closely resembles the true cod. Exceedingly voracious also, in taking it the Indians use no hook; they simply secure a small fish, usually a perch or sculpin, to the line, and when the cod closes its jaws upon the bait, it holds with bulldog tenacity, and is hauled into the canoe and knocked on the head. The Indian name for it is *tush-kaii*. A fish closely resembling this, and perhaps of the same species, is sold in the San Francisco market under the name of cod. At certain seasons, particularly during the spring, it is found around the rocks and in coves of shallow water, and is then easily speared. The Indians seldom dry it, preferring to boil and eat it fresh. The true cod, ka-datl, is taken in limited quantities. In some seasons it is more plentiful than at others. It is caught on banks and shoals, in from thirty to forty fathoms of water. This fish abounds in the more northern waters of the Pacific coast; but the extreme depth and swift currents of Fuca Strait make it difficult to fish for them there, except at those times during the summer months, when it approaches near the shore. Another fish, termed by the Indians *be-sho-we*, or black [29] cod, although not a codfish, has not been described in any work that I have seen. It is a deep water fish, being caught in eighty fathoms. I have never been able to get one perfect. They are rarely taken, and those that I have seen had been split for curing. The color of the skin is black, and the flesh white and fat like mackerel. I have eaten some broiled, and the flavor was like that of halibut fins, extremely rich and fat. The weight varies from four to twelve pounds.

The dogfish (*ya-cha*) *Acanthias suckleyi*, is taken in great quantities for the sake of the oil contained in the liver, which forms the principal article of traffic between these Indians and the whites. Although this fish is plentiful on the coast south of Cape Flattery, I have never known the Indians there to make a business of fishing for them. Even at Kwilleyute {Quileute}, where I saw great quantities of dogfish in the summer of 1861, the Indians of that tribe and locality did not know how to extract the oil, and we had to send a Makah Indian, who was on board the vessel, ashore to show them how to try out the livers of a lot of fish we had caught.

The Indians on Vancouver Island, on the contrary, make a lucrative business of extracting the oil, and sell large quantities to the Makahs in exchange for whale oil, which they eat. The Clyoquots and Nootkans eat dogfish oil, but prefer whale oil when they can obtain it. The method of extracting as practised by the Makahs is to collect the livers, which are put into a tub and kept until a considerable quantity has accumulated. They are then put into iron pots, and set to simmer near the fire; or else hot stones are placed among them and they are cooked by the heat until all the oil is extracted, which is then carefully skimmed off and stored in receptacles, made of the paunches and intestines of whales, fish, or seals. In the fall of the year the flesh of the dogfish contains a considerable proportion of oil, which at other times it does not appear to possess; this is extracted in the following manner: When the livers are taken out, the head and back bone are also removed, and the rest of the body, being first slightly dried in the smoke, is steamed on hot stones till it is thoroughly cooked. It is then put into little baskets, made for the purpose, of soft cedar bark, and rolled and squeezed till all the liquid is extracted. This in color resembles dirty milk. It is boiled and allowed to cool and settle, and the oil is then skimmed off. After the oil is extracted, the flesh is washed in fresh water and again squeezed in the baskets, and in this state it is eaten by the Indians when other food is scarce. But dog fish is seldom tasted by the Makahs, and never until the oil has been thoroughly removed. The oil has a nauseous taste, and is not relished by these Indians, who are epicures in their way, and prefer the oil of whales and seals. The quality of dogfish oil for burning is very good, quite superior to whale oil. In astral lamps it burns with a clear, strong flame, and, when properly refined, is second only to sperm oil. Dr. Suckley states that while he was on service as surgeon at the US military station at Fort Steilacoom, he used dogfish oil with great success in pulmonary affections, and considered it, when fresh, equal to cod-liver oil. A very large species of shark, known among whalemen as "bone shark," is occasionally killed by the Makahs, and its liver yields great quantities of oil. I saw one in October, 1862, killed in Neeah Bay, twenty-six feet long, and its liver yielded nearly seven barrels of oil, or over two hundred gallons. These sharks are very abundant [30] during the summer and fall, but the Indians rarely attack them except when they come in shore to feed, which they do at certain times. They are easily seen by the long dorsal fin projecting above the water, and, as they appear to be quite sluggish in their movements, are readily killed with harpoons or lances. The flesh is never eaten.

A fish of the *Anarrhichthys* tribe is frequently killed during the summer months at low tide among the rocks. This is called the "doctor fish" by the Indians, and is never eaten except by some medicine-man who wishes to increase his skill in pharmacy.

Of the porpoise family there are three varieties in the waters of Fuca Strait. The large black kind called by the Makahs *a-ikh-pet'hl*; white fin porpoise, called *kwak-watl*, and the "puffing pig," *tsailt h-ko*. These are killed with harpoons of a smaller size than those used for whales, and are highly esteemed as food.

Seals also abound. The sea-lion, the largest variety, is called *a-ka-wad-dish*; the fur-seal, *kat-hla-dos*, and the hair-seal, *kas-cho-we*. The skin of the hair-seal is always taken off whole, and, after the head and feet have been removed and the orifices firmly secured, it is blown full of air and dried with the hair side in. This is the buoy used for the whale fishery, and is usually painted on the outside with rude devices in red vermilion or ochre. The skins of the fur-seal are sold to the whites. The sea otter, *ti-juk*, is very rarely found around the cape, but is plentiful further down the coast in the vicinity of Point Grenville. During the summer of 1864 the fur-seals were more numerous in Fuca Strait than they had been for many years, and great numbers were taken by the Indians. Sometimes they kill seals with spears; but the common mode is to shoot them with guns. The flesh of all the species is eaten. There are several deep caverns in the cliffs at Cape Flattery in which the seals congregate during the breeding season. At such times the Indians go in with a torch and club, and kill numbers by knocking them on the head.

The ease with which these Indians can obtain their subsistence from the ocean makes them improvident in laying in supplies for winter use, except of halibut; for, on any day in the year when the weather will permit, they can procure, in a few hours, provisions enough to last them for several days.

Trade. – The Makahs, from their peculiar locality, have been for many years the medium of conducting the traffic between the Columbia River and Coast tribes south of Cape Flattery, and the Indians north as far as Nootka. They are emphatically a trading, as well as a producing people; and in these respects are far superior to the Clallams and other tribes on Fuca Strait and Puget Sound. Before the white men came to this part of the country, and when the Indian population on the Pacific coast had not been reduced in numbers as it has been of late years, they traded largely with the Chinooks at the mouth of the Columbia, making excursions as far as the Kwinaiult tribe at Point Grenville, where they met the Chinook traders; and some of the more venturesome would even continue on to the Columbia, passing through the Chihalis country at Gray's Harbor and Shoalwater Bay. The Chinooks and Chihalis would in like manner come north as far as Cape Flattery; and these trading excursions were kept up pretty regularly, with only the interruption [31] of occasional feuds and rivalries between the different tribes, when the intercourse would be suspended, or carried on by means of intermediate bands; for instance, the Chinooks would venture up as far as Chihalis, or perhaps Kwinaiult; they would go as far as the Kwilleyute, and these last in turn to Cape Flattery. After a while peace would be restored, and the long voyages again resumed. The Makahs took down canoes, oil, dried halibut, and hai-kwa, or dentalium shells. The large canoes were almost invariably made on Vancouver Island; for, although craft of this model are called "Chinook" canoes, very few in reality, except small ones, were made at Chinook, the cedar there not being of suitable size or quality for the largest sizes, and the best trees being found on the Island. The Makahs in return received sea-otter skins from Kwinaiult; vermilion or cinnabar from the Chinooks, which they in turn had procured from the more southern tribes of Oregon; and such articles of Indian value as might be manufactured or produced by the tribes living south of the cape. Their trade with the northern Indians was for dentalium, dried cedar bark for making mats, canoes, and dried salmon; paying for the same with dried halibut, blubber, and whale oil. Slaves also constituted an important article of traffic; they were purchased by the Makahs from the Vancouver Island Indians, and sold to the coast Indians south.

The northern Indians did not formerly, nor do they now, care to go further south on their trading excursions than Cape Flattery; and the Columbia River and other coast tribes seem to have extended their excursions no further north than that point. Isolated excursions are attributed to certain chiefs. Comcomly, for instance, the celebrated Chinook chief, would occasionally go north as far as Nootka; while Maquinna, Klallakum, and Tatooshatticus, of the Clyoquots, made visits to Chinook; but, as a general practice, the Makahs at Cape Flattery conducted the trade from north to south. In those early days, when so many more Indians were in every tribe than at present, and when they were so often at variance with each other, it is not probable that the trade conducted by the coast tribes was of any great value. But when the white traders began to settle at the mouth of the Columbia, the desire to obtain their goods, which had been awakened by the early fur traders at Nootka, caused a more active traffic to spring up, the Makahs wishing to get from Chinook the blankets, beads, brass kettles, and other commodities obtained at the trading post at Astoria. The entire supply was drawn from that settlement, until the Hudson's Bay Company established a trading post at Victoria, and, as trade could be conducted so much more readily at that place than at Astoria, the coast traffic was nearly stopped, or confined to the

Makah

summer excursions of those Indians who had intermarried with the Kwinaiults or Chihalis. The coast trade south at present is confined to the exchange of a few canoes for the sea-otter skins of tin. Kwinaiults, but the amount is very small. Their trade with the Vancouver Island Indians is to exchange whale oil and dried halibut, for dog fish oil, which is procured in large quantities by the Nittinat and Clyoquot tribes. The dog-fish oil is sold by the Makahs to the white traders. Formerly it went to those who traded with them at Neeah Bay; but of late years the greater portion is carried either to Victoria, or else to the different lumber mills on the Sound, where it finds a ready sale at prices averaging about fifty cents per gallon. They also trade [32] off considerable quantities of dried halibut and whale oil to the Clallams and the Victoria Indians receiving in return from these Indians blankets, guns, beads, &c, and from the whites either blankets, flour, hard bread, rice, and molasses, or money, which they usually expend before their return, in the purchase of those articles either at Victoria or at the villages on the Sound.

Blankets are the principal item of wealth, and the value of anything is fixed by the number of blankets it is worth. In the early days of the Hudson's Bay Company, and until within the past ten years, a blanket was considered equal in trade to five dollars; but since so many different traders have settled on the Sound, with such a variety of qualities and prices, the Indian in naming the number of blankets he expects to receive (as for a canoe), will state what kind he demands. Thus, if the price is to be twenty blankets, he will say, "how many large blue ones," which are the most costly, "how many red, and how many white ones" and the purchaser must be acquainted with the value of the several kinds before he can tell what the canoe will really cost. Also in their trades among themselves they will pay for a slave, for instance, from one to two hundred blankets, but the number of each quality is always stated. They are very shrewd in their bargains, and from their long intercourse with the white traders are as well informed of the money-value of every commodity they wish to purchase, as most white people are.

I have no trustworthy statistics from which to derive information respecting the amount of their yearly barter; for, as I before remarked, only a portion of their oil is sold to the traders in the bay, the remainder being carried to Victoria, or the saw-mills; nor have I any means of ascertaining the value of the oil and dried fish they trade to other Indians I think, however, I am not far from the truth when I assert that their yearly produce of oil of all kinds will amount, on an average, to five thousand gallons. I have seen it stated in some reports of the Indian Department that the Makahs sold to the whites annually about sixteen thousand gallons of oil. They may possibly have done so in former years, but since my residence among them, I doubt if their sales have ever reached that amount. They, nevertheless, produce more than any other tribe I know of in the Territory, not of oil alone, but of the various products of the ocean; and were they a little more industrious, and more capable of realizing the advantage of taking care of their earnings, they would not only be a self-supporting tribe, completely independent of any assistance from the Government, but might actually become a wealthy community in the sense in which we employ the term. But they are, like all Indians, careless, indolent, and improvident, seeking only to obtain a temporary supply of food, or to get oil enough to purchase a superfluity of blankets, hard bread, rice, and molasses; and then have a big feast and give everything away. By judicious management on the part of the Government and its agents, these Indians might easily be taught to improve their fisheries of all kinds, so as to reap more lucrative returns; but as far as the Makahs are concerned, there are two very serious obstacles which will forever prevent them from being an agricultural people; and these two obstacles are soil and climate.

Makah

I have already shown that the whole of the reservation is a rocky, mountainous, forest-covered region, with no arable land except the low swamp and marsh, extending [33] from Neeah Bay to Wäatch, and a small prairie at Tsuess. And not only are these lands too wet for the cultivation of anything but roots, but the climate is so exceedingly humid that cereals will not ripen. The only sure, repaying crop is potatoes. But Indians cannot live on potatoes alone, any more than the white men; they require animal food, and prefer the products of the ocean to the farina of the land. It will take many years, and cost the Government large sums of money to induce these savages to abandon their old habits of life and acquire new ones. In fact, these Coast Indians are an anomaly in their general style of living, as compared with the tribes of the plains, and as such, I think they should be encouraged in their fisheries, and taught to prepare fish for sale, to make barrels to hold their stock and oil, and helped, by means of the white men's experience, to take more whales and fish than they do now.

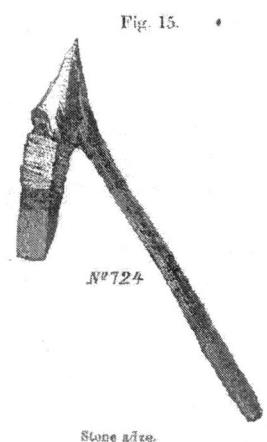

*Fig. 15. Stone adze.

There is one article, and but one that I know of, which I think might be cultivated with profit, and that is the osier willow. If anything will grow in this wet climate, it appears to me it must be this, and, as these people are very expert in making baskets, they could easily be taught to manufacture an article from osiers suitable for our markets, or to prepare the osiers alone for sale to basket-makers. Agricultural labor is very odious to them all; still, a few will work, but they must be paid for everything they do. They are so accustomed to trade with white people and to receive gifts, that they will neither perform labor, however trivial, nor part with the least article of property, without exacting payment. They carried this practice so far as to demand compensation for allowing their children to attend the reservation school. They know the use and value of money, and are generally willing to do anything required of them if they can look for tangible results that will be of advantage to themselves. But they are profoundly indifferent to the benefits of education, and cannot be made to believe that clearing land, making roads, or draining swamps is of any use. When the season for planting arrives they are willing to put a few potatoes into the ground, because their experience has taught them that they can reasonably expect a harvest. But potatoes are esteemed by them rather as a luxury than as ordinary food, and, when they know how easily they can draw their subsistence from the ocean, and how much labor is required to till the earth, they prefer to continue in their old course, and let the white man's agriculture alone.

*Fig. 16. Chisel.

There are other articles of traffic, such as miniature canoes, baskets, mats, berries, &c; but the principal source of wealth is oil and dried fish; the rest is only sold as the chance presents, on the arrival of strangers in the bay, or when they make their excursions up the Strait to the white settlements.

Tools. – The Makahs display considerable ingenuity in the manufacture of the knives, tools, and weapons they use, and are quite expert in forging a piece of iron with no greater heat than that of their ordinary fire, with a large stone for an anvil and a smaller one for a hammer. Their knives, which are employed either as weapons of defence or for cutting blubber or sticks, are made of rasps and files, which they procure at the saw-mills after they have been used in sharpening the mill-saws; or, not uncommonly, they purchase new ones of the traders in Victoria. They are first rudely fashioned with the stone hammer into the required shape, [34] brought to an edge by means of files, and finely sharpened on stones; they are always two-edged, so as to be used as daggers. The handles are of bone riveted, and sometimes ornamented with inserted strips of brass or copper. As they are experienced in the use of heat, they are able to temper these knives very well. The chisels are made of rasps, or of any kind of steel that can be obtained. Some times they take an old axe, and, after excessive labor, succeed in filing it in two, so as to make as it were two narrow axes; these are then heated and forged into the required shape, and handles attached similar to that shown in *Fig. 16. They are not all carved alike, but the mode of fastening the iron to the handle is the same. The instrument for boring holes in the canoes to receive nails or wooden pegs is simply an iron or steel wire flattened at the point and sharpened; this wire or gimlet is inserted into the end of a long stick which serves as a handle; and the manner of using it is to place the point of iron on the spot where a hole is required, and then roll the stick briskly between the palms of the hands.

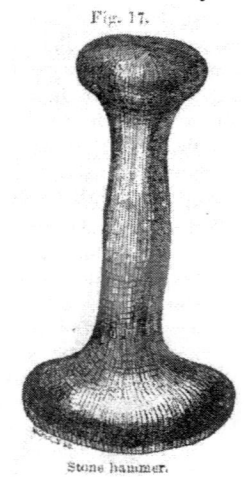

Knives somewhat resembling a round-pointed cobbler's knife are also used, the end being bent into a hook. This tool is used in carving, or for work where a gouge would be required, the workman invariably drawing the knife toward instead of thrusting it from him. All the native tools are made to operate on this principle. Cutting with a knife of any kind, or with a chisel, is done by working toward instead of from the person, and it is only when they get hold of an old plane that they work as white men do. They also make knife-blades from half an inch to two inches long, which are inserted into wooden handles, and used either for whittling or for scarifying their bodies during their medicine or *ta-ma-na-was* performances. Some of them have managed to procure hammers and cold chisels from the various wrecks that have been thrown on the coast from time to time; and the wreck of the steamer *Southerner*, in 1855, about 30 miles south of Cape Flattery, afforded a rich harvest of old iron and copper, as well as engineer's tools, [35]

Fig. 17. Stone Hammer which have been extensively distributed and used among the coast tribes of the vicinity. Those who have been so fortunate as to obtain iron hammers use them in preference to those made of stone; but they generally use a smooth stone like a cobbler's lap-stone for an anvil. The common hammer is simply a paving stone. They, however, make hammers, or, more properly speaking, pestles, with which to drive their wooden wedges in splitting fire wood or making boards. These pestles are shaped like that shown in *Fig. 17. They are made of the hardest jade that can be procured, and are wrought into shape by the slow drudgery of striking them with a smaller fragment, which knocks off a little bit at each blow. Months are consumed in the process, and it is one of their superstitions that from first to last no woman must touch the materials, nor the work be done except at night, when the maker can toil in solitude unnoticed by others. If a woman should handle the pestle, it would break; or if other persons should look on while the work was in progress the stone would split or clip off. The night is preferred, because they imagine the stone is softer then than during the day. Any one can form an idea of the nature of this manufacture and its tedious labor by taking two nodules of flint or a couple of paving stones and attempting to reduce one of them to a required shape by striking them together. Yet these Indians not only fashion their hammers in this manner, but they make very nice jobs, and some that I have seen had quite a smooth surface with a degree of polish. They are valued, according to the hardness of the stone, at from one to three blankets.

A canoe-maker's stock of tools is quite small, consisting only of an axe, a stone hammer, some wooden wedges, a chisel, a knife, and a gimlet. Those who are so fortunate as to possess a saw will use it occasionally; but the common method of cutting off a piece of wood or a board is with the axe or chisel. And yet with these simple and primitive tools they contrive to do all the carpenter work required.

The principal articles manufactured by the Makahs are canoes and whaling implements, conical hats, bark mats, fishing lines, fish-hooks, knives and daggers, bows and arrows, dog's hair blankets, feather capes, and various other articles which will hereafter be named and described. As I before remarked, the largest and best canoes are made by the Clyoquots and Nittinats on Vancouver Island; the cedar there being of a quality greatly superior to that found on or near Cape Flattery. Canoes of the medium and small sizes are made by the Makahs from cedar procured a short distance up the Strait or on the Tsuess River. After the tree is cut down and the bark stripped, the log is cut at the length required for the canoes, and the upper portion removed by splitting it oft with wedges, until the greatest width is attained. The two ends are then rough-hewed [36] to a tapering form and a portion of the inside dug out. The log is next turned over and properly shaped for a bottom, then turned back and more chopped from the inside, until enough has been removed from both inside and out to permit it to be easily handled, when it is slid into the water and taken to the lodge of the maker, where he finishes it at his leisure. In some cases they finish a canoe in the woods, but generally it is brought home as soon as they can haul it to the stream. Before the introduction of iron tools, the making of a canoe was a work of much difficulty. Their hatchets were made of stone, and their chisels of mussel shells ground to a sharp edge by rubbing them on a piece of sandstone. It required much time and extreme labor to cut down a large cedar, and it was only the chiefs who had a number of slaves at their disposal who attempted such large operations. Their method was to gather round a tree as many as could work, and these chipped away with their stone hatchets till the tree was literally gnawed down, after the fashion of beavers. Then to shape it and hollow it out was also a tedious job, and many a month would intervene between the times of commencing to fell the tree, and finishing the canoe. The implements they use at present are axes to do the rough-hewing, and chisels fitted to handles, as shown in Figure 15; these last are used like a cooper's adze, and remove the wood in small chips. The process of finishing is very slow. A white carpenter could smooth off the hull of a canoe with a plane, and do more in two hours than the Indian with his chisel can do in a week. The outside, when it is completed, serves as a guide for finishing the inside, the workman gauging the requisite thickness by placing one hand on the outside and the other on the inside and passing them over the work. He is guided in modelling by the eye, seldom if ever using a measure of any kind; and some are so expert in this that they make lines as true as the most skilful mechanic can. If the tree is not sufficiently thick to give the required width, they spring the top of the sides apart, in the middle of the canoes, by steaming the wood. The inside is filled with water which is heated by means of red hot stones, and a slow fire is made on the outside by rows of bark laid on the ground, a short distance off, but near enough to warm the cedar without burning it. This renders the wood very flexible in a short time, so that the sides can be opened from six to twelve inches. The canoe is now strengthened, and kept in form by sticks or stretchers, similar to a boat's thwarts. The ends of these stretchers are fastened with withes made from tapering cedar limbs, twisted, and used instead of cords, and the water is then emptied out; this process is not often employed, however, the log being usually sufficiently wide in the first instance. As the projections for the head and stern pieces cannot be cut from the log, they are carved from separate pieces and fastened on by means of withes and wooden pegs. A very neat and peculiar scarph is used in joining these pieces to the body of the canoe, and the parts are fitted together in a simple and effectual manner. First the scarph is made on the canoe; this is rubbed over with grease and charcoal; next the piece to be fitted is hewn as nearly like the scarph as the eye can guide, and applied to the part which has the grease on it. It is then removed, and the inequalities being at once discovered and chipped off with the chisel, the process is repeated until the whole of the *scarph* or the piece to be fitted is uniformly marked with the blackened [37] grease. The joints are by this method perfectly matched, and so neat as to be water tight without any calking. The head and stern pieces being fastened on, the whole of the inside is then chipped over again, and the smaller and more indistinct the chisel marks are, the better the workmanship is considered. Until very recently it was the custom to ornament all canoes, except the small ones, with rows of the pearly valve of a species of sea-snail. These shells are procured in large quantities at Nittinat and Clyoquot, and formerly were in great demand as an article of traffic. They are inserted in the inside of the edge of the canoe by driving them into holes bored to receive them. But at present, they are not much used by the Makahs, for the reason, I presume, that they are continually trading off their canoes, and find they bring quite as good a price without these ornaments as with them. I have noticed, however, among some of the Clallams, who are apt to keep a canoe much longer than the Makahs, that the shell ornaments are still used. When the canoe is finished it is painted inside with a mixture of oil and red ochre. Sometimes charcoal and oil are rubbed on the outside, but more commonly it is simply charred by means of long fagots of cedar splints, set on fire at one end like a torch, and held against the side of the canoe. The surface is then rubbed smooth with a wisp of grass or a branch of cedar twigs. When the bottom of the canoe gets foul from long use, it is dried and charred by the same process.

*Fig. 18. Canoe showing method of scarphing.

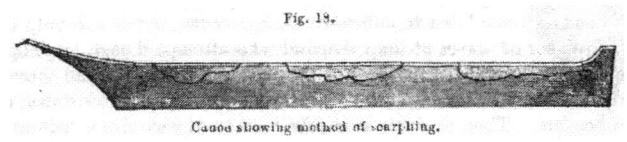

*Fig. 19. Clyoquot paddle.

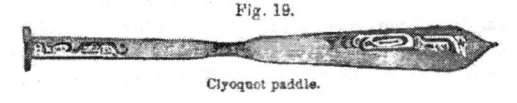

*Fig. 20. Canoe under sail.

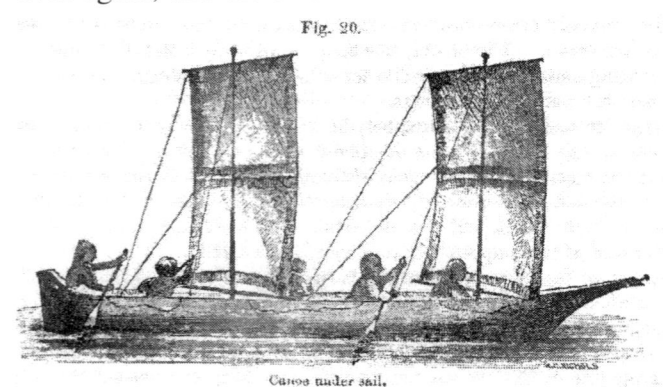

The small canoes sold to the white people as curiosities are made from aider; they vary in size, from two to three feet in length; but they are not good models of the great canoes, the head and stern pieces being too large in proportion to the whole, and generally the breadth is too great. Still they afford an idea of the general form. These miniature boats usually painted in a fanciful style according to the taste of the maker. Some have in them grotesquely carved figures

Makah

resembling men in various attitudes, but these do not really represent anything that may be recognized as a custom peculiar to canoe service. I have seen one with the effigy of a man on horseback standing in it, a sight that of course was never seen. Not only are there no horses at Cape Flattery, but it is quite impossible for a man on horseback to get into, and stand in, one of these canoes. I have seen others with figures of owls, eagles, and bears in them. The Indians assured me they were merely fancy work, and I mention the fact lest any one seeing these rude carvings elsewhere, might be led to suppose that they were seriously designed to represent [38] certain customs of the tribe. Neither the paintings nor carvings on these miniature canoes have any symbolical value or other significance attached to them. All the large canoes, in fact all except the miniature ones, are invariably painted red inside, and charred or painted black outside.

Fig. 24.

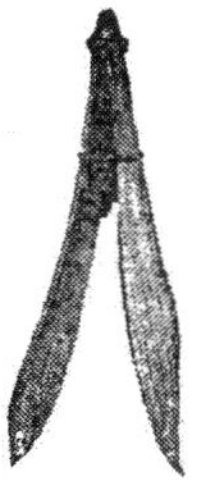

The paddles are made of yew, and are usually procured by barter with the Clyoquot Indians. The blade is broad like an oar blade, and the end rounded in an oval or lanceolate form. The handle is a separate piece fitted transversely with the length of the paddle, and sufficiently long to afford a good hold for the hand. These paddles when new are blackened by slightly charring them in the fire, and then rubbed smooth and slightly polished.

*Fig. 24. fish lure.

The sails were formerly made of mats of cedar bark, which are still used by some of the Clyoquots, although most of the tribes in the vicinity now use cotton. The usual form is square, with sticks at the top and bottom like a vessel's yards; a line passes through a hole in the top of the mast, rigged from the lower stick, and the sail is easily and quickly hoisted or lowered. When taken in it is rolled round the lower yard, and can be enlarged to its full size or reduced to adjust it to the force of the wind. Some Indians have adopted sprit-sails, but they are not in general use, nor are they as safe or convenient for the canoe as the square sail.

In cruising on the Strait they usually keep well in shore, unless they intend to cross to the opposite side; and, if the canoe is large and heavily laden, they always anchor at night, and for this purpose use a large stone tied to a stout line. Some times they moor for the night by tying the canoe to the kelp. When the craft is not heavily burdened it is invariably hauled on the beach whenever the object is to encamp. If the wind is fair, or they have white men on board, they will travel all night, but on their trading excursions they usually encamp, which causes much delay in a journey. I have been seven days in the winter season making the passage between Neeah Bay and Port Townsend, about one hundred miles, and in the summer have made the same trip in but little over twenty-four hours. [39] The average passage, however, is about three days for the distance named, which includes camping two nights.

Fig. 21.

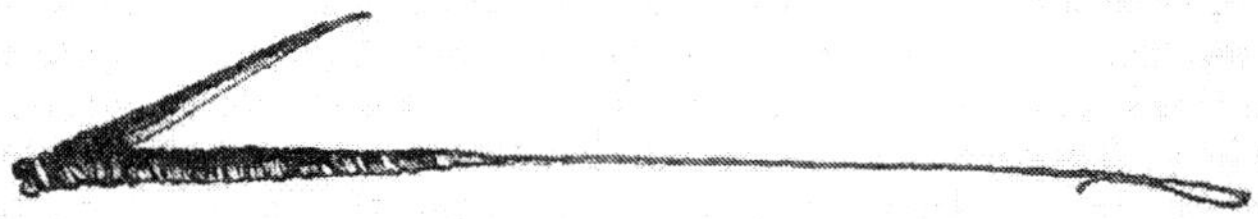

Codfish hook. No. 2629.

*Fig. 21. Codfish hook. No. 2629.

Whaling And Fishing Gear. – This is a most interesting and important portion of the manufacture of the Makahs, and consists of harpoons, ropes, lines, buoys, fish-hooks, spears, &c.

The harpoon has been partly described before. Its head is made of sheet copper or sheet iron, cut as shown in *Fig. 4, a. The barbs are of elk or deer horn, and shaped as shown in *Fig. 4, b. These are fixed on each side of the blade or point, fitted tightly, and kept in place by cords or strips of bark. The whole is then covered with spruce *Fig. 22. Fish club. gum, which is

39

Makah

obtained by setting a fat pitch-knot by the fire, and catching the melted pitch in a shell placed beneath. It is then kneaded till it acquires the consistency of soft cobbler's wax, and is applied and distributed with the fingers. The whole blade and a portion of the barbs are covered with this pitch, which when cool is hard and smooth, and forms a tapering wedge-shaped spear-head. The pitch is then scraped from the edge of the blade, which is ground very sharp. The lanyard attached to the spear-head is made of the sinews of the whale, twisted into a rope and covered with twine. It is made fast to the head by unlaying the strands, fitting them around the barbs, and winding the cord and bark over them while fastening the barbs on. The fisherman is careful to have the lanyard securely fastened to the barbs, for on it depends the hold of the buoy on the whale. The blades, not being so securely fastened, frequently get loose after being imbedded in a whale for a long time, although some that were shown to me have been used for years.

This species of harpoon would scarcely be strong enough to bear the strain of a whale boat towing by it, as is the practice with our whalemen; but as they have only to bear the tension of the buoyancy of the float which is attached to the lanyard, they answer the double purpose of impeding the progress of the whale, so as to enable the Indian to kill it, and also of keeping the body from sinking after it is dead. The staff of the harpoon I have already described.

The method of making ropes and cords from sinews of the whale is as follows: The sinews, after being well dried, are separated into small fibres, and when ready for twisting resemble finely dressed flax. The threads are spun by twisting them between the palm of the hand and the naked thigh, and, as they are twisted, they are rolled up into balls. When unrolled for use they are twisted in the same manner by rolling them on the thigh. The strands are prepared from fine or coarse fibres, as the size of the cord or rope may require. Twine too is made by the process just described; but ropes are first made into strands, and these strands are twisted by hand and laid together with much hard work, which might the use of the most primitive machinery of our rope factories. But the Makahs use nothing but their hands, and, although the work is slow and hard, yet they manufacture as handsome ropes as any of the "hand-laid" articles of the whites.

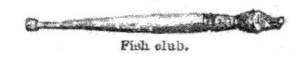

*Fig. 23. Fish club

Ropes of greater size, such as are required for towing whales, are made of the tapering limbs of the cedar, first twisted like withes; and from the long fibrous roots of the spruce. These are first cut in lengths of three or four feet, and then [40] subjected to a process of roasting or steaming in the ashes, which renders them extremely tough and pliable and easy to split. They are reduced to fine strands or threads with knives, and are then twisted and laid in ropes by the same process as that described for making the rope of sinews. Those that are attached to the buoys have one end very neatly the tapered down, as shown in *Fig. 4. This is to enable the whalemen to tie the rope with facility, and to pass it readily through the loop in the end of the harpoon lanyard. In making ropes, it is customary for quite a number of persons assist. They are invited by the man who wishes to get ready his whaling gear, and each prepares a portion of the roots or sinews, so as to have as much as may be required at once. The next operation is to twist the fibres into threads. Another party, perhaps the same individuals, will meet on another day and work till the strands are completed. Then there may be a resting spell, probably because the provisions are exhausted and more must be obtained. The operation is often interrupted, and

Makah

resumed at intervals, consequently much time is consumed in completing the work, a rope of thirty fathoms occupying frequently a whole winter in its manufacture.

Fig. 25. No. 2566.

Fishing lines, as already described, are made of the kelp stem. This is collected by means of two sticks joined like the letter Y. At the bottom a stone is secured as a sinker; five or six inches above the stone a knife-blade is fastened between the two sticks, and a line is then fastened to the upper ends. This instrument is to *Fig. 25. No. 2566. slipped over the bulb of kelp and lowered to the bottom, and a slight pull severs the stem close to the ground. They usually prefer the kelp growing in ten or twelve fathoms of water; most of the stems, however, that they procure rarely exceed ten fathoms in length, and many are not over five. The lower portion of the kelp stem is solid and cylindrical, and about a fourth of an inch in diameter. It retains this size for five or six fathoms, and then increases very gradually to the surface of the water, where it terminates in a globular head from four to six inches in diameter, from which float long streamer-like leaves. For more than half its length the stem is hollow, but this section is not taken for lines. The bulbs are frequently used to hold bait, or as water-bottles for fishermen. When a sufficient number of stems have been cut they are placed in fresh water a running brook being always preferred where they remain for five or six days, or until they become bleached nearly white. They are then partially dried in the smoke, and knotted together at the ends, and further dried in the sun, after being *Fig. 26. stretched to their full length, and to their utmost tension. This process reduces the size to that of a cod-line. They require several days exposure to the sun and air before they are sufficiently cured They are taken in every night while curing, and are coiled up very neatly each time. When perfectly dry they are brittle, and break easily, but, when wet, they are exceedingly strong, fully equal to the best of hemp cod-lines. The usual length is from eighty to one hundred fathoms, although it is seldom that fishing is attempted at that depth, except for the "*be-sho-we*" or black cod; and the probable reason for their being so long is to guard against accidents by which a portion of the line may be lost.

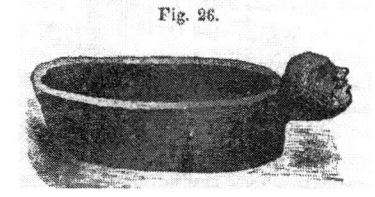

When fishing in shoal water, it is usual to untie a portion of the line at the required depth, and lay the remainder on one side, so as not to endanger its being entangled by the fish that may be caught. [41] Lines for small fish are made from kelp stems of the first year's growth, which are about as large as pipe-stems, with heads perfectly round and of the size of billiard balls. I supposed from the dissimilarity in the appearance of the kelp that it was a different variety, till the Indians assured me that it was all the same, but that it did not attain its full growth the first year. I have had no means of making observations to satisfy myself on this point; but as they make so much use of kelp, and seem to know so much about it, I am inclined to think they must be correct.

*Fig. 28. Wooden bowls and dishes.

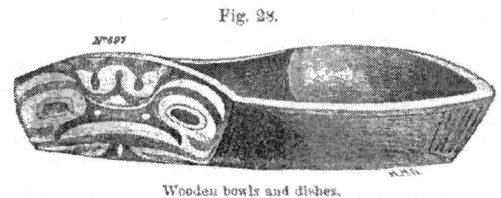

The halibut hook (Fig. 9) is a peculiarly shaped instrument, and is made of splints from hemlock knots bent in a form somewhat resembling an ox bow. These knots remain perfectly

41

sound long after the body of the tree has decayed, and are exceedingly tough. They are selected in preference to those of spruce because there is no pitch in them to offend the fish, which will not bite at a hook that smells of resin. The knots are first split into small pieces, and after being shaped with a knife, are inserted into a hollow piece of the stem of the kelp and roasted or steamed in the hot ashes until they are pliable; they are then bent into the required form, and tied until they are cold, when they retain the shape given them. A barb made of a piece of bone is firmly lashed on the lower side of the hook with slips of spruce cut thin like a ribbon, or with strips of bark of the wild cherry. The upper arm of the hook is slightly curved outward, and wound around with bark to keep it from splitting. A thread made of whale sinews is usually fastened to the hook for the purpose of tying on the bait, and another of the same material loosely twisted, serves to fasten the hook to the kelp line. As the halibut's *Fig. 27. No. 1137. Wooden trencher. mouth is vertical, instead of horizontal like that of most other fish, it readily takes the hook, the upper portion of which passes outside and over the corner of the mouth, and acts as a sort of spring to fasten the barb into the fish's jaw. The Indians prefer this kind of hook for halibut fishing, although they can readily procure metal ones from the white traders. Smaller hooks for codfish are made of a single straight piece of wood from four to six inches long, with a bone barb lashed on in a manner similar to the barb of the halibut hook.

For very small fish, like perch or rock fish, they simply fasten a small piece of bone to a line of sinews. The bone is made sharp as a needle at both ends, and is tied in the middle. Many of the old men will not use any other than native madehooks and lines; while a few are very glad to obtain fish hooks and lines from the whites, tn every canoe is a club for killing fish, which is usually nothing more than a billet of wood roughly fashioned, though sometimes rudely carved, as seen in [42] *Figs. 22, 23. This club is about a foot long, and is commonly made of yew, and its use is to stun the fish by striking it on the head before the hook is removed from the mouth. Another instrument used in fishing is called the *kak-te-wahd-de* (Fig 24).

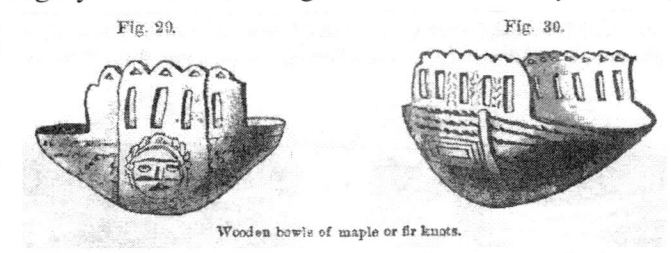

This is formed of two slender   *Fig. 29. *Fig. 30. Wooden bowls of maple or fir knots. slips of cedar something in the shape of feathers. What would be the quill part is fastened to a bit of wood with a stone in it, to keep instrument in an upright position. It is used for attracting fish when they do not bite readily. The Indian takes his fishing spear, thrusts the *kak-te-wahd-de* to the bottom, and when he releases it, its buoyancy brings it to the surface, while the wooden blades or feathers create a rotary or gyratory motion which attracts the fish.

Boxes, Mats, &c. – Vessels for carrying water, and large boxes for containing blankets or clothing, are made in the following manner: a board as wide as the box is intended to be high, is carefully smoothed with a chisel, then marked off into four divisions, and at each of the marks cut nearly in two. The wood is then wet with warm water, and gently bent around until the corners are fully formed. Thus three corners of the box are made, and the remaining one formed by the meeting of the two ends of the board, is fastened by wooden pegs. The bottom is then tightly fitted in by pins, and the box is made. The water box or bucketconsists of one of these, and the chest is simply two large boxes, one shutting down over the other. These boxes are manufactured principally by the Clyoquot Indians, very few being made by the Makahs, on account of the scarcity of good cedar. They procure these by barter, and every lodge has a greater or less number of them according to the wealth of the occupants. Many have trunks purchased from the whites, either of Chinese or American manufacture, but although they can readily supply themselves at cheap rates with these as well as bowls with water pails, they prefer those used by their ancestors. Wooden bowls and dishes are usually manufactured from alder (Figs. 25 to 28). Some are of an oblong [43] shape and used as chopping trays (Figs. 27 and 28). The wood of the alder, when freshly cut, is soft and white and easily worked, but a short exposure to the air hardens and turns it to a red color. The bark chewed and spit into a dish forms a bright red dye pigment of a permanent color, which is used for dyeing cedar bark or grass. I have tried to extract this color by other means, but find that no process produces so good a dye as chewing. Alcohol gives an orange color, and boiling water, dark brown or black. I think, however, if it were macerated or ground in warm water, with, perhaps, the addition of certain salts, a very useful dye might be obtained.

Bowls are sometimes made of knots taken from decayed logs of maple or fir, as represented in *Figs. 29 and 30.

Feather and Dog's-Hair Blankets. – Blankets are not only made of feathers, or rather down, and of dog's hair, but also of cedar bark. The method of manufacturing the first named is to select a bird that has plenty of down, and, first picking out all the feathers carefully, to skin it, and then dry the skin with the down on. When a sufficient number have been prepared they are slightly moistened, [44] then cut into narrow strips, each one of which is twisted around a thread, leaving the down outside, which thus forms a round cord of down resembling a lady's fur boa. This is woven with twine and forms a compact, light, and very warm blanket. The hair blankets are made from the woolly covering of a species of dog of a yellowish-white color, which, after having been sheared off, is packed away with dry pulverized pipe clay, for the purpose of extracting the oil or grease. When a sufficient quantity has been obtained, and has remained long enough in the pipe clay, it is carefully picked over by hand, and beaten with a stick to knock out the dirt. It is then twisted on strong threads, and finally woven into a thick, strong, and heavy blanket. The pipe clay[5] is procured at Kwilleyute. The weaving process does not clean out all this substance, since its presence can be readily noticed at any time by shaking or beating the blanket. Bark blankets and capes are made from the inner bark of the cedar, dried and beaten into a fine mass of fibres, which are then spun into threads, and woven into the required forms, the edges of which are trimmed with fur. Very nice ones are also made by the Clyoquot Indians from the inner bark of the white pine, which is whiter and softer than cedar bark.

---

[5] Diatomaccous earth. GG

Makah

Gambling Implements. – Of these one form consists of disks made from the wood of a hazel which grows at Cape Flattery and vicinity. The shrub is from ten to fifteen feet high, and with limbs from two to three inches in diameter. The name in Makah is *hul-li-a-ko-bupt*, the disks *hul-liak*, and the game *la-hul-lum*. The game is common among all the Indians of this territory, and is called in the jargon *la-hull*. The disks are circular like checkers, about two inches in diameter, and the fourth of an inch thick; and are usually smoothed off and polished with care. They are first cut off transversely from the end of a stick which has been selected and properly prepared, then smoothed and polished, and marked on the outer edge with the color that designates their value. They are used in sets of ten, one of which is entirely black on the outer edge, another entirely white, and the rest of all degrees from black to white. Two persons play at the game, each having a mat before him, with the end next his opponent slightly raised, so that the disks cannot roll out of reach. Each player has ten disks which he covers with a quantity of the finely-beaten bark, and then separates the heap into two equal parts, shifting them rapidly on the mat from hand to hand. The opposing player guesses which heap contains the white or black, and on making his selection the disks are rolled down the mat, when each piece is separately seen. If he has guessed right, he wins; if not, he loses. Another game consists in passing a stick rapidly from hand to hand, and the object is to guess in which hand it may be. A third game, played by females, is with marked beaver teeth, which are thrown like dice. Four teeth are used; one side of each has marks, and the other is plain. If all four marked sides come up, or all four plain sides, the throw forms a double; if two marked and two plain ones come up, it is a single; uneven numbers lose. Both males and females are passionately fond of these games, and continue them for days, or until one or the other loses all that can be staked. [45]

Mats, Baskets, Ornaments, &c. – Mats constitute one of the principal manufactures of the females during the winter months. With the Makahs, cedar bark is the only material used. Other tribes, who can obtain bulrushes and flags, make their mats of these plants, which, however, do not grow in the vicinity of Cape Flattery. Cedar bark, which constitutes an important item in their domestic economy, is prepared by first removing the outer bark from young trees, then peeling the inner bark off in long strips, which are dried in the sun, folded in a compact form, and used as articles of trade or barter. When wanted for use, if for making mats, the strips are split into strands varying from an eighth to a quarter of an inch in width, and as thick as stout wrapping-paper. These are then neatly woven together, so as to form a mat six feet long by three wide. Formerly mats were used as canoe sails, but at present they are employed for wrapping up blankets, for protecting the cargoes in canoes, and for sale to the whites, who use them as lining of rooms, or as floor coverings. Baskets for various uses are also made of this bark; but, as it is not very strong, those used for carrying burdens are made from spruce roots.

The bark is reduced to fine fibres by being broken across the edge of a paddle, and, when perfectly prepared in this way, is put to a variety of uses. It serves to make the beds of infants, for gun-wadding, as a substitute for towels,

Fig. 31. conical hat. and for gambling in the game of la-hull. It is often dyed red with alder bark, and worn like a turban around the head during tamanawas performances. In the mat manufacture some is dyed black by soaking it in mud, and woven in as a sort of ornament around the edge, or as the dividing line across the centre. The Kwilleyute tribe manufacture very neat

44

Makah

mats of a species of coarse grass, and excellent baskets from ash, which grows upon the banks of the river. These are common among the Makahs, being received in the way of trade.

Conical-shaped hats are made of spruce roots split into fine fibres, and plaited so as to be impervious to water. They are very ingeniously manufactured, and it requires some skill and experience to make one nicely. These hats are painted with rude devices on the outside, the colors being a black ground with red figures. The black is produced by grinding a piece of bituminous coal with salmon eggs, which have been chewed and spit on a, stone; the red, by a mixture of vermilion and chewed salmon eggs. These eggs, after having been first dried, form a glutinous substance when chewed, which easily mixes with the colors, and forms a paint that dries readily and is very durable. The designs are drawn with brushes made of sticks, with the ends chewed. Some Indians, however, use brushes or pencils of human hair a for these designs as well as those on the miniature canoes; but the most common brush is simply stick. The process, with these rude implements, is very slow.

Beside the conical hats worn by themselves, they have also, of late years, manufactured hats which they sell to the white men. These are shaped like the common straw hat, and are made of spruce roots, and, although rather heavy, are strong and durable. Some have designs of various kinds woven in them, while others [46] are plain, the color being of a buff, somewhat resembling the Mexican wool hats. This color cannot be removed by bleaching, attempts for this purpose having been made in San Francisco and Victoria; but the experiment proved a failure. The color, however, is no objection, and is indeed rather preferred; the hats being more generally purchased as curiosities than as articles for wear. Within a few years past they have taken a fancy to cover with basket-work any bottles or vials they can obtain, and, as they do this sort of work very well, they find "ready sale for it among the seekers after Indian curiosities.

During rainy weather they make use of capes worn over the shoulders while in the canoes. These are woven whole, with a single opening in the centre for the head to pass through, something like a poncho. They come down from the neck to the elbow, and are usually trimmed with fur around the edges. Some are woven from cedar bark, and others from strips of cloth or old blankets. They are warm, and impervious to water, and when an Indian has on one of these and his conical hat, his head and shoulders are well protected from wet. The rest of his body he seems to care little about, and he paddles round in his canoe with bare legs and arms, seemingly as indifferent to the rain or the water as a seal or an otter.

The baskets made by the Makahs are classed according to the material of which they are formed, and the uses to which they are put. The large ones, made of bark, which are used for holding dried fish, or blankets, are called *klap-pairk*. Carrying-baskets, worn on the back, with a strap around the fore head, are made of spruce roots or cedar twigs. They are woven quite open, and much larger at the top than at the bottom, the form tapering down in something of a wedge-shape. This enables them to carry loads with greater ease, as the weight is kept well up on the shoulders. These baskets are called *bo-he-vi*. Small baskets are made of bark and grass, dyed of various colors. Some are woven with designs intended to represent birds or animals; others in simple checks of various patterns. Other small ones are of bark, and a species of eel grass that bleaches of a beautiful white. These small baskets are called *pe-ko*. The various colors are produced thus: black, by immersing the material in the salt-water mud, where it remains several weeks, usually during the summer months; a place being selected where the mud is rich with marine alga?, and emits a fetid smell, the sulphuretted hydrogen undoubtedly being the agent that imparts the color to the vegetable fibres of the bark or grass; red is procured from the alder bark by the process already described; yellow from the bark of the root of the Oregon grape (Berberis), which is boiled, and the grass immersed in it. Bark is not dyed yellow, that color only being imparted to beach grass, which is used for weaving into baskets, and around the edges of some kinds of mats as an ornament. Grass in its natural state, by contrast with the other colors, appears white; but a pure white is obtained from the eel grass, or sea weed, which is procured in the bay, and bleached in the sun. [47]

*Fig 32. Bark basket.

Their ornaments consist mainly of the head and ear decorations worn by young girls, and of pieces of variegated shell inserted in their noses and ears. The first are made of the Dentalium, which is procured by barter with the Nootkan and other Indians of Vancouver Island. The shape of these ornaments is shown in *Fig. 3, the shells being run on strings separated by pieces of leather, and so arranged as to form a fillet to surround the head. The shells, in the ear ornaments, generally have their tapering or small end up. These last are usually finished off with a quantity of glass beads of various sizes, shapes, and colors. They are not, however, attached to the head ornament, as shown in the drawing, unless they are very heavy; but usually tied to the ear, which is pierced all round the edge with holes, into which the strings are inserted. When the ornaments are laid aside, these holes in the ear usually have a piece of twine tied in them, and sometimes brass buttons are attached to the twine. This head ornament is very pretty, and when a squaw is in full dress she has quite a picturesque appearance. The shell ornaments for the nose are made of the Haliotis, which is procured on Vancouver Island. The largest specimens I have seen came from the Cowitchan district, on the eastern side; smaller ones are found at Clyoquot and Nootka. The pieces worn in the nose are of various shapes, circular, oval, or triangular, and hang pendent by means of a string; others are cut in the form of rings, with a small opening on one side, so they can be inserted or removed at pleasure; the size varies from a dime to a quarter of a dollar. Some of the ear ornaments, however, and particularly those worn by children, are much larger not unfrequently two inches square. These are fastened to the rim of the ear by strings; they are not very attractive ornaments, as they serve to give the wearer a very savage appearance. Bracelets are made of brass wire, bent to the form of the wrist; some are rudely ornamented by notches filed in them, but most of them are plain. Finger rings are manufactured out of silver coin by first beating it flat, and then cutting it into strips, which are bent into a circular form and smoothed. The ends are not joined together, probably from the fact that they do not understand the art of brazing; although among the Haida and Chimsyan tribes the art of working in precious metals has attained a considerable degree of perfection.

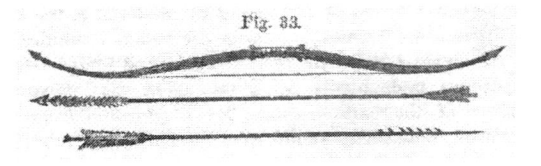

*Fig. 33. Bow & Arrow.

Bows and Arrows, Fish, and Bird-Spears. The bow is usually made from yew, and bent in the form shown in *Fig. 33; but many are straight, simply acquiring a curved form when bent for use. Those that are made with care have usually a lock of hair fastened to the middle by means of a strip of bark wound around it. The string is made of whale sinews or seal gut, and is very strong. Inferior bows are made of a species of dog-wood which grows around Neeah Bay. This wood is white and tough, and also makes excellent hoops for barrels. The bow is used [48] principally by the boys, who are not very dexterous in its use, but manage to kill birds and other small game; as a weapon of defence it is scarcely ever used, fire arms entirely superseding it, most, if not all, of the men having guns. The arrows are made of cedar split into the required size and finished with a knife. It is usual when making arrows to be seated holding one end of the stick with the toes of the left foot, and the other end in the left hand, and to use the knife by drawing it towards the person. The arrow-heads are of various patterns; some are made of a piece of iron wire, which is usually obtained from the rim of some old tin pan or kettle; this is flattened at the point, sharpened, and a barb filed on one side, and driven into the end of the shaft; a strip of bark is wound around it to keep the wood from splitting. Some are made of bone with jagged edges, like barbs; others of two pieces of wood or bone so attached as to form a very acute angle to the shaft; others again are regularly shaped, double-barbed, and with triangular heads of iron or copper, of very neat workmanship. All the arrows are winged or tipped with feathers to give them a steady flight through the air. They are all buoyant, so as to be readily recovered after having been shot at waterfowl, for the aim while shooting from a canoe can no more be relied on than in throwing a stone. Frequently five or six arrows will be shot at a duck before it is hit, and they will often miss it altogether.

Fig. 34.

Bird spear.

The bird spears are made of three or four prongs of different lengths, jagged, and barbed, and fastened to a pole or staff ten or twelve feet long, with a place at the upper end for the hand to press against. This spear is used at night, when the natives go in a canoe with fire to attract the birds. The prongs are made either of wood or bone. Fish spears have longer poles, and barbs of iron or bone, and are used for spearing fish, echini {sea urchins}, and crabs. The manufacture of implements is practised by all; some, however, producing neater articles, are more employed in this way. The manufacture of whaling implements, particularly the staff of the harpoon and the harpoon head, is confined to individuals who dispose of them to the others. This is also the case with rope making; although all understand the process, some are peculiarly expert, and generally do the most of the work. Canoe making is another branch that is confined to certain persons who have more skill than others in forming the model and in finishing the work. Although they do not seem to have regular trades in these manufactures, yet the most expert principally confine themselves to certain branches. Some are quite skilful in working iron and copper, others in carving, or in painting; while others, again, are more expert in catching fish or killing whales.

*Fig 34 Bird spear.

Although clay is found at Neeah Bay, the Indians do not know how to manufacture earthen or pottery ware. Their ancient utensils for boiling were simply wooden troughs, and the method of cooking in them being by hot stones, with which they could boil or steam whatever they desired to prepare. These troughs are used by many at the present day, and are preferred for cooking fish and potatoes to boiling in kettles; particularly on occasions of feasting, where a large quantity of [49] food is to be prepared; but for ordinary purposes pots and kettles are used. Iron pots and brass kettles, with a goodly display of tin pans, are to be found in every lodge, all of which are purchased from the white traders.[6]

---

[6] Arrow and spear-heads of stone seem not to have been used by the tribes in this part of the coast. Basket work and wood take the place of pottery, the manufacture of which article, however, again prevails among some of the tribes of Alaska. – GG

Songs. – The songs of the Makahs are in great variety, and vary from that of the mother lulling her infant to sleep, to barbarous war cries and horribly discordant "medicine" refrains. Some of the tunes are sung in chorus, and many of the airs of the children do not sound badly when heard in the distance. They are good imitators, and readily learn the songs of the white men, particularly the popular negro melodies. Some of their best tunes are a mixture of our popular airs with notes of their own, and of these they sing several bars, and while one is expecting to hear them finish as they began, they will suddenly change into a barbarous discord. Their songs at ceremonials consist of a recitative and chorus, in which it would be difficult for any one to represent in musical characters the wild, savage sounds to which they gave utterance.

Some of the tribes sing the songs that have been composed by other tribes, and as they cannot always pronounce the words accurately, a person is liable to be misled as to the meaning. I was present, with several other white persons, at the opening ceremonies of the Clallams, at Port Townsend, a few years since. The chorus was a repetition of the words (as we all understood them) "*a new-kushu ah yah yah.*" *Kushu* in the jargon means hog, and we supposed they were referring to that animal. The words, however, which they did pronounce were "*wah-noo-koo-choo ah yah yah*," but they said they did not know their meaning, they were "*tamanawas.*" I subsequently ascertained that the song originated with the Clyoquots, and by them it is pronounced "*wa-na-ka-chee-ah ya yah*," and signifies a disposition to break things, or to kill their friends; and is in evidence of a bold and fearless spirit. Sometimes the young men assemble in the evening and sing some simple air in chorus, the words being generally improvised. They keep time with a drum or tambourine, which is simply a skin stretched tightly on a hoop. These songs sound very well, and are melodious when compared to some of their other chants. Many, both males and females, have good voices, and could be taught to sing, but their own native songs have nothing to recommend them to civilized ears. The words used are very few, seldom extending beyond those of a single sentence, and generally not more than one or two, which are repeated and sung by the hour. Sometimes they take the name of an individual, and repeat this over and over. A single instance will suffice as an illustration: There was a young Nittinat Indian, by the name of Bah-die, who was quite a favorite with the Makah boys. Some prank that he played caused his name to be frequently mentioned, and finally some one sang it to a tune with a rousing chorus. All the words used were "*ah Bah-die,*" and this would be roared through all the changes in the gamut. This was a popular and favorite tune till *Bah-die* died, and then it was dropped, as they would not mention his name after he was dead. [50]

Method of Warfare. – The causes of feuds and hostilities between the coast tribes are usually of a trivial nature, generally originating in a theft, either of canoes, slaves, or blankets, or sometimes a dispute about a barter; but as these difficulties, no matter how they originate, are never confined to the principals, but are taken up by friends and relatives on both sides, reprisals are made on any one who may chance to fall in the way. For instance, a Makah visiting a neighboring tribe may perhaps steal something. He will not be pursued and the property taken away, but an opportunity will be embraced at some other time to steal from any Makah who may visit the same tribe. He in return may possibly kill some one, and then the whole tribe is held responsible. Sometimes several years may intervene between the commission of the first offence and the breaking out of hostilities; but every offence is remembered, and if not settled in an amicable manner,

Makah

is avenged sooner or later. Since I have been among the Makahs, I have known but one war expedition, and a description of that will illustrate their general system of warfare.

An Indian belonging to the Makah tribe had a difficulty with an Elwha Indian belonging to a band of Clallams, who reside at the mouth of the Elwha River, emptying into the Strait of Fuca, near Port Angeles. The difficulty was about a squaw, and the ill-feeling had lasted for a year or two when the Elwha waylaid the Makah, and shot him. As the murdered man was a chief, the whole tribe were determined to avenge the murder; but first they referred the affair to the agents of the Indian Department, who promised that the murderer should be arrested and hung; nothing, however, was done about it, and at last the tribe, getting tired of waiting the action of the white men, concluded to settle the affair in their own way. After several meetings had been held, and the matter decided upon, they prepared themselves for war. The plan of approach to the Elwha village was first drawn on the sand, and the method of attack decided on. They then prepared great torches of dried pitch-wood made into fagots, and tied on the ends of poles. These were to set the houses of the Elwhas on fire. Knives were also sharpened, bows and arrows prepared, bullets cast, and guns cleaned. The largest canoes were put in war trim to convey the party, were blackened by burning fagots of cedar splints passed along under the bottom, freshly painted red in the inside, and decorated with branches of spruce limbs tied to the head and stern. There were twelve of these canoes, containing in all about eighty men, dressed with their blankets girt tight about the waist, in such a manner as to leave both arms free. Their faces were painted black, and their hair tied up in a club-knot behind, and bound round with sprigs of evergreen. They assembled on the beach previous to starting, where speeches were made and war dances performed; they then embarked precipitately and set off at the full speed of their boats up the Strait for Elwha village. As soon as they had gone, the women and children assembled on the roofs of the lodges and commenced a dismal chant, which they continued for a couple of hours, accompanying their music with beating the roof boards with sticks to mark the time. Each day, during the absence of the men, the women went through this perform ance at sunrise and sunset. On the third day the party returned, bringing with them the heads of two Elwhas they had killed. They came with songs of victory, [51] with shouts, and firing volleys of musketry. When they had landed on the beach, they formed a circle, and having placed the two heads on the sand in the centre, they danced and howled around them like fiends. Speeches were then made, another volley fired, and the heads taken from village to village, at each of which the same scenes were repeated, until they finally arrived at Tsuess, the residence of the chief of the expedition, where they were stuck on two poles, and remained several months, presenting a weather-beaten and very ghastly appearance. From the parade the Indians made on starting, and after their return, one would be led to suppose that they had boldly attacked their enemies and burned their village; but such was not the fact. They crept along the coast, and after they had reached a point a few miles from Elwha, they hid themselves and sent a canoe to reconnoitre. This party discovered a couple of Elwhas fishing, and getting between them and the shore, killed them, cut off their heads, and returned to the main body, who, con sidering the murder of the chief fully avenged, returned without making any further demonstrations. Formerly, however, these battles were very sanguinary, numbers being killed on both sides and prisoners taken, who were invariably made slaves; but of late years they have confined themselves to occasional murders only, fearing lest any more extensive warfare would call down upon them the vengeance of the whites. They do not appear to have practised scalping, their custom being to cut off the heads of their enemies, which they bring home as trophies.

Since the system of reservations has been established, with officials residing upon them, there have been no attempts made by the Makahs to go. on these war parties; but they refer all their grievances instead to their agent; they have, however, been threatened with an attack from some of the Vancouver Island Indians, and during the time the apprehension lasted they put themselves in a state of defence by erecting stockades of poles and brush about their houses, which they pierced with loop holes, and by keeping a constant watch night and day. Formerly they had stockade forts at Tatoosh Island, and on one of the rocky islets composing Flattery Rocks, where on an attack by their enemies, or during any alarm, they retired as to strong holds, in which they could easily defend themselves. These forts have been done away with for several years, and the only one that I know of at present, between the Columbia River and Cape Flattery, is at Kwilleyute. A precipitous rock, several hundred feet high, situated at the mouth of that river, is still fortified, and to all Indian attack is perfectly impregnable. I visited this rock a few years since, and found it several acres in extent on the surface, and with quite a growth of large spruce trees upon it, which are used both for firewood and for defence. There is but one path by which the summit can be gained, and to defend this they roll great logs to the brink of the descent, whence they can be easily thrown down on any force attacking them. As the approach is steep and slippery, nothing could prevent a log from sweeping down as many as might be in its path. The only way they could be subdued would be by siege and starvation; but that species of warfare does not seem to be practised among the coast tribes, their plan being to go in a body in their canoes, surprise their enemies, and return as soon as possible whether successful or not.

It has been customary to kill the men who fall into their hands, and to make [52] slaves of the women and children; but very few if any slaves have been gained by the Makahs in this manner for several years past; all they have acquired being by purchase. They never bury their enemies slain in battle, as they have a superstition that the bodies would come to life again, and attack them; so they leave them exposed to the wolves; but the heads are stuck on poles, in order to be readily seen at all times. Thus, if the enemy should recover the bodies of his slain, and bury them, it would not matter so long as the heads were drying in the air. The two heads of the Elwhas that I have mentioned had remained on poles for several months, when the relatives requested permission to purchase them of the old chief who had them in charge, and offered ten blankets apiece; but the old savage refused the offer with the greatest disgust, and being fearful that I might possibly get hold of them for specimens, he hid them away in the woods, and I saw them no more. This chief, whose name was *Kobetsi*, or *Kabatsat*, was a powerful man, possessed of great strength and personal bravery. He was celebrated for his prowess in killing whales, and that, together with his being an hereditary chief, had given him the pre-eminence on all war parties. The other chief who headed the expedition was also a celebrated whale-killer named *Haahtse*, or *Sowsom*.

Government. – Formerly the tribe had chiefs and head men whose word was law. The strongest man, who had the most friends or relatives, was the head chief, but of late years there has been no head. In every village there are several who claim a descent from chiefs of note, and call themselves chiefs ana owners of the land, but their claims are seldom recognized, excepting that they are considered as belonging to the aristocracy, and are superior to the *mis-che-mas* or common people, or the *kōt-hlo* or slaves. They are listened to in counsel, and always invited to feasts; are sure of a share of all presents, and of their proportion of any whales that are killed; but no one takes precedence of the rest, although many, if not all, would be very glad to be considered as the head chief provided the rest would consent. The eldest son of a chief succeeds to the title and property of the father, and in case of several children, of whom only one is a boy, he takes the property whether he is the eldest or youngest child. In case of a chief who died leaving one child, a son, the widow took for a second husband the brother of the one who died. By the last one she had a girl, and the father told me that his property too would descend to his brother's son, and not to the girl who was his own and only child. In the event of his having a son, the bulk of the property would still go to the nephew, whom he considered as his eldest son. The dignity of chief or head man can be attained by any one who possesses personal prowess, and who may be fortunate enough to accumulate property. An instance of this kind is in the case of Sekówt'hl, the head chief of the tribe, who was appointed such by Governor Stevens at the time of making the treaty. Sekówt'hl's mother was a slave, and his father a common person, but he was very brave and very successful in killing whales, and having accumulated much wealth in blankets, canoes, and slaves, was enabled to marry the daughter of a chief, by whom he had a son, who is also celebrated for his strength and bravery, and his success in the whale fishery, and is now considered as one of the principal chiefs of the village at Flattery Rocks, where both father and son reside. [53]

In the government of the tribe at present, all matters of importance are submitted to a council, which is held whenever any one gives a feast, or during the time of the ceremonials of the *tamanawas*. The old men on these occasions generally do all the talking, although women are permitted to speak on matters where they are concerned. I have known of but two or three instances where they have inflicted punishment, and on those occasions their mode was a pretty rough one. The first case was that of a man who was noted for his quarrelsome disposition; always in trouble, and always finding fault. Having become offended with his squaw, he turned her off and took another, a practice which is very common, both men and women leaving their partners on the most trivial occasions. Some time afterward the squaw got another husband, at which the first one was very indignant; and after much wordy warfare finally stabbed the new husband in the back. This was considered a gross outrage by the rest of the tribe; not the stabbing, but doing it without sufficient cause. The head men deliberated, and at last gathering together a band of friends, they proceeded to the village where the culprit resided, and after first securing him, they pulled out his hair and scarified the top of his head. The women finished the scene by pouring salt water on him, and rubbing his head with sand. One of the performers in this strange mode of punishment told me that the man felt very much ashamed, and would probably hereafter be more civil in his speech, and try and improve his fractious temper, a result very likely to be attained, as they promised upon a repetition of any more acts of violence to treat him to another and a severer dose. I have observed that he has been remarkably quiet in his deportment ever since. The other instances were for offences committed during the tamanawas ceremonies, and the punishment consisted in having sharp skewers of bone thrust through the fleshy part of the arms between the elbows and shoulders. After they had thus remained a short time, they were pulled out, and stuck in the bark head band, where they were obliged to be worn during the remainder of the ceremonies. In some instances they close the mouth by thrusting these skewers through the lips. This punishment is inflicted on those who laugh at or ridicule the ceremonials. In cases of theft, adultery, or murder, an opportunity is always offered to compromise the affair by restitution of the stolen property; and by the payment of a certain amount of blankets, guns, or canoes for the other offences; the amount of such payment being decided by the friends of the plaintiff in the case. If no such compromise is made, the aggrieved party will take his revenge either on the person who has committed the offence, or on any of his relatives; this revenge will be satisfied by breaking up a valuable canoe, taking forcible possession of any blankets or guns that may be had; or, if the offence consists in murder, by shooting or stabbing the offender or his nearest relative.

With the exceptions I have already noticed, there have been no instances, during my residence, of the tribe, or a number of them, being concerned in the punishment of offenders. All other cases that have come under my observation have been settled by individuals after their own fashion. In one instance a sort of bloodless duel was fought between two men, one of whom had stolen the other one's ~~squaw~~ wife. They were both slaves, and had the will to kill each other with knives, but the [54] presence of the white men prevented resort to such extreme measures, and they were obliged to content themselves with seizing each other by the hair, and scuffling for a fall. After they had pulled one another about till they were tired, the victor, who in this instance was the man to whom the squaw really belonged, was considered entitled to her by the voice of the collected crowd. The affair was then considered satisfactorily settled. Others have been more serious. One young chief who had a grudge of long standing against another of equal rank, satisfied himself by shooting a brother of his adversary with a pistol, inflicting a serious though not a mortal wound. This affair, which caused much excitement, was finally compromised by the payment of certain articles. A common and favorite means of revenge consists in defacing or destroying canoes, and in other wanton acts of malice which would disgrace school boys; but as a general thing they have very few quarrels among themselves, compared with the breaches of the peace which so frequently occur in white settlements containing an equal number of individuals. This fact can be attributed to their freedom from the use of in toxicating liquor, which has been .entirely prohibited on the reservation by the exertions of the agent. When, in former times, they had access to liquor, they were quite as quarrelsome as any other savages. Whenever, a slave commits an offence, the owner administers punishment according to his own fancy, without consulting with others, or being held responsible for his acts. Two instances came within my knowledge where the slaves were killed. In one of these a slave went to Kwilleyute and murdered a man and woman, and on his return home was shot by his master. Peace was thus preserved between the two tribes, the murderer being rightly punished. In the other, a woman used abusive language toward her master, which he bore for a long time, till, finally, becoming exa perated, he struck her a blow on the head with a club, which stunned, but did not quite kill her. She remained in that state all night, and tpward morning partially recovered; but the owner's wrath was not appeased, and he killed her with his knife. No notice was taken of this affair by the tribe. The owner, however, for this and several other crimes, was taken to Fort Steilacoom, and imprisoned for several months by order of the Indian agent. The Indians say, that formerly when slaves were more numerous, and more easily obtained, they were oftener punished. Instances are related in which an offender has been bound hand and foot, placed in a canoe and set adrift, while a strong east wind was blowing, which would carry him out to sea, and insure a miserable death by starvation. Others have been hung, and others tortured; but they are getting more moderate of late years, and extreme measures are seldom resorted to. The presence of white men has exerted a salutary influence in this respect, and the fear of being held responsible renders them more gentle in their deportment to their slaves.

The authority of the chief is respected relative to anything cast ashore by the tide, whether drift lumber, dead whales, or wrecks. Formerly, when each village contained but one head chief, he claimed and owned all the land between certain points, and everything cast ashore became his by right of seigniorage, and of this he could make distribution among his friends as he saw fit. The chief, for instance, who owned the land around Neeah Bay, was named Deeaht or Deeah, [55] who, with his brother Obiee, claimed all the shore to the Hoko River, a distance of about eight miles. Deeaht died without issue, and his brother Obiee or Odiee succeeded to his property, and his descendants still claim this right of seigniorage. The same custom prevails not only in all the villages of this tribe, but with every tribe on the coast; arid as it is the custom, and agreed to by all, there is no dispute relative to any property acquired by jetsam. This right is not insisted on at present, except when a whale is cast ashore, or in case of wrecked property. Drift lumber, particularly mill logs, are so frequently brought down the straits, and cast ashore about the Cape, that any one who finds them has only to cut a notch in them with his axe, and his right is respected. The chief who receives any wrecked property invariably pays the finder something, or makes him a present of some kind. The chiefs also claimed the right to make prisoners of all who were cast ashore by shipwreck, whether Indians or white men; and, unless they could ransom themselves, they were detained as slaves. Hence we can readily account for, the avidity with which they possessed themselves of the persons and property of shipwrecked mariners who have from time to time been cast upon their shores. They looked upon everything thrown up by the waves as theirs, and it is but very recently that they have been led to respect the rights of white men, and to account to their agent for any wrecked materials coming into their possession. They still demand payment for anything they save, and, on the principle of salvage, such demands are just; but these claims are now arbitrated by the agent, instead of being left to the savages, as has always been the case heretofore.

History, Traditions, etc. – The history of this tribe, as far as their knowledge extends, is a confused mass of fables, legends, myths, and allegories. Nothing that they can state prior to the existence of a few generations back is clear or wholly to be relied upon. There are a few prominent events that have been remembered as having occurred; but the detail is confused, and it is very rare that two Indians tell the same story alike, unless it may be some wild and improbable legend, like the fairy tales related in nurseries, which are remembered in after life. A notable instance of this unreliability is in their version of the account of the Spanish settlement attempted at Neeah Bay by Lieut. Quimper, in 1792, by order of the commandant of the Spanish forces at Nootka. All they really know about it, is that they have been told by their fathers that the Spaniards were here, and they can point out the locality where yet may be found pieces of tile used by the Spaniards in building. But although that occurrence was only seventy-three years ago, there is but one man living in the tribe who remembers the circumstances, and he is in his dotage. Almost every Indian I have questioned upon the subject gives a different version of the detail. Now, as they cannot relate correctly matters given in our history, and of a comparatively recent date, but little dependence can be placed upon the tales of their origin, which are interesting only for their fabulous and superstitious nature. In the matter of the Spaniards, I have been told by one that they built a brick house with a shingle roof, and surrounded it with palisades. Another stated that the house was of wood, with a brick chimney; another that they built no house at all, but simply landed some bricks and other materials; and, before they could build the house, were driven away by the Indians. More recent events, such as the murder of the crews of the ship Boston, in 1803, and of the *Tonquin*, in 1811, and the captivity of Jewett among the Nootkans, they remember hearing about, and relate with tolerable accuracy. As events recede in years, however, they become obscured with legends and fables, so that the truth is exceedingly difficult to discover.

The legend respecting their own origin is, that they were created on the Cape. First, animals were produced, and from the union of some of these with a star which fell from heaven, came the first men, and from them sprang all the race of Nittinats, Clyoquots, and Makahs. Indians were also created on Vancouver Island at the same time. They claim for themselves and the Nittinats a greater antiquity than the Clyoquots or Nootkans, so-called, which were originally a mere band of the Nittinat tribe. The name Nootka, which was given by the first discoverers to the band of Indians called *Mowitchat*, or, as the Makahs pronounce it, *Bo-wat-chat*, has been most singularly accepted by all the authors; and not only is the tribe or band, and the Sound they live near, called Nootka, and the treaty of 1790, between Great Britain and Spain, relative to its possession, called the Nootka convention, but recent ethnologists class all these tribes as belonging to the Nootkan family. Had Captains Cook and Vancouver, and the early Spanish explorers made Neeah Bay their headquarters, there is no reason to doubt that the Makahs, or Classets, as they were called, would have been considered the parent stock, and the other coast tribes classed as of the Makah family. My own impression is that the Nittinats were originally the principal and most powerful tribe; and that the Clyoquot, Nootka, Ahosett, and other bands on the southwest portion of Vancouver Island, as well as the Makahs at Cape Flattery, were bands or offshoots from that tribe. We have seen that the name "Nootka" is not the name of any tribe on the northwest coast, but one given in mistake by the whites, and since adhered to. Still, it may perhaps be as well to class all these tribes as the Nootkan family, since that name has come into such general use; though there is no evidence that the tribe called Nootkas were the parent stock, nor can any proof of ancestry be obtained from any of the tribes, of which each claims an antiquity as great as the others.

There is, however, a marked similarity among all the coast tribes from the Columbia River to Nootka. But, farther north, the Haida, Stikine, Chimsyan, and other tribes are very different in appearance. This great dissimilarity can be noticed by the most casual observer in the streets of Victoria at any time. All these different tribes resort there for purposes of trade; and the northern Indians for so those three are termed can at a glance be distinguished from the Nootka family, or from the Flatheads. The northern Indians, so-called, are much taller, more robust, and with features more like the Tartar hordes of the Siberian coast. The women are much larger, better shaped, and with lighter complexions than the Flatheads, among which may be classed of those who frequent Victoria, and with whom a comparison may be formed the Cowitchins, Songish, Clallams, and the various tribes on Puget Sound, who all resemble the coast tribes in general appearance, manners, and customs. A northern Indian can as readily be distinguished and marked, among a crowd of Flatheads, as a Chinaman among white men. That the northern tribes have originated from wandering hordes from the Asiatic side of the Pacific, coming by way of the Aleutian Islands and Behring Strait, is in my opinion the most probable hypothesis, for there is as strong a resemblance to each other among all the Indians

Makah

north of Vancouver Island, as far as Sitka, as there is among the so-called Nootkan family. Whether the Flatheads originally travelled by the same route, cannot be shown, either by their own traditions, or any other evidence that I have been able to get, during a very careful investigation among them, and the truth respecting their origin, if ever found, must be by evidence derived from other sources. The only tradition that I have heard respecting any migratory movement among the Makahs, is relative to a deluge or flood which occurred many years ago, but seems to have been local, and to have had no connection with the Noachic deluge which they know nothing about, as a casual visitor might suppose they did, on hearing them relate the story of their flood. This I give as stated to me by an intelligent chief; and the statement was repeated on different occasions by several others, with a slight variation in detail.

"A long time ago," said my informant, "but not at a very remote period, the water of the Pacific flowed through what is now the swamp and prairie between Wäatch village and Neeah Bay, making an island of Cape Flattery. The water suddenly receded, leaving Neeah Bay perfectly dry. It was four days reaching its lowest ebb, and then rose again without any waves or breakers, till it had submerged the Cape, and in fact the whole country, excepting the tops of the mountains at Clyoquot. The water on its rise became very warm, and as it came up to the houses, those who had canoes put their effects into them, and floated off with the current, which set very strongly to the north. Some drifted one way, some another; and when the waters assumed their accustomed level, a portion of the tribe found themselves beyond Nootka, where their descendants now reside, and are known by the same name as the Makahs in Classet, or *Kwenaitchcchat*. Many canoes came down in the trees and were destroyed, and numerous lives were lost. The water was four days regaining its accustomed level."

The same tradition was related to me by the Kwilleyutes, who stated that a portion of that tribe made their way to the region in the vicinity of Port Townsend, where their descendants are known as the Chemakum tribe. I have also received the same tradition from the Chemakum Indians, who claim to have originally sprung from the Kwilleyutes. There is no doubt in my mind of the truth of this tradition. The Wiiatch prairie shows conclusively that the water of the Pacific once flowed through it; and on cutting through the turf at any place between Neeah Bay and Wäatch, the whole substratum is found to be pure beach sand. In some places the turf is not more than a foot thick; at others the alluvial deposit is two or three feet.

As this portion of the country shows conclusive evidence of volcanic action, there is every reason to believe that there was a gradual depression and subsequent upheaval of the earth's crust, which made the waters rise and recede as the Indians stated. Fossil remains of whales are said by the Indians to be found around a lake [58] near Clyoquot, which were possibly deposited at the time of this flood. I have not seen these remains, but I have been told of their existence by so many different Indians who professed to have seen them, that I think the story probably correct. The Indians do not think they got there by means of the flood, but that, as before stated, they are the remains of the feasts of the *T'hlukloots*, or thunder bird, who carried the whales there in his claws, and devoured them at his leisure. With the single exception of this legend of the flood, I have never learned from them that they have any tradition respecting the tribe coming to or going from the place where they now reside, and this is the only one which they relate of ancient times that is corroborated by geological or other evidence.[7]

The only genealogical record that has been related to me is one commencing twelve generations ago, beginning with Deeaht and his brother Obiee, or Odice. This was told me by an old chief, named Kolchotc, or Kalchote, who died two years ago. He was a very intelligent Indian, and held high rank among his people. According to his account he was a direct descendant, on his mother's side, from Odiee Deeaht (or, as it is sometimes pronounced, Deeahks, or Deeah, and by the Nittinats and Clyoquots Neeah), was the principal chief, and owned the land and resided at Neeah Bay, where Neeah village now stands. The bay takes its name from the village, and the village from its being the residence of, and owned by Deeah, who, dying without issue, was succeeded by his brother Odiee. His descendants were in the following order: *Kat hl-che-da*, *Wa-wa-tsoo-pa*, *Wat-lai-waih-kose*, *Kla-che-tis-sub*, *How-e-sub*, *Ko-shah-sit*, *Tai-is-sub*, *Kloo-kwa-kay*, *Yah-hie*, and *Kow-e-das*. The daughter of *Kow-e-das* was the mother of *Kalchote*. Thus from Obiee to *Kalchote* are twelve generations. Some of the other Indians, who claim a descent on the male side, have told me that this story of *Kalchote* is incorrect, and that Neeah Bay was not named from *Deeaht*; but as they could assign no reason for the word, except that it was in use many years ago, I am inclined to think his version correct, particularly as he gave it to me just before his death, and it was interpreted to me on two different days by two different Indians, and was told me as an evidence that his only child, a daughter, was of high rank, and was to have his property, which he wished me to see distributed according to directions given at the time.[8]

The legend about Deeaht, and his tragical end, is as follows: The Nittinats came over with a mighty host and attacked the Makahs, driving them away from all their villages, and forcing them to retire to their strongholds at Flattery Rocks. *Deeaht*, who was a young man, very brave and influential, ventured back alone and built a house near the brook at Neeah village. He was shortly joined by his brother Obiee, and soon had a large number of friends and retainers around him. The Hosett Indians at Flattery Rocks, becoming jealous of his prosperity, came up and attacked him; but he defeated them and drove them back, discomfiting them so badly that they were glad to sue for peace, which he granted on condition of receiving for a wife the daughter of a chief residing at Hosett village. [59] This chief had a boy and girl who wore twins, and could scarcely be told apart; so they dressed the boy in his sister's clothes, and delivered him to Deeaht; but as soon as it became night the young savage, who had concealed a knife in his dress, cut Deeah's throat, and then made his escape to Hosett {Ozette}. *Odiee* then succeeded his brother, and is the ancestor of a great portion of the Makahs who reside at Neeah Bay.

In one of the lodges at Neeah Bay are three carved figures, on whose heads rests the huge beam that supports the roof; of these one is intended to represent *Decahks*, or *Deeaht*. Another figure, in the centre, is named *Klessakady*, and is symbolical of sunrise. His head is surmounted with a crescent-shaped cap, and between his feet is a head representing night. The beam above is marked with circular holes, to represent stars, and, according to *Kalchote*, the old chief, who placed it there, it may be said to show the manner in which the sun, when rising, thrusts the stars

---

[7] Traditions of a deluge are also universal among the Flathead tribes, each claiming to have its particular Ararat. GG

[8] The earlier names in this genealogy are probably of mythical personages. GG

away with his head and tramples the night under his feet. A figure at the remote end of the lodge is named *Billaksakut'hl*, and represents a fabled giant of antiquity, who could spread his feet apart, leaving a space between his legs wide enough to pass the largest canoes through. These are the only carvings of any note in the village, but as to their significance, as stated to me by *Kalchote*, there is good reason to doubt its correctness. I recently asked the Indian who carved them, whose name is Dick, what he intended to represent! He said he had no other idea than to cut some posts to look like men, and that so far as the head between the feet of *Klessakady* was concerned, it simply meant nothing; but there happened to be a big knot in the wood, which made it difficult to carve, so he made a head of it; and after it was done, *Kalchote* painted it and set it up in his lodge with the other two, and gave them names, and invented the allegory himself. He explained himself further by remarking that he would carve me a figure if I would like, and that I could make any meaning to it I chose. Although *Kalchote* undoubtedly associated in his mind the allegories which he related to me with the images, the other Indians ridicule the idea, and say they are only Dick's work, which he did, with no particular object in view.

Each village has its own local traditions and genealogies, and each claims to have had, at former times, great men, who were head chiefs of the tribe. But it would appear that really each village was a community by itself, and they were often engaged in feuds among themselves; nor is this feeling wholly extinct; they speak of each other as they do of other tribes, and it is only on questions affecting the whole that they admit themselves to be all one. It is a common practice with all the chiefs of these tribes, Makahs, Nittinats, Clyoquots, Nootkans, etc., to claim great possessions, particularly when relating their talcs to white men. Thus, if one's father or mother, or even the grandparents, belonged to another tribe, it is customary to claim the land of that tribe as theirs. For instance, one, whose mother was a Nittinat, will say: "That is my land at Nittinat". The chief of the Clyoquots, named Cedakanim, who frequently comes to Neeah Bay, told me that Cape Flattery was his land, because his mother was a Makah. His wife, who was the daughter of a Makah chief formerly residing at Neeah Bay, lays claim, in behalf of her son, to the land around the bay, as a portion of his grandfather's estate. Such claims, however, are ignored by the Makahs, or looked upon [60] as merely complimentary titles. It was thus that the great chiefs of the Nootkans and Clyoquots made the early discoverers helieve that they owned all the land south of Nootka and about Cape Flattery; and undoubtedly it was with this impression that Meares named the island at the entrance of the strait Tatoosh, supposing it to belong to *Tatooshatticus*, one of the Clyoquot or Nootkan chiefs. The Indian name of the island and village is *Chahdi*, and it is either called by that name, or *Opa-jek-ta*, meaning island in the same manner as we would say, "We will go to Tatoosh," or "We will go to the island."

Taken in connection with the allegory of the thunder bird, Tatoosh or *Tootootsh*, which is the Clyoquot name of the thunder bird, seems singularly appropriate. The roaring of the waves reverberating in the caverns of the island, reminding them of thunder, and the bright flashes from the thunder cloud of the *Ha-hek-to-ak* the producer of fire. But however amusing such an application of the name might appear, it has no foundation in reality, as the Indians do not, nor have they ever called the island by any other name than *Chahdi*. It is worthy of remark at this place that Maquinna or Maquilla, the great Nootkan chief mentioned by Vancouver, Meares, and others, is claimed by *Cedakanim* to have been a Clyoquot; while *Kwistoh*, a very intelligent chief among the Nittinats, has assured me that he was a Nittinat, who resided at Mowatchat, or Nootka. It is from conversation with these chiefs, as well as the Makahs, that I have formed the

Makah

opinion that the Nittinat tribe was in reality the parent stock, and that the Indians of the south western portion of Vancouver Island, and at Cape Flattery, should be termed the Nittinat family, instead of the Nootkan or Clyoquot. I have not been able to prepare vocabularies of all these tribes, but their language, so far as I can judge from hearing them speak, is sufficiently alike to be recognized, and to leave no doubt that it was originally the same in all.

The changes that have been introduced among the Makahs by intercourse with the whites, can be summed up in a few words. Formerly they were clothed in robes of furs or skins, or with blankets made from cedar bark, dog's-hair, or bird skins; their weapons consisted of bows and arrows, spears, and stone-knives, and hatchets. Their food was the product of the ocean, the roots and berries indige nous to the Cape, and such wild animals and birds as they could destroy. Their trade was confined to barter among themselves, or the tribes of the coast. They were almost constantly at variance with other tribes, and lived in a state of fear and apprehension. They were cruel, ferocious, and treacherous, particularly to any so unfortunate as to be thrown among them, either by the fortunes of war, or other wise. With the advent of white men blankets were substituted for their robes of skins and bark, and calico used for the simple cincture of bark worn about the loins; guns and knives were substituted for bows and spears; and potatoes, flour, bread, with other articles of food, replaced in a measure their fish, game, and roots. They acquired the knowledge of trade, and learned the value of money; but farther than this their progress has been slow. They have learned enough during their inter course with the whites to make them careful about committing hostilities, knowing that the good-will of the white men, and the benefits of their trade, were means of enriching themselves and procuring many comforts; but their savage natures [61] have never changed; they are as wild and treacherous as ever; and, but for the fear of punishment and the love of gain, would exterminate every settler that attempted to make his residence among them. Frequently, since the establishment of the reservation, they have made threats of hostilities; but the councils of those who desired to acquire property or hoped for favors have prevailed, and they have contented themselves with simple threats. Improvement in their customs, and habits, must be gradual, and the work of time and patient perseverance on the part of those delegated by the Government to reside among them and look after their welfare. They have steadily opposed everything that has been done or attempted for their benefit, and even now, though they see that the promises made to them by their agent have been, in great part, realized, they are totally indifferent as to whether anything more is to be done, and in no case volunteer a helping hand. Their ancient history is wrapped in an impene trable obscurity that of a more recent date I have endeavored to exhibit; their future can be read in the annals of the New England emigrants. The steady wave setting to our western shores will have its due effect upon the Indian races, and in the lapse of another century the places that now know them will know them no more.

MYTHOLOGY. – The Makahs believe in a Supreme Being, who is termed by them *Cha-batt-*a *Ha-tartstl*, or *Ha-tartstl Cha-batt-a*, the Great Chief who resides above. The name of this Great Chief, or Divine Being, is never given, although they have a name; but they must not speak it to any except those who have been initiated into their secret rites and ceremonies. They have no outward forms of religion, but each one addresses the Supreme Being by himself, and generally retires to the depth of the woods, or some cave, for the purpose. Intermediate spirits, or familiars, are supposed to guard the destinies of individuals, and to manifest themselves at certain times by visions, signs, and dreams. These are called in the jargon *Tamanawas*, and the receiving of a revelation is termed "seeing the *Tamanawas*."[9] I never with certainty have known an Indian to address himself to the Supreme Being until recently, while in a canoe with a chief named *Klaplanhie*, or Captain John. He was taken with a violent fit of sneezing, and as soon as he re covered he repeated aloud several short sentences, accompanying each with a blowing noise from his mouth. I asked him what he was saying"? He replied that he was asking the *Ha-tartstl Cha-batt-a* not to kill him by sneezing, but to let him live longer. I have on other occasions, however, noticed that the Indians, upon sneezing, repeat a few words, and think it very probable they all do as John said he did ask the Great Spirit not to kill them. John told me that, if they did not utter this brief petition, the top of their heads would be blown off when they sneezed.[10] The same chief informed me, during a recent conversation [62] respecting their religious belief, that they think the sun is the representative of the Great Spirit, and to him they make their secret prayer. He also said that "The Indian Sunday is not one day, like your Sunday, but it is many days. When we want to talk with the Great Chief, we wait till the moon is full, and then go into the mountain, and rub our bodies with cedar twigs, after having first washed them clean. The cedar makes us smell sweet, and that the Great Chief likes. We watch for the sun, and when he first makes his appearance, we ask him to let us live long, to be strong to defend ourselves or attack our enemies, to be successful in our fisheries, or in the pursuit of game; and to give us everything we want. Every night we wash and rub ourselves with cedar, and every morning talk to the Great Chief, or his representative, the sun, whose name is Kle-sea-kark-tl."[11] 1 We continue praying daily for one week, or from full moon to the quarter. The only instruction the children have as to the Supreme Being, of rather the only form of address taught them, is during the same period, when they are waked up at daylight and made to wash themselves before sunrise, and to ask the sun to let them live. Their tamanawas ceremonies are in reference to events they believe to have happened on the earth, and they try to represent them. But the doings of the Great Supreme they do not dare to attempt to represent, and only address him in private and at stated times. Their prayer is simply a selfish petition; they do not ask to be made wiser or better, but simply for long life, and strength, and skill, and cunning, so that they may be able to enrich themselves and obtain an ascend ancy over their fellow-men.

At certain periods, generally during the winter months, they have ceremonies, or mystical performances, of which there are three distinct kinds. The *Dukwally*, or black *tamanawas*; the *Tsiark*, or medicine *tamanawas*, and the *Dothlub*. The latter is seldom performed, the great

---

[9] This word, which in Chinook means the practice of shamanism, in the jargon of the coast embraces everything supernatural. GG

[10] A similar custom existed among the Peruvians, and runs through nearly all modern Europe. For the antiquity and universality of some superstition connected with sneezing, v. Encycl. Brit. also Encycl. Metrop., and Roes Encycl. GG

[11] Among the western Selish, or Flathead tribes of the Sound, I have not detected any direct worship of the sun, though he forms one of their mythological characters. He is by them represented as the younger brother of the moon. According to Father Mengarini he is, however, the principal object of worship among the Flatheads of the Rocky Mountains, or Selish proper, as well as by the Blackfeet. Among both the tribes mentioned he was supposed to be the creation of a superior being. GG

Makah

variety of scenes to be enacted requiring a large number of persons, and a much greater expense on the part of the individual who gives them. All these ceremonies are commenced in secret, none but the initiated being allowed to be present; and it is then, if ever, that they make common supplication to the Deity. Although I have never been able to ascertain the real facts in the case, it would seem that they address themselves to some intermediate being. Certain other ceremonies are performed in public, and spectators admitted. From those that I have seen, I infer that the Dukwally is a ceremonial to propitiate the Thlukloots, or thunder bird, who seems with the Makahs to take precedence over all other mythological beings. Into all these mysteries persons of both sexes, and even children, are initiated; but the initiation does not endow them with medicine or tamanawas qualities until they have gone through the private ordeal, of finding their own tamanawas, or guardian [63] spirit. At such times they are supposed to receive some manifestation which guides them in their after life. This ceremony is performed as follows: The candidate retires to some place of concealment near the salt water, where he bathes himself, remaining till he is pretty well chilled; then returns to his hiding place, and warms himself by rubbing his body and limbs with bark or cedar twigs, and again returns to the water; keeping up this alternate bathing and friction day and night, without eating, and with no interval of sleep. Both body and mind becoming thus exhausted, he lies down in a sort of trance, during which, in his disordered fancy, he sees visions and receives revelations. What he sees he makes known to no one, but ever after addresses himself in secret to that being that has presented itself to him, whether in form of bird, beast, or fish, though the animal representing this guardian spirit is sometimes indicated by carvings or paintings made by the Indian. Such animals as would be most likely to come around him while thus alone are owls, wolves, minks, and mice, during the night; or eagles, crows, ravens, blue-jays, cranes, elk, deer, or seals, during the day. These are all considered tamanawas animals, some possessing more powerful influence than others; and, as an Indian could scarcely be several days or nights without seeing something of the kind, their ceremonies are generally successful in obtaining a manifestation. They do not imagine, however, that the animal they may see is the Guardian Spirit, but only the form in which he shows himself. Of the above, owls, bears, and wolves seem to be those most generally seen, and heads of these are more frequently carved than any others. To illustrate their superstitious belief in animals connected with their Guardian Spirit, I will relate an incident told me by Captain John, one of the chiefs. About three years ago he had lost the use of one of his feet, probably from paralysis, but which he attributed to a "*skookoom*," or evil spirit, entering into it one day while he was bathing. He had been confined to his house for several months, and was reduced to a skeleton. I saw him during this sickness, and thought he could not recover. One pleasant day, however, according to his account, he managed to crawl to a brook near his house, and, while bathing, heard a rustling sound in the air, at which he became frightened, and covered his face with his blanket, whereupon a raven alighted within a few feet of him and uttered a hoarse croak. He then peeped through a corner of his blanket, and saw the raven with its head erect, its feathers bristled, and a great swelling in its throat. After two or three unsuccessful efforts, it finally threw up a piece of bone about three inches long, then uttering another croak it flew away. Remaining quiet a few minutes, till he was satisfied that the raven had gone, he picked up the bone, which he gravely informed me was of the *Ha-hek-to-ak*. He hid this bone near by, and returned to his lodge, and, after relating the occurrence, was informed by the Indian doctors that it was a medicine sent to him by his tamanawas, and this proved to be true, as he entirely recovered in three days. I knew that this man had recovered very speedily, but do not know the actual cause. He says he shall keep the bone hid till his son is old enough to kill whales, when he will give it to him to take in his canoe, as a powerful medicine to insure success. The tale of the raven alighting near him is not improbable, as ravens as well as crows are very plenty and very tame; nor is it impossible that the raven might have had [64] a bone in its mouth, and finally dropped it; nor is it entirely uncertain that the circumstance so affected his superstitious imagination that it caused a reaction in his system, and promoted his recovery. The same effect might perhaps have been produced by a smart shock from a galvanic battery. It is thus, without doubt, that the persons going through the ordeal of becoming *tamunawas*, or medicine men, have their minds excited by any animal they may see, or even by the creak ing of a limb in the forest, and their imaginations are sufficiently fertile to add to natural causes, fancies that appear to them to be real. If there is anything connected with their ceremonials approaching to our ideas of worship, it must be during the secret portion, from which all except the initiated are rigorously ex cluded; but I have no evidence that such is the fact, and believe, as the Indians state to me, that the only time they address the Supreme Being is by themselves and in secret.

As their general tamanawas ceremonies are based upon their mythological fables, it will perhaps be well first to relate some of those legends before describing their public performances. The Makahs believe in a transmigration of souls;[12]* that every living thing, even trees, and all sorts of birds and fishes as well as animals, were formerly Indians who for their bad conduct were transformed into the shapes in which they now appear. These ancient Indians, said my informant, were so very bad, that at length two men, brothers of the sun and moon, who are termed *Ho-ho-e-ap-bess* or the "men who changed things" came on earth and made the transformations. The seal was a very bad, thieving Indian, for which reason his arms were shortened, and his legs tied so that only his feet could move, and he was cast into the sea and told to catch fish for his food. The mink, *Kwahtie*, was a great liar, but a very shrewd Indian, full of rascalities which he practised on every one, and many are the tales told of his acts. His mother was the blue-jay, *Kwish-kwishee*. Once, while *Kwahtie* was making an arrow, his mother directed him to get some water, but he refused until he should have finished his work. His mother told him to make haste, for she felt that she was turning into a bird. While she was talking she turned into a blue jay and flew into a bush. *Kwahtie* tried to shoot her, but his arrow passed behind her neck, glancing over the top of her head, ruffling up the feathers, as they have always remained in the head of the blue-jay. Those Indians that were turned into wolves formerly resided at Clallam Bay. One day their chief *Chu-chu-hu-uks-th*l, came to *Kwahtie*'s house, who pretended to be sick, and invited the wolf to come in and take a nap. This he did, as he was quite tired. When he was fast asleep *Kwahtie* got up and with a sharp mussel shell cut the wolf's throat and buried him in the sand. Two days after this a deputation of the wolf tribe came to look for their chief. "I have not seen him," said *Kwahtie*. "I am sick and have not left my house." The wolves retired; and shortly another, and then another deputation came. To all of these he gave the same answer. At last one of the [65] wolves said, "*Kwahtie*, you tell lies, for I can smell something, and my nose tells me that you have killed our chief." "Well," says

---

[12] The term " transmigration of souls" is not strictly correct. The idea is that the pre-human, or demon race, was transformed into the animals and other objects whose names they bore and still bear. The souls of the present race are not supposed to undergo transmigration. GG

Makah

Kwahtie, "if you think so, call all your tribe here, and I will work spells, and you can then see whether I have killed him or not." Accordingly they all came. *Kwahtie* told them to form a circle, leaving an opening on one side, which they did. He then took a bottle or bladder of oil in one hand, and a comb with very long teeth in the other, and commenced a song in which he at first denied all knowledge of the chief, but at length admitted the fact, upon which he started and ran out of the circle, dashing down the bladder of oil which turned into water. He also stuck his comb into the sand, which was immediately changed into the rocks from Clyoquot to Flattery rocks. He then dived into the water and escaped. It was in this manner, said my informant, that Neeah Bay and the Straits were formed; for the land formerly was level and good, till *Kwahtie* turned it into rocks and water. *Kwahtie* was a great magician till the *Ho-ho-e-ap-bess* transformed him. He had the choice offered him of being a bird or a fish, but declined both. He was then told that as he was fond of fish he might live on land and eat what fish he could catch or pick up.

The raven, *Klook-shood*, was a strong Indian very fond of flesh, a sort of cannibal, as was his wife *Cha-ka-do*, the crow, and their strong beaks were given them to tear their food, whether fish, flesh, or vegetable, for they had great appetites, and devoured everything they could find. The crane, *Kwah-less*, was a great fisherman, always on the rocks, or wading about, with his long fish spear ready to transfix his prey. He constantly wore the *tsa-sa-ka-dup*, or little circular cape, worn by the Makahs during wet weather while fishing. This was turned into the feathers about his neck, and his fish spear into his long bill. The kingfisher, *Chesh-kully*, was also a fisherman, but a thief, and had stolen a necklace of the *Che-toh-dook* or dentalium shells; these were turned into the ring of white feathers about his neck.

At the time of the transformation of Indians into animals, there was no wood in the land, nothing but grass and sand, so the *Ho-ho-e-ap-bess*, mindful of the wants of the future inhabitants, prepared for them fuel. To one they said, you are old, and your heart is dry, you will make good kindling wood, for your grease has turned hard and will make pitch (*kluk-ait-a-biss*), your name is *Do-ho-bupt*, and you shall be the spruce tree, which when it grows old will always make dry wood. To another, your name is *Kla-ka-bupt*, and you shall be the hemlock. The Indians will want some harder wood, and therefore *Kwahk-sa-bupt*, you shall be the alder, and you, *Dopt-ko-bupt*, shall be the crab apple, and as you have a cross temper you shall bear sour fruit. The Indians will likewise want tough wood to make bows, and wedges with which to split logs; you *Kla-haik'-tle-bup* are tough and strong, and therefore you shall be the yew tree. They will also require soft lasting wood to make canoes, you *Kla-ae-sook* shall be the cedar. And thus they give the origin of every tree, shrub, or herb.

The cause of the ebb and flow of the tides is accounted for in this manner. The raven, *Klook-shood*, not being contented with his one wife, the crow, went up the straits and stole the daughter of *Tu-chee*, the east wind. *Tu-chee*, after searching twenty days, found him, and a compromise was effected, by which the raven was to [66] receive some land as a present. At that time the tide did not ebb and flow, so *Tu-chee* promised he would make the waters retire for twenty days, and during that time *Klook-shood* might pick up what he could find on the flats to eat. *Klook-shood* was not satisfied with this, but wanted the land to be made bare as far as the cape. *Tu-chee* said no, he would only make it dry for a few feet. *Klook-shood* told him he was a very mean fellow, and that he had better take his daughter back again. At last the matter was settled by *Tu-chee** agreeing to make the water leave the flats twice every twenty-four hours.

Makah

This was deemed satisfactory, and thus it was that the ebb and flow of the tide was caused, to enable the ravens and crows to go on the flats and pick up the food left by the water.

The *Dukwally* and other *tamanawas* performances are exhibitions intended to represent incidents connected with their mythological legends. There are a great variety, and they seem to take the place, in a measure, of theatrical performances or games during the season of the religious festivals. There are no persons especially set apart as priests for the performance of these ceremonies, although some, who seem more expert than others, are usually hired to give life to the scenes, but these performers are quite as often found among the slaves or common people as among the chiefs, and excepting during the continuance of the festivities are not looked on as of any particular importance. On inquiring the origin of these ceremonies, I was informed that they did not originate with the Indians, but were revelations of the guardian spirits, who made known what they wished to be performed. An Indian, for instance, who has been consulting with his guardian spirit, which is done by going through the washing and fasting process before described, will imagine or think he is called upon to represent the owl; he arranges in his mind the style of dress, the number of performers, the songs and dances or other movements, and having the plan perfected, announces at a tamanawas meeting that he has had a revelation which he will impart to a select few. These are then taught and drilled in strict secrecy, and when they have perfected themselves, will suddenly make their appearance and perform before the astonished tribe. Another Indian gets up the representation of the whale, others do the same of birds, and in fact of every thing that they can think of. If any performance is a success, it is repeated, and gradually comes to be looked upon as one of the regular order in the ceremonies; if it does not satisfy the audience, it is laid aside. Thus they have performances that have been handed down from remote ages, while others are of a more recent date. My residence in the school building, but a stone's throw from the houses at Neeah village, gave me an excellent opportunity to see all the performances that the uninitiated are permitted to witness, and to hear all the din of their out-door and in-door operations.

The ceremony of the great *Dukwally*, or the Thunder bird, originated with the *Hesh-kwi-et* {*Hesquiath*} Indians, a band of Nittinats living near Barclay Sound, Vancouver Island, and is ascribed to the following legend: Two men had fallen in love with one woman, and as she would give neither the preference, at last they came to a quarrel. But one of them, who had better sense than the other, said, Don't let us fight about that ~~squaw~~; I will go out and see the chief of the wolves, and he will tell me what is to be done; but I cannot get to his [67] lodge except by stratagem. Now they know we are at variance, so do you take me by the hair, and drag me over these sharp rocks which are covered with barnacles, and I shall bleed, and I will pretend to be dead, and the wolves will come and carry me away to their house. The other agreed, and dragged him over the rocks till he was lacerated from head to foot, and then left him out of reach of the tide. The wolves came, and supposing him dead, carried him to the lodge of their chief; but when they got ready to eat him, he jumped up and astonished them at his boldness. The chief wolf was so much pleased with his bravery, that he imparted to him all the mysteries of the Thunder bird performance, and on his return home he instructed his friends, and the Dukwally was the result. The laceration of the arms and legs among the Makahs, during the performance to be described, is to represent the laceration of the founder of the ceremony from being dragged over the sharp stones.

Makah

A person intending to give one of these performances first gathers together as much property as he can obtain, in blankets, guns, brass kettles, beads, tin pans, and other articles intended as presents for his guests, and procures a sufficient quantity of food, which of late years consists of flour, biscuit, rice, potatoes, molasses, dried fish, and roots. He keeps his intention a secret until he is nearly ready, and then imparts it to a few of his friends, who if need be assist him by adding to his stock of presents or food. The first

*Fig. 35. No. 2714.

intimation the village has of the intended ceremonies is on the night previous to the first day's performance. After the community have retired for the night, which is usually between nine and ten o clock, the performers commence by hooting like owls, howling like wolves, and uttering a sharp whistling sound intended to represent the blowing and whistling of the wind. Guns are then fired, and all the initiated collect in the lodge where the ceremonies are to be performed, and drum with their heels on boxes or boards, producing a sound resembling thunder. The torches of pitch wood are flashed through the roof of the house, and at each flash the thunder rolls, and then the whole assemblage whistles like the wind. As soon as the noise of the performers commences, the uninitiated fly in terror and hide themselves, so great being their superstitious belief in the supernatural powers of the *Dukwally*, that they have frequently fled to my house for protection, knowing very well that the tamanawas performers would not come near a white man. They then visit every house in the village, and extend an invitation for all to attend the ceremonies. This having been done, the

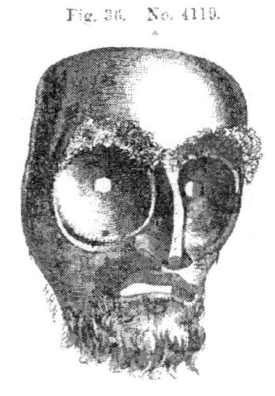

*Fig. 36. No. 4119.

crowd retire to the lodge of ceremonies, where the drumming and singing are kept up till near daylight, when they are quiet for a short time, and at sunrise begin again. The first five days are usually devoted to secret ceremonies, such as initiating candidates, and a variety of performances which consist chiefly in songs and chorus and drumming to imitate thunder. They do this part very well, and their imitation of thunder is quite equal to that produced in the best equipped theatre.

What the ceremony of initiation is I have never learned. That of the Clallams, whiqh I have witnessed, consists in putting the initiates into a mesmeric sleep; but if the Makahs use mesmerism, or any such influence, they do not keep the candidates under it for any great length of time, as I saw them every day [68] during the ceremonies, walking out during the intervals. The first out-door performance usually commences on the fifth day, and this consists of the procession of males and females, with their legs and arms, and sometimes their bodies, scarified

*Fig. 37.

with knives, and every wound bleeding freely. The men are entirely naked, but the women have on a short petticoat. I had seen this performance several times, and had always been told by the Indians that the cutting was done by the principal performers, or medicine men, who seized all they could get hold of, and thus lacerated them; but I have since been admitted to a lodge to witness the operation. I expected the performers would be in a half

64

frantic state, cutting and slashing regardless of whom they might wound; I, however, found it otherwise. A bucket of water was placed in the centre of the lodge, and the candidates squatting around it washed their arms and legs. The persons who did the cutting, and who appeared to be any one who had sharp knives, butcher-knives being preferred, grasped them firmly in the right hand with the thumb placed along the blade, so as to leave but an eighth or quarter of an inch of the edge bare; then, taking hold of the arm or leg of the candidate, made gashes five or six inches long transversely, and parallel with the limb, four or five gashes being cut each way. Cuts were thus madeon each

*Fig. 38.   arm above and below the elbow, on each thigh, and the calves of the legs; some, but not all, were likewise cut on their backs. The wounds were then washed with water to make the blood run freely. The persons operated on did not seem to mind it all, but laughed and chatted with each other until all were ready to go out, and then they set up a dismal howling; but I think the pain they felt could not be very great, for two Indians who went in with me, seeing there were but few in the procession, asked me if I would like to see them join in. I told them I should like very well to see the performance; upon which they deliberately pulled off their blankets and shirts, and continued in conversation with me while their arms and legs were gashed in the same manner. An Indian must be possessed of a much lower degree of nervous organization than a white man to suffer such operations and show no more feeling. Some may think it stoical indifference, but certainly such a scoring of the body would throw a white man into a fever. The same two Indians came to me   *Fig. 39.   about an hour after the performance had closed, and although their wounds had bled freely, they assured me they felt no pain. Sometimes, however, the cuts are accidentally made deep, and produce sores. When all was ready the procession left the lodge, and marched in single file down to the beach; their naked bodies streaming with blood presenting a bar barous spectacle. A circle was formed at the water's edge, round which this bloody procession marched slowly, making gesticulations and uttering howling cries.

Five men now came out of the lodge carrying the principal performer. One held him by the hair, and the others by the arms and legs. He too was cut and bleeding profusely. They laid him down on the beach on the wet sand, and left him, while they marched off and visited every lodge in the village, making a circuit in each lodge. At last the man on the beach jumped up, and seizing a club laid about him in a violent manner, hitting everything in his way. He too went the same round as the others, and after every lodge had been visited they all returned to the lodge from which they had issued, and the performances, [69] outdoor, were closed for that day. In the meanwhile a deputation of fifteen or twenty men, with faces painted black and sprigs of evergreen in their hair, had been sent to the other villages with invitations for guests to come and receive presents. They went in a body to each lodge, and

*Fig. 40.   after a song and a chorus, the spokesman of the party in a loud voice announced the object of their visit, and called the names of the invited persons. Any one has a right to be present at the distribution, but only those specially invited will receive any presents.

Makah

Fig. 41. No 4117

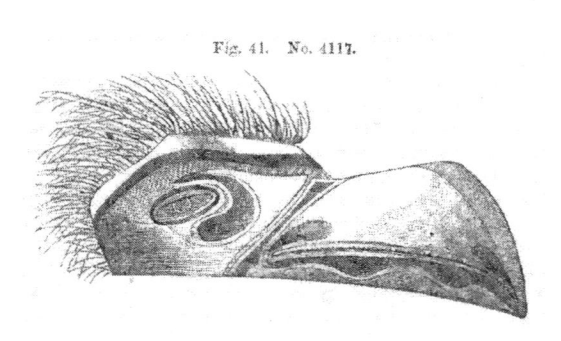

Every evening during the ceremonies, excepting those of the first few days, is devoted to masquerade and other amusements, when each lodge is visited and a performance enacted. Some of the masks are frightful objects, as may be seen in Figures 35-41. They are made principally by the Clyoquot and Nittinat Indians and sold to the Makahs, who paint them to suit their own fancies. They are made of alder, maple, and cottonwood; some are very ingeniously executed, [70] having the eyes and lower jaw movable. By means of a string the performer can make the eyes roll about, and the jaws gnash together with a fearful clatter. As these masks are kept strictly concealed until the time of the performances, and as they are generally produced at night, they are viewed with awe by the spectators; and certainly the scene in one of these lodges, dimly lighted by the fires which show the faces of the assembled spectators and illuminate the performers, presents a most weird and savage spectacle when the masked dancers issue forth from behind a screen of mats, and go through their barbarous pantomimes. The Indians themselves, even accustomed as they are to these masks, feel very much afraid of them, and a white man, viewing the scene for the first time, can only liken it to a carnival of demons.

Among the masquerade performances that I have seen was a representation of mice. This was performed by a dozen or more young men who were entirely naked. Their bodies, limbs, and faces were painted with stripes of red, blue, and black; red bark wreaths were twisted around their heads, and bows and arrows in their hands. They made a squealing noise, but otherwise they did nothing that reminded me of mice in the least. Another party was composed of naked boys, with bark fringes, like veils, covering their faces, and armed with sticks having [71] needles in one end; they made a buzzing noise, and stuck the needles into any of the spectators who came in their way. This was a representation of hornets. These processions followed each other at an interval of half an hour, and each made a circuit round the lodge, performed some antics, sang some songs, shouted, and left. Another party then came in, composed of men with frightful masks, bear-skins on their backs, and heads covered with down. They had clubs in their hands, and as they danced around a big fire blazing in the centre of the lodge, they struck wildly with them, caring little whom or what they hit. One of their number was naked, with a rope round his waist, a knife in each hand, and making a fearful howling. Two others had hold of the end of the rope as if to keep him from doing any harm. This was the most ferocious exhibition I had seen, and the spectators got out of their reach as far as they could. They did no harm, however, excepting that one with his club knocked a hole through a brass kettle; after which they left and went to the other lodges, when I learned that they smashed boxes and did much mischief. After they had gone the owner examined his kettle, and quaintly remarked that it was worth more to him than the pleasure he had experienced by their visit, and he should look to the man who broke it for remuneration.

On a subsequent evening I was present at another performance. This consisted of dancing, jumping, firing of guns, etc. A large fire was first built in the centre of the lodge, and the performers, with painted faces, and many with masks resembling owls, wolves, and bears, crouched down with their arms clasped about their knees, their blankets trailing on the ground, and fastened around the neck with a single pin. After forming in a circle with their faces towards the fire, they commenced jumping sideways round the blaze, their arms still about their knees. In this manner they whirled around for several minutes, producing a most remarkable appearance. These performers, who were male, were succeeded by some thirty women with blackened faces, their heads covered with down, and a girdle around their blankets drawing them in tight at the waist. These danced around the fire with a shuffling, ungainly gait, singing a song as loud as they could scream, which was accompanied by every one in the lodge, and beating time with sticks on boards placed before them for the purpose. When the dance was over, some five or six men, with wreaths of sea-weed around their heads, blackened faces, and bear-skins over their shoulders, rushed in and fired a volley of musketry through the roof. One of them then made a speech, the purport of which was that the ceremonies had progressed favorably thus far, that their hearts had become strong, and that they felt ready to attack their enemies, or to repel any attack upon themselves. Their guns having in the meanwhile been loaded, another volley was fired and the whole assembly uttered a shout to signify approval. The performances during the daytime consisted of representations on the beach of various kinds. There was one representing a whaling scene. An Indian on all fours, covered with a bear-skin, imitated the motion of a whale while blowing. He was followed by a party of eight men armed with harpoons and lances, and carrying all the implements of whaling. Two boys, naked, with bodies rubbed over with flour, and white cloths around their [72] heads, represented cold weather; others represented cranes, moving slowly at the water's edge, and occasionally dipping their heads down as if seizing a fish. They wore masks resembling a bird's beak, and bunches of eagle's feathers stuck in their hair. During all of these scenes the spectators kept up a continual singing and drumming. Every day during these performances feasts were given at different lodges to those Indians who had come from the other villages, at which great quantities of food were eaten and many cords of wood burned, the giver of the feast being very prodigal of his winter's supply of food and fuel. The latter, however, is procured quite easily from the forest, and only causes a little extra labor to obtain a sufficiency.

*Fig. 42.

The final exhibition of the ceremonies was the *T'hlukloots* representation, after which the presents were distributed. From daylight in the morning till about eleven o clock in the forenoon was occupied by indoor performances, consisting of singing and drumming, and occasional speeches. When these were over, some twenty performers dressed up in masks and feathers, some with naked bodies, others covered with bear skins, and accompanied by the whole assembly, went down on the beach and danced and howled in the most frightful manner. After making as much uproar as they could, they returned to the lodge, and shortly after every one mounted on the roofs of the houses to see the performance of the *T'hlukloots*. First, a young girl came out upon the roof of a lodge wearing a mask representing the head of the thunder bird, which was surmounted by a top-knot of cedar bark dyed red and stuck full of white feathers from eagles tails. Over her shoulders she wore a red blanket covered with a profusion of white buttons, brass thimbles and blue beads; her hair hung down her back covered with white down. The upper half of her face was painted black and the lower red. Another girl with a similar headdress, was naked except a skirt about her hips. Her arms and legs had rings of blue beads, and she wore bracelets of brass wire around her wrists; her face being painted like the other. A smaller girl had a black mask to resemble the ha-hek-to-ak. The masks did not cover the face, but were on the forehead, from which they projected like horns. The last girl's face was also painted black and red. From her ears hung large ornaments made of the haikwa or dentalium, and blue and red beads, and around her neck was an immense necklace of blue beads. Her skirt was also covered with strings of beads, giving her quite a picturesque appearance. A little boy with a black mask and head-band of red bark, the ends of which hung down over his shoulders, and eagles feathers in a top-knot, was the remaining performer. They moved around in a slow and stately manner, occasionally spreading out their arms to represent flying and uttering a sound to imitate thunder, but which resembled the noise made by the nighthawk when swooping for its prey, the spectators meanwhile beating drums, pounding the roofs with sticks, and rattling with shells. This show lasted half an hour, when all again went into the lodge to witness the distribution of presents and the grand finale. The company all being arranged, the performers at one end of the lodge and the women, children, and spectators at the other, they commenced by putting out the fires and removing the brands and cinders. A quantity of feathers were strewed over the ground floor of the lodge, and a dance and song commenced, every one joining in the latter, each [73] seeming to try to make as much noise as possible. A large box, suspended by a rope from the roof, served as a bass drum, and other drums were improvised from the brass and sheet-iron kettles and tin pans belonging to the domestic furniture of the house, while those who had no kettles, pans, or boxes, banged with their clubs on the roof and sides of the house till the noise was almost deafening. In this uproar there was a pause, then the din commenced anew. This time the dancers brought out blankets, and with them beat the feathers on the floor till the whole air was filled with down, like flakes of snow during a heavy winter's storm. Another lull succeeded, then another dance, and another shaking up of feathers, till I was half choked with dust and down. Next the presents were distributed, consisting of blankets, guns, shirts, beads., and a variety of trinkets, and the whole affair wound up with a feast.

*Fig. 43.

This was the *Dukwally* or "black *tamanawas*" ceremony. It is exhibited every winter, sometimes at only one village and sometimes at all.

The other performance is termed *Tsiahk*, and is a medicine performance, quite as interesting, but not as savage in its detail. It is only occasionally performed, when some person, either a chief or a member of his family, is sick. The Makahs believe in the existence of a supernatural being, who is represented to be an Indian of a dwarfish size, with long hair of a yellowish color flowing down his back and covering his shoulders. From his head grow four perpendicular horns, two at the temple and two back of the cars. When people are sick of any chronic complaint and much debilitated, they imagine they see this being in the night, who promises relief if the ceremonies he prescribes, are well performed. The principal performer is a doctor, whose duties are to manipulate the patient, who is first initiated by secret rites into the mysteries of the ceremony. What these secret rites consist of I have not ascertained, but there is a continual singing and drumming during the day and evening for three days before spectators

Makah

are admitted. From the haggard and feeble appearance of some patients I have seen, I judge the ordeal must have been severe. The peculiarity of this ceremony consists in the dress worn alike by patients, novitiates, and performers. Both men and women assist, but the proportion of females is greater than of males. *Fig. 42 shows a back view of a female performer in full dress; on her head is worn a sort of coronet made of bark, surmounted by four upright bunches or little pillars, made of bark wound round with the same material, and, sometimes threads from red blankets to give a variety of color. From the top of each of the four pillars, which represent the horns of the *tsiahk*, are bunches of eagles quills, which have been notched, and one side of the feather edge stripped off. In front is a band, which is variously decorated, according to the taste of the wearer, with beads, brass buttons, or any trinkets they may have. From each side of this band project bunches of quills similar to those on the top of the head. The long hair of the Tsiahk is represented by a heavy and thick fringe of bark, which covers the back and shoulders to the elbow. Necklaces composed of a great many strings of beads of all sizes and colors, and strung in various forms, are also worn, and serve to add to the effect of the costume. The paint for the face is red for the forehead and for the lower part, from the root of the nose to the cars; the portion between the forehead and the lower part is black [74] with two or three red marks on each cheek. The dress of the novitiate females is similar, with the exception of there being no feathers or ornaments on the bark headdress, and with the addition of black or bine stripes on the red paint covering the forehead and lower portion of the face. The headdress of the men (Fig. 43) consists of a circular band of bark and colored worsted, from the back part of which are two bunches of bark, like horses tails. Two upright sticks are fastened to the band behind the ears, and on top of these sticks are two white feathers tipped with red; the quill portion is inserted into a piece of elder stick with the pith extracted, and then put on the band sticks. These sockets give the feathers the charm of vibrating as the wearer moves his head; when dancing or moving in procession the hands are raised as high as the face, and the fingers spread out.

The doctor or principal performer has on his head a dress of plain bark similar to the female novitiate. He is naked except a piece of blanket about his loins, and his body is covered with stripes of red paint. The out-door performance consists of a procession which moves from the lodge to the beach; the principal actor or conductor being at the head, followed by all the males in single file, the last one being the doctor. Immediately behind the doctor the patient follows, supported on each side by a female assistant. The females close up the procession. All parties, male and female, have their hands raised as high as their faces, and the motion of the procession is a sort of shuffling dance. They move in a circle which gradually closes around the patient, who, with the novitiate, is left seated on the ground in the centre; songs with choruses by the whole of the spectators, drumming, shaking rattles, and firing of guns wind up the performance, and all [75] retire to the lodge, where dancing and singing are kept up for several days. Finally, presents are distributed, a feast is held, and the friends retire. The patient and novitiates are obliged to wear their dress for one month. It consists of the bark headdress, having, instead of feathers, two thin strips of wood, feather-shaped, but differently painted. Those of the patient are red at each end and white in the centre, with narrow transverse bars of blue. Those of the noviciate have blue ends and the centre unpainted. The patient's face is painted red, with perpendicular marks of blue on the forehead and the lower part of the face. The noviciate's forehead and lower portion of face is painted with alternate stripes of red and blue, the remainder of the face blue; the head band is also wound with blue yarn and yellow bark. The

Makah

head-band of the patient is wound with red. The tails of bark of both headdresses are dyed red. The patient carries in his hand a staff which can be used as a support while walking; this has red bark tied at each end and around the middle.

The *Dukwally* and *Tsiahk* are the performances more frequently exhibited among the Makahs than any others, although they have several different ones. The ancient *tamanawas* is termed *Do-thlub* or *Do-thlum*, and was formerly the favorite one. But after they had learned the T'hulkloots or Thunder Bird, they laid aside the *Do-thlub*, as its performance, from the great mimber of ceremonies, was attended with too much trouble and expense. The origin of the *Do-thlub* was, as stated to me by the Indians, in this manner: many years ago, an Indian while fishing in deep water for codfish, hauled up on his hook an immense haliotis shell. He had scarcely got it into his canoe when he fell into a trance which lasted a few minutes, and on his recovery he commenced paddling home, but before reaching land he had several of these trances, and on reaching the shore his friends took him up for dead, and carried him into his house, where he presently recovered, and stated, that while in the state of stupor he had a vision of *Do-thlub*, one of their mythological beings, and that he must be dressed as *Do-thlub* was and then he would have revelations. He described the appearance, as he saw it in his vision, in which Do-thlub presented himself with hands like deer's feet. He was naked to his hips, around which was a petticoat of cedar bark dyed red, which reached to his knees. His body and arms were red; his face painted red and black; his hair tied up in bunches with cedar twigs, and cedar twigs reaching down his back. When his friends had dressed him according to his direction, he fell into another trance, in which he saw the dances which were to be performed, heard the songs which were to be sung, and learned all the secret ceremonies to be observed. It was also revealed that each performer must have a piece of the haliotis shell in his nose, and pieces in his ears. He taught the rites to certain of his friends, and then performed before the tribe, who were so well pleased that they adopted the ceremony as their tamanawas, and retained its observance for many years, till it was superseded by the *Dukwally*. The haliotis shell worn by the Makahs in their noses is a custom originating from the *Do-thlub*. Other ceremonies are occasion ally gone through with, but the description above given will serve to illustrate all those observed by the Makahs. Different tribes have some peculiar to themselves, the general character of which is, however, the same. It will be seen that the [76] public part of these performances are rather in the nature of amusements akin to our theatrical pantomimes than of religious observances, though they are religiously observed.

The Makahs, like all other Indians, are exceedingly superstitious {?!}, believing in dreams, in revelations, necromancy, and in the power of individuals over the elements. An instance of the latter fell under my own observation. Early in April, 1864, there was a continuance of stormy weather which prevented them from going after whales or fishing. At length an Indian, who came from the Hosett village at Flattery Rocks informed me that his people had found out that Keyattie, an old man living with them, had caused the bad weather. A woman and a boy had found him at his incantations and reported him to the tribe; where upon the whole village went to *Keyattie's* lodge, and told him that if he did not immediately stop and make fair weather, they would hang him. He promised to do so, and they gave him two days to calm the wind and sea. The Indian added with great gravity that now we should have fair weather. I told him that it was foolish talk. He said no, that the Indians in former times were capable of making it rain or blow at pleasure, and cited a recent case of a Kwilleyute Indian, who only a few summers previous had made bad weather during the halibut season. The Kwilleyutes hung him, and immediately the weather became fair. In the present instance we did have fair weather in two days after, and the Indians were confirmed in the belief that old Keyattie had caused the storm that prevented their going out in canoes, and that the fear of death had forced him to allay it. Through dreams they think they can foretell events and predict the sickness or death of their friends. Some are supposed to be more gifted in this respect than others, and many a marvellous tale has been related to me by these dreamers; but in every instance the events had already taken place which they pretended to have predicted. Their necromancy consists in the performance of the doctors, which will be alluded to more at length under the heading of "medicine."

It will be seen that though the Makahs are heathens in the fullest sense, they are not idolaters or worshippers of images, but that their secret addresses are to the sun as the representative of the Great Spirit. They seem, on the other hand, perfectly indifferent to teaching. They will not believe that the white man's God is the same as their Great Chief, nor give any attention to the truths of Christianity. If the children could be removed from their parents and the influences of the tribe, and placed in a civilized community, they might be led to embrace our religion as well as customs; but any efforts of a missionary on the spot, opposed as they would be by prejudice, superstition, and indifference, would be futile. The most that can be hoped for, at present, is to keep them at peace, and gradually teach them such simple matters as they can be made to take an interest in, and will tend to ameliorate their condition.

Magic and "Medicine". – The Makahs have, as usual, certain persons, both male and female, who are supposed to be skilled in the art of healing. The male practitioners alone, however, go through an ordeal or *tamanawas* to constitute them "doctors." An ancient ceremony called *Ka-haip* was formerly always observed to endow them with supernatural powers, but it is seldom used of late years, and there [77] are but three persons living in the tribe at present who have undertaken it. They obtain notoriety by occasional good fortune in apparently performing remarkable cures, and each is celebrated for some faculty peculiar to himself in removing disease. Every sickness for which they cannot assign some obvious cause is supposed to be the work of a "*skoo-koom*," or demon, who enters the mouth when

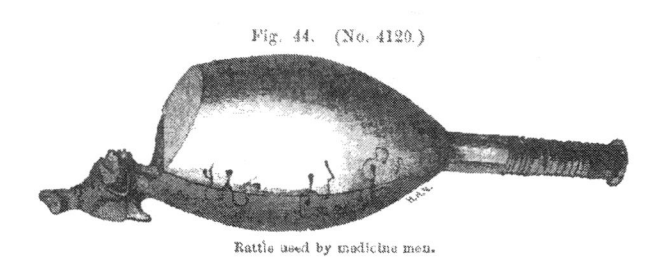

Fig. 44. (No. 4120.) Rattle used by medicine men. drinking at a brook, or pierces the skin while bathing in salt water. These evil spirits assume the form of a little white worm which the doctor extracts by means of manipulations, and the patient recovers. Although I have repeatedly seen them at work on their patients, and pretending to take out these animals, I have never seen the object itself, which, as they generally informed me, is only seen by the doctor. In extracting these pretended evil spirits, he manipulates the part affected, frequently washing the hands during the operation, and warming them at the fire. This, he states, is to make the hands sensitive, so that on pressing them upon the patient's body he can the more easily feel where the evil is located. Sometimes he is an hour or two in finding the *skookoom*, particularly if the patient be a chief, as then not only the doctor's fees will be larger, but there will probably be a great company of friends assembled to sing and drum, and afterwards to feast. When the doctor thinks that he has worked enough, he will then try to catch the thodkoom and squeeze it out. If

he succeeds, he blows through his hand toward the roof of the lodge, and assures the patient that it has gone. An instance occurred about Christmas time, 1864, of an old man who had been sick for two or three years of lingering consumption. He had exerted himself very much at a *Dukwally* performance, and by some violent strain had burst an abscess on his lungs and was in a very critical condition. I was sent for, and told he was dying, and went immediately to his lodge, where I found him under the immediate charge of an Indian doctor. By virtue of my position as dispenser of medicines for the reservation, I was permitted to remain as a sort of consulting physician. I was perfectly well aware of the circumstances attending the case, and that the patient was dying, and simply took with me an anodyne to relieve the pain of his last moments; but as I could do nothing while the Indian doctor was at work, I remained a spectator of the scene. The patient was upon his knees, his head supported by an Indian who was in front of him. The doctor, a muscular, powerful man, having washed his hands and warmed them, grasped the patient by the back of the neck, pressing his thumbs against the spinal column, and moving them with [78] all his might as though he was trying to separate the skull from the backbone. He exerted himself to such a degree that every muscle and vein was distended, and drops of perspiration ran freely from his face. At length he gave a wrench and a twist, the patient uttered a yell, when it was announced to me by the doctor that the skookoom had been caught, and that the man would recover. I told him the man would die in half an hour, but if he had not been squeezed so hard, and had taken my medicine, he would possibly have lived two or three days. The doctor laughed, and replied that I did not know as well as the Indians did; but it proved as I predicted. The man did die, and in less than two hours from the time I had made the remark he was buried, myself assisting in the ceremonies, as I desired to see how they were performed.

They have a variety of songs and chants during the performance, each doctor seeming to have a tune of his own. But the method adopted by all, is first to remove the skookoom by manipulation, and after that administer other remedies. Some of the old women are skilled as physicians both in the above method and in the preparation of medicinal herbs. I saw the application of a most singular remedy in the case of a young man who had been shot through the left arm by a dragoon pistol, in the hand of another Indian who was drunk. The ball passed through the arm between the shoulder and the elbow, injuring, but not breaking the bone, and lodged in the muscles of the back, from whence it was extracted in a rude manner by an incision made with a jack-knife. I advised the friends to take him immediately to Port Angeles or Victoria, where he could have surgical advice, but they concluded to try their own remedies first. They attempted to stop the bleeding by applying hemlock bark chewed fine, which seemed to have the desired effect. They next went to where the young man's father was buried, and dug up the bone of the upper part of the left arm, which they washed, and then sawed or split in two, lengthwise, and formed splints of it. These were scraped, and the scrapings of the bone applied as a dressing. The bone splints were applied and the arm bandaged firmly. The Indians assured me that the bone from the father's arm would renew or replace the wounded one in the boy's arm; that they always tried it in the case of a broken bone, and it always effected a cure. Thus, if a leg, an arm, or a rib is broken, they take a similar one from the body of the nearest relative who has been dead over a year, and apply it either as a dressing by scraping, or in the form of splints. I have, however, seen none but the instance above quoted where the splints were applied. In this case fragments of the bone continually coming away, the remedy proved worthless, and after several months suffering, the young man was carried to Victoria, where the arm was attended to by a skilful surgeon, and he shortly recovered. There is not an instance in the whole tribe where an amputation has been performed, although I have known several cases where life would have been saved had the patient or his friends submitted to or allowed the operation. But as they know nothing of the practice themselves, they are very reluctant to have any such operations performed, preferring death to the loss of a limb. Incised wounds and lacerations are treated either with a poultice of chewed hemlock, or elder bark, or wood ashes strewed on, which absorbs the discharge and forms a crust or scab. Wounds of this description [79] heal very readily, which is to be wondered at, since their systems are so full of humors, but it is very rare that suppuration occurs; although in several instances of bruises on the leg, or the skin, I have seen bad ulcers that were a long time healing.

The whole tribe are pervaded by a scrofulous or strumous diathesis which shows itself in all its various forms; enlargement and suppuration of the cervical glands; strumous ulcers in the armpits, and swelling and suppuration in the groin and thigh. The strumous bubo is of common occurrence in infants, children of all ages, and adults. These are invariably cut, I cannot say lanced, for the instrument in all cases is a knife, and the wounds allowed to take care of themselves. Sores of this description are considered by most of the white people of the territory to be of syphilitic origin, but I am of opinion that such is not the case. This tribe is remarkably exempt from diseases of a venereal nature; and in a residence of three years among them, during two of which I have dispensed medicines, but three cases have come to my observation of syphilitic bubo. One was a squaw, who had contracted the disease in Victoria; the other two, men of the tribe to whom on her return she had imparted it; but I think I can safely assert that there is scarcely an individual in the whole tribe but what has had strumous buboes or ulcerations of the cervical glands at some period of life. Eruptive diseases, such as scald head, ringworm, and a species of itch, are very common among infants; all of which, and their scrofulous tumors, may be attributed to filthy habits and the nature of their food, which consists chiefly of fish and oil. A variety of the thorn oyster is frequently thrown ashore after, heavy storms; or is found in the root of the kelp which has grown upon it, and, being torn up by the breakers, brings the oyster ashore in its grasp. These are not eaten, but I have seen the fresh ones made use of as a sort of poultice for boils, and also raw fish is occasionally applied to the same purpose. Sometimes, when they wish to apply a rubefacient to tumors, they use *Pyrola elliptic*, which is bruised into a pulpy mass, and applied by means of a bandage. This little plant is very common in the woods, and is capable of producing a blister on the skin of a white person; but the Indians seldom retain it long enough to create anything more than a redness or inflammation of the part.

One of their remedies to reduce a strumous tumor is by means of actual cautery, prepared from the dried inner bark of the white pine, which is applied by a *moxa* or cone. The skin is first wet with saliva at the desired point; the moxa then placed upon it and set on fire. The bark burns very rapidly and causes a deep sore, which is kept open by removing the scab as often as it forms, until relief is felt. Sometimes they apply several of these moxas to the person at one time. I have seen them give relief in many instances. This practice seems to be a common one among all the coast tribes in the vicinity, and it is rare to see an adult who has not scars produced by its means.

Burning the flesh is also resorted to for other purposes. Boys will apply moxas made of dried and partially charred pitch, to the back of the thumbs from the nail to the wrist. When the sores heal, they leave scars or callous spots, which are supposed not only to keep the bow-strings from hurting the hand, but to give a steadiness of aim, so that they can throw their arrow's with more precision. I have [80] seen school-boys sit down of an evening by the fire and amuse themselves in this manner, holding out their hands with the burning pitch singeing into the flesh, and showing their bravery by the amount of pain they could bear. I usually found, however, that they were very willing for me to dress their hands with salve when ever they had attempted this performance. Blood-letting is not practised according to our methods, but in case of bruises when there is swelling and much pain, they scarify the skin by cutting longitudinal and transverse gashes just deep enough to make the blood flow by keeping the part moistened with water. Cauterizing the flesh is, however, the favorite and most generally practised remedy for all internal complaints, and answers with the Inxlian the double purpose of blisters and bleeding. There are many cases of deformity arising from strumous disease of hip-joint, white swelling of the knee, and rheumatic affection of feet. These cripples go about with the aid of a stick or pole, which they hold with both hands. I have made crutches for some, but they could never be persuaded to use them. There is one case of enlargement of the scrotum to an enormous size. The patient is a man about forty years of age, who has been troubled with the complaint for about twenty years, the sac gradually enlarging, so that now it reaches four inches below the knee and is of the size of a five gallon keg. He assures me that he suffers no pain from it, but the enormous size is quite inconvenient, and causes him to walk with a very peculiar gait. As his only covering is a blanket, the parts are frequently exposed. The complaint does not appear to be dropsical, but rather an adipose secretion. Doctor Davies, formerly physician and surgeon to the reservation, was desirous of making an examination, but the man was exceedingly opposed to it, and no opportunity has been had of ascertaining its real character.

The most common complaints are diarrhoea and dysentery, coughs, colds, and consumption. The first two are most frequent, and have been formerly very fatal. I find, however, that taken in their early stages they readily yield to simple treat ment, and a dose of castor oil, followed by Dover's powder from five to ten grains, is quite sufficient in most cases to effect a cure. During my experience among the coast Indians for a period of more than twelve years, I have noticed, as a general rule, that they require less medicine than white men, and invariably when administering any (with the exception of castor oil), I have given but one-half the amount that would be given to one of the latter. There seem to be no general remedies among themselves, each doctor or doctress having his or her own peculiar herbs, roots, or bark which they prepare in secret and administer with ceremony. I have seen a woman pulverize charcoal and mix it with water for her child to drink, who had a diarrhoea. Some make a tea of hemlock bark for an astringent, others scrape that of the wild currant, elder, or wild cherry, and make tea of it.

The *Polypodium falcatum* ? or, as it is commonly called, the sweet liquorice fern, is a most excellent alterative, and is much used by both white persons and. Indians in the territory, having acquired a reputation in venereal complaints. In the form of a decoction it is an excellent medicine combined with iodide of potassium. There are two varieties found at Cape Flattery; one growing on the trunks of trees or old mossy logs; the other on the rocks. The plants are similar in general appearance, except that those growing on rocks have a stout, fleshy leaf. The [81] taste of the roots and their medicinal virtues appear to be the same. From the very many evidences I have had of their beneficial effects, I am led to conclude that their virtues far surpass those of the *P. vulgare*, which was formerly of great repute, but which has been laid aside in modern practice. Perhaps the Polypodium growing upon the immediate sea-coast derives some peculiar quality from the atmosphere of the ocean, but it certainly seems to be as efficacious and to take the place in this latitude of the sarsaparilla of the equatorial regions. By the white settlers it is often mixed with the root of the "Oregon grape" (*Mahonia*), but the Makahs use it alone, either simply chewing it and swallowing the juice, or boiling it with water and drinking the decoction. A number of species of liverwort are found at Cape Flattery, one of which grows upon the ground, and when freshly gathered has the taste of spruce leaves. The Indians use this for coughs, and as a diuretic. When chewed it appears to be of a mucilaginous nature, somewhat like slippery elm. It loses its peculiar spruce flavor on being dried, and I think its virtues are greatest when the plant is green. A variety of bittersweet or wintergreen is used for derangement of the stomach and intestinal canal. This is simply chewed and swallowed. I was shown one day by a sick chief, a great medicine which he had received from a Clyoquot doctor. It was kept very secret, and I was permitted to examine it as a mark of great confidence and friendship. After a number of rags had been unrolled, a little calico bag was produced, and in this bag, very carefully wrapped up in another rag, were several slices of a dried root, which the Indian informed me was very potent. I tasted it and found it to be the Indian turnip (*Arisoema*). Dr Bigelow (Am. Medical Botany) says "the root loses nearly all its acrimony by drying, and in a short time becomes quite inert." But this which the Indian showed me was intensely acrid, and it had been dried for several months. I have not seen the plant growing in this vicinity, but if it is not a different variety from the eastern species, it certainly retains its potency for a much longer period.

The Indians have shown me at different times other plants which they said were good for certain complaints, but I have never seen them exhibited as medicine. It is to be observed, however, that there is scarcely an herb of any kind which grows on the Cape or its vicinity, but is considered a medicine in the hands of some one or other, and so what one considers good another ridicules, for as they have no knowledge of the diagnosis of disease, they are apt to think that what is good in one case is good in all. Thus, one doctor acquired quite a reputation by administering a pasty mass composed of the shell of the Natica, ground with water on a stone. This was useful in cases of acidity of the stomach arising from surfeits of butter and oil. Another tried the same remedy in the case of an abscess on the liver, but the patient died and the medicine was ridiculed. I think, as a general rule, they have but little confidence in their own preparations, as they invariably come to me after a trial of a day or two of their native remedies; and the whole of their materia medica is employed after the manner of the old women of all countries. But their ceremonials and tamanawas, and the manipulations and juggling feats of the doctor they have great faith in, and will probably continue them for a long time to come, if indeed they ever relinquish the practice.

Various plants have been shown me by the Indians as valuable during parturition, [82] but I do not think they are in general use. As a rule the Indian women require but little assistance during labor, and it is very rare that one dies during childbirth. I saw an instance of one who was taken with labor pains while on her way to the brook for water. This was a very unusual occurrence, as they generally keep in the house at such times. My attention was called to the circumstance by seeing her sitting on the ground and another ~~squaw~~ supporting her back. I went out to learn the cause, and found that she had just been delivered of a child. The woman sat still for a few moments longer, then got up and walked into the house without assistance. They are seldom confined to the house over a day, and often not over a couple of hours. That the process is somewhat shorter, and apparently attended with less suffering than among white women, is probably owing to a much lower degree of nervous sensibility, rather than to any material

Makah

physical difference. The children are, as a usual thing, well formed. I have heard of cases of malformation, but during three years past have not seen a single one. Twins are of rare occurrence, and during the same period I knew of but one instance, which happened on Tattoosh Island during the summer of 1864. The Indians did not seem to know what to do about it. They considered it as a sort of evil which would affect in some way the summer fisheries. So the woman and her husband were sent back to Neeah Bay, and prohibited from eating fish of any description for two or three months; and had it not been for the food procured at the Agency she must have starved. The twins died shortly after their birth, and I strongly suspect that they were killed by the Indians to get rid of the demons which were supposed to have come with them.[13]

In cases of sickness where the doctors consider that the patient cannot recover, it was formerly the custom to turn the sufferer out of doors to die, particularly if it was something they did not understand; the belief being, that if suffered to die in a house all the other occupants would die of the same disease. An instance came under my observation of a woman who was paralyzed so as to be utterly helpless. They dragged her out upon the beach on a cold wintry day, and left her on the snow to perish. The sympathies of the white residents were aroused, and several Indians were appealed to to take the woman into their lodges, and payment offered them for the performance of this simple act of humanity; but all refused through fear. They were, however, finally induced by promise of reward, and with the assistance of myself and another white person, to construct a rude hovel, in which she was placed, and food and fuel supplied her; but the Indians would do nothing more, and she was attended by the white residents and made as comfortable as the circumstances would admit, until death relieved her. Since then, and for the past two years, no instances of like inhumanity have occurred; the Indians fearing lest the agent would punish them for a repetition of the offence. But I have been frequently assured that, except for this, they would have treated several other patients in a similar manner. [83]

Funeral Ceremonies. – When a person dies the body is immediately rolled up in blankets and firmly bound with ropes and cords, then doubled up into the smallest possible compass and placed in a box which is also firmly secured with ropes. When all is ready, the boards of a portion of the roof are removed, and the box with the body taken out at the top of the house and lowered to the ground, from a superstition that if a dead body is carried through the doorway, any person passing through it afterwards would sicken and die. The box is then removed to a short distance from the house, and sometimes placed in a tree; but of late years the prevailing custom is to bury it in the earth. A hole is first dug with sticks and shells deep enough to admit the box, leaving the top level with the surface. Boards are then set up perpendicularly all around so as to completely inclose it, their ends rising above the ground from four to five feet. A portion of the property of the deceased is placed on top of the box; this, in the case of a man, consists of his fishing or whaling gear, or a gun with the lock removed, his clothing, and bedding. If a female, beads and bracelets of brass, iron, calico, baskets, and her apparel. A little earth is thrown on top, and then the whole space filled up with stones. Blankets, calico, shawls, handkerchiefs, looking glasses, crockery and tin ware, are then placed around and on the grave

---

[13] The same superstition exists among other tribes. Some years ago a woman belonging to a party who were being conveyed on a California river steamer to their reservation, gave birth to twins, which were immediately thrown overboard. GG

for show, no particular order being observed, but each being arranged according to the fancy of the relatives ef the deceased. The implements used in digging the grave are also left and placed among the other articles. A description of a few of these graves may not be out of place. One was that of a woman who was buried at Baäda, the eastern extremity of Necah Bay. The husband was a young chief, who decorated it as became his ideas of his dignity. In front of the grave was a board on which was painted the representation of a rainbow, which they believe has great claws at each end with which it grasps any one so unfortunate as to come within its reach. On top of the board, which formed its edge, was a sort of shelf containing the crockery ware of the deceased; and on the left corner a carved head of an owl, wrapped up with a white cloth. A short stick wound with calico at the right corner bore a handkerchief at its top, and from two tall poles similarly wound around with calico a shawl, a dress pattern, and some red flannel were displayed like flags. At the expiration of a year the cloth disappeared, having been rotted by the rains and torn into shreds by the wind.

Another was the grave of a chief named *Hure-tall*, known by the whites as "Swell," and who was killed by an Elwha Indian in 1861 while engaged in bringing supplies from Port Townsend for the trading post at Neeah Bay. As he was an Indian well known and very much respected by the whites, his body was received by some settlers at Port Angeles, and placed in a box, and was brought from thence to Neeah Bay by a brother of the deceased, assisted by myself and another white man. The box was deposited in the ground, after the custom of the Indians, and over his remains a monument was raised by the relatives. It is built of cedar boards, and surmounted by a pole on the top of which is a tin oil can. Around its base are the painted tamanawas boards which he had in his lodge. A third grave is that of an Indian boy, at Bäada. A couple of posts were set up at the ends, and boards fastened to them which were covered with blankets. In the [84] centre of the upper edge of the boards an eagle's tail was fastened, spread out like a fan; two guns without locks were hung up at the ends, and a stick with a piece of calico served as a streamer. All these graves, with the exception of Swell's, are now denuded of their covering of cloth, nothing being replaced when once destroyed by the elements.

The tying a corpse in its blanket is of recent date. Formerly it was not considered necessary to be so particular, but a case of suspended animation, where the patient recovered, having occurred some ten years ago, they adopted it to prevent any future instances of the same kind. The circumstance, as related to me by some Indians, is as follows: The Indian, whose name was Harshlah, resided at Bäada village, and died, or was supposed to have died, after a very brief illness. He was buried in the usual manner, but in two days after he managed to free himself and to make his appearance among his friends, greatly to their consternation. After having assured them that he was no spirit, but really alive, they were induced to listen to his statement. He said that he had been down to the centre of the earth, which the Indians suppose to be the abode of the departed, and there he saw his relatives and friends, who were seated in a large and comfortable lodge enjoying themselves. They told him that he smelled bad like the live people, and that he must not remain among them. So they sent him back. The people he saw there had no bones; these they had left behind them on the earth; all they had taken with them was their flesh and skin, which, as it gradually disappeared by decomposition after death, was removed every nignt to their new abode, and when all was carried there, it assumed the shape each one wore on earth. It is one of the avocations of the dead to visit the bodies of their [78] friends who have died, and gradually, night by night, remove the flesh from the bones, and carry it to the great resting-place, the lodge in the centre of the earth. He further stated that on his return to where he had been buried he struggled and freed himself from his grave-cloth and the box, and then discovered that he had been dead.[14]

This man *Harshlah* afterwards died of small-pox, and my informant remarked that the second time he was tied up so securely that he never came to life again. Since then they have been very particular to secure all bodies so firmly that a revival is hopeless. This circumstance, so fresh in the minds of all the adults of the tribe, and the revelations respecting the other world, which correspond so exactly with their ancient ideas, make it impossible to teach them our views of a future state. They do not doubt the white man's statement, but they say that his heaven, which is represented to be in the sky, is not intended for the Indian, whose abode is in the earth. I have known several instances where, from the attending circumstances, there is little doubt that persons have been buried while in a swoon, or in a simply comatose state, and I have repeatedly urged upon them the folly of burying such persons before means could be tried to resuscitate them; but I never have been able to get them to wait a single moment after they think the breath has left the body. On the 10th of October, 1864, Sierchy, a middle-aged man of general good health, was reported to me as having just died. It appeared that the evening previous he had eaten a raw carrot, which the farmer on the reservation had given him, and towards morning he complained of a pain in his breast, but as he made no request for assistance, his squaw took no notice of him, and at sunrise went about preparing the usual meal. While thus engaged, she noticed Sierchy to exhibit a slight convulsive motion, and as she supposed instantly die. She at once began to howl, and in this was joined by the rest of the squaws. I was sent for and went over to the lodge, which was only four or five rods from my quarters; but when I arrived, which could not have been over ten minutes from the time the man was supposed to have died, the others had wrapped him up in his blanket, and wound a stout cord tight around him from head to foot, drawing it so firmly about the neck that it would have suffocated a well person in five minutes. I tried to induce them to undo the face and let me attempt to restore him, for I thought he had only swooned away, or at the worst had but a fit from eating the carrot, which they had told me about, but I could not persuade them. "It was very bad to look on the face of the dead, and they must be covered from sight as soon as they cease to breathe." So they carried him out and buried him. I shall always, however, think that if proper means had been tried, he would have speedily revived. Another case was that of a ~~squaw~~ who had suddenly lost her husband a few days before. He had been sick for a long time and had apparently recovered; but taking a severe cold, he died from its effects in about twenty-four hours from the time of the attack. The woman was remarkably stout, and in good health. I saw her sitting by the bank of the brook, lamenting the death of her husband, and passed by to the upper village, about a quarter of a mile distance, where having attended some sick persons, I was about returning to the school building, when I heard the wailing cry of women announcing death. I quickened my steps and soon learned that it was the same woman I had passed but a short time previously, weeping for her husband, who was now also announced as dead. By the time I could get into the lodge, she too was tied up and in a box, ready to be buried, nor would the friends listen to a word I said, or

---

[14] Cases of apparent death, sometimes, perhaps, feigned for the purpose of acquiring influence, or notoriety, are not unfrequent among these coast tribes, and in all those I have known, a similar story lias been told of a visit to the dead country. GG

permit me to use any measures for her recovery. Dead she was, they were sure, or if not, they took good means to insure that she should be so shortly.

As soon as an Indian dies the property, if there be any, is divided at once among the relations and friends. The time of mourning is one year, and at the expiration of the period, or on the return of the same season, or the same moon, the nearest surviving relative gives a feast and distributes presents, both to appease the spirit of the departed and to give notice that mourning is over. During the interval it is considered disrespectful to mention the name of the deceased in the hearing of relatives or friends, and whenever it is necessary to speak the name to a white person, it is invariably done in an undertone or whisper.

Although I have stated that it is the general custom to place the dead in a box, yet it is not the invariable practice, as, in case of persons of inferior rank who are either old or poor, it not unfrequently occurs that they are simply wrapped in a blanket and a mat and buried in the ground. The bodies of slaves are dragged a [86] short distance from the lodge and covered over with a mat. In the case of the old man whom I mentioned in connection with the performance of the doctor, and whose body I assisted to bury, he was simply rolled in his blanket, lashed up firmly in a mat, and buried in a shallow grave. Over the remains were piled broken boxes, mats, old blankets, and the clothing he had worn. Care is always taken to render worthless everything left about a grave, so that the cupidity of the evil minded may not tempt them to rob the dead. Blankets are cut into strips, crockery ware is cracked or broken, and tin pans and kettles have holes punched through them.

No monuments of a lasting character mark the last resting place of even the greatest chief. Whatever of display there may be made at the time of burial is of an ephemeral nature calculated to last but for a year, and after that but little care or respect is shown the remains. As time elapses the graves go to decay, and the bones of the dead lie scattered around. During the clearing of land at Neeah Bay for the uses of the Agency a large number of bones and skulls were found, which were all gathered and burned, the sight of such relics of humanity being offensive to the feelings of the whites.

There are no antiquities connected with this tribe; such as earthworks, mounds, or other evidences of the usages of former generations. All that the antiquarian can find to repay him for his researches are arrow-heads of stone, and ancient daggers and hatchets of the same material, which are occasionally thrown up by the plough or occasionally found on the surface. The mounds of shells and other debris of ancient feasts are but the refuse of the lodges, and whatever may be found in them has not been so deposited from any design, but simply lost or thrown away. The only fortifications they have used as a defence against enemies were the rude stockades or pickets of poles, which I have before alluded to, and which have gradually decayed or have been used as firewood.

Superstitions. {?!} – Besides the legends I have already related, there are others which may serve to convey an idea of the mental character of the tribe, and throw some light upon statements made by early explorers on the northwest coast. There is a remarkable rock standing detached from the cliff at the northwest extremity of the Cape, a little south of the passage between the main land and Tatoosh Island. This rock, the Indian name of which is *Tsa-tsa-dak*, rises like a pillar from the ocean over a hundred feet almost perpendicularly, leaning, however, a little to the northwest. Its base is irregular in form, and about sixty feet in diameter at its widest portion near the surface of the water. It decreases in size till at the top it is but a few yards across, and on its summit are low stunted bushes and grass. It is entirely inaccessible except on its southeastern side, where a person possessed of strength and nerve could, with great difficulty, ascend, but to get down by the same way would be impossible. The Indians have a tradition respecting this Pillar Rock, that many years ago an Indian climbed to its summit in search of young cormorants and gulls, which make it a resort during the breeding season; but after he had reached the top he could not again descend. All the attempts he made were fruitless, and at length his friends went to his relief, every expedient they could think of being resorted to without success. They tied strings to their arrows and tried to shoot them over, but they could not make them ascend sufficiently [87] high. They caught gulls and fastened threads to their feet, and tried to make them fly over and draw the string across the rock, but all was of no avail. Six days were wasted in the vain attempt to save him, and on the seventh he lay down and died. His spirit, say the Indians, still lives upon the rock, and gives them warning when a storm is coming on, which will make it unsafe for them to go out to sea in pursuit of their usual avocations of killing whales or seals, or catching fish. Duncan, one of the early explorers, mentions this rock and gives a drawing of it, but he places it between the island and the main land. Vancouver, in alluding to Duncan's statement, says he saw no such rock. It does not exist where Duncan states he saw it, but it does exist about one mile a little east of south of Tatoosh Island. It is easily seen when sailing up the coast close in land; but when opposite to it at a short distance off it is so overtopped by the cliffs of the Cape as not to be particularly noticeable. The passage between the island and the main land is half a mile wide, and is not, as is stated by various authors, obstructed by a reef connecting the island and the cape, but has a depth of four and five fathoms of water through its entire distance; and although there are several rocks which are bare at low water, yet vessels can pass through at any stage of the tide, providing the wind is fair, for the ebb and flood tides rush through with great velocity, making tide rips which have been mistaken for shoals. I have passed through the passage in a schooner twice, and I know of several other vessels that have gone through without the slightest difficulty.

There is another rock not far from the Pillar Rock, near the top of which is a sort of cavity, across which rests a large spar which has been borne on the crest of some stupendous wave and tossed into its present resting place. It had been there long before the memory of the present generation of Indians, and is believed by them to have been placed there by supernatural agency, and is consequently regarded with superstitious awe. They think that any one who should attempt to climb up and dislodge it would instantly fall off the rock and be drowned. All down the coast from Cape Flattery to Point Grenville, pillar rocks are seen of various heights and sizes, and most fantastic shapes, and for each and all of them the Indians have a name and a traditionary legend. About midway between the cape and Flattery Hocks is one of these pillars, looking in the distance like a sloop with all sail set. The tide sets strongly round it both at flood and ebb. The Indians believe a spirit resides upon it, whose name is *Se-ka-jec-ta*, and to propitiate it, and give them a good wind and smooth sea, they throw overboard a small present of dried fish or any other food they may have whenever they pass by.

The aurora borealis they think is the light caused by the fires of a mannikin tribe of Indians who live near the north pole, and boil out blubber on the ice. On one occasion while in a canoe on the Strait of Fuca at night, there was a magnificent display of the aurora, and I asked the chief who had charge of the canoe, if he knew what it was. He said, far beyond north, many moons journey, live a race of little Indians not taller than half the length of this paddle. They live on the ice and eat seals and whales. They are so strong that they dive into the water and catch whales with their hands, and the light we saw was from the fires of those little people boiling blubber. They were *skookooms*, and he did not dare speak [88] their names.[15] Drowned persons they supposed to turn into owls, and several years since a party of Indians having been lost by the accidental demolishing of their canoe by the tail of a whale they were killing, I was gravely assured that the night after the accident eight owls were seen perched on the houses of the drowned men, and each had suspended from his bill the shell worn in the nose of the man while alive.

A most ludicrous instance of their superstition occurred while I was making a survey of the reservation during the summer of 1862. A chief, *Kobetsi*, who lived at Tsuess village, owned a large cranberry meadow, of the possession of which he was very jealous. Among the Indians who accompanied me on the survey was a young man who had quite recently had a difficulty with *Kobetsi*, in which he felt that the chief was the aggressor. The Indians, who are very fertile in inventing tales, informed Kobetsi that the fellow had sold the cranberry meadow to me, and that I had a great medicine which I could set in the field which would gather all the cranberries. This medicine was a field compass. They had seen the mariner's compass, but a field compass on a Jacob staff was something they could not comprehend. Old *Kobetsi* believed the tale, and sent a party, armed and painted, from the island where he was then residing, to attack me and the surveying party at Tsuess. We did not happen to be there on their arrival, so they returned; but the following day I went down and finished the survey, and after returning home the old chief, who had been informed of the fact, came himself from Tatoosh Island with his warriors to demand redress for the supposed loss of his cranberries. He was soon convinced of the real facts, and left, quite mortified that he had worked himself up into such a state of excitement about nothing; but he still believed that the compass possessed great and mysterious properties, and requested me not to place it on his land again. Another instance of superstition was during the time of my taking a census of the tribe in 1861. The Indians at Hosett village were much opposed to giving me their names, from the belief that every man, woman, or child whose names were entered in my book, would have the small-pox and die.

The cliffs at the extreme point of Cape Flattery are pierced by deep caverns and arches that admit the passage of canoes, not only saving the distance of going around or outside the rocks during rough weather, but affording snug coves and shelter during high wind, and secure passages for the Indian to skulk along unseen. Some of the caverns extend a great distance under the cliff, and afford hiding places for seals, which, however, are not allowed to remain always in peace; for the Indian, watching an opportunity when it is calm, boldly ventures in as far as his canoe can be managed; then with a torch in one hand, and a knife in the other, he dashes into the water and wades or swims to where the seals are lying on the sandy bottom at the remote end of the cave. The light partially blinding and stupefying the [89] animals, and the Indian, taking

---

[15] Traditions of the Eskimos as a race of dwarfs, possessing supernatural powers, who dwell in the "always night country," are current among the Indians of Puget Sound also. One of the incentives to desperate resistance by them during the war of 1855-56, was the circulation by their chiefs of a story that it was the intention of the whites to take them all there in a steamer. The idea of eternal cold and darkness carried with it indescribable horrors to their imaginations. GG

advantage of this, is enabled to kill as many as he can reach. But this is an exploit attended with great danger, for occasionally the torch will go out, and leave the cavern in the profoundest darkness. At such times the cries of the seals, mingled with the roar of the billows as it echoes through the caves, inspire the Indian with a mortal terror; and should he escape with his life, he will have most fearful tales to relate of the dark doings and still darker and mysterious sayings of the beings -who are believed to inhabit these caverns and dens of the earth, and who being angry because their secret retreats were invaded, blew out the torch, and filled the air with the horrid sounds he heard. It is, however, but seldom that the usually turbulent waters in the vicinity of the cape are quiet enough to permit of such expeditions.

The craggy sides of the perpendicular cliffs afford resting places for numerous sea fowl, particularly the violet-green cormorant, which here builds its nest wherever it can find a hole left by some pebble or boulder fallen from the cliff, or where it can scratch or burrow into any loose soil that may form the summit. Harlequin ducks, mokes {?}, guillemots, petrels and gulls abound, and during the breeding season the air is filled with their discordant cries. These birds are all considered as departed Indians, and the cries they utter in an approaching storm, are supposed to be warnings of dead friends not to venture around the cape till it shall have abated.

Lichens and moss collect on the sides of the cliffs above the direct action of the waves, and where the tides reach, the rocks are covered with barnacles and mussels, or else entirely hidden by sea-weeds which grow in rich profusion. In some places there are beds of clay slate in the conglomerate which have been bored full of holes by the borer clam (*Parapholas*), and present a singular appearance; elsewhere they are the resting places of a great variety of star fish, sea slugs, limpets, etc. Some of these to the Indian mind are great medicines, others of them are noxious, and some are used for food. The jutting promontories, the rocky islets, and detached boulders, the caverns and archways about the Cape have all some incident or legend, and in one large cave, opposite Tatoosh Island where the breakers make an unusual sound, which becomes fearful on the approaching of a storm, they think a demon lives, who, coming forth during the tempest, seizes upon any canoes that may be so unfortunate as to pass at the time, and takes them and their crews into the cave, from whence they issue forth as birds or animals, but never again in human shape. The grandeur of the scenery about Cape Flattery, and the strange contortions and fantastic shapes into which its cliffs have been thrown by some former convulsion of nature, or worn and abraded by the ceaseless surge of the waves; the wild and varied sounds which fill the air, from the dash of water into the caverns and fissures of the rocks, mingled with the living cries of innumerable fowl, the great waves of the ocean coming in with majestic roll and seemingly irresistible force, yet broken into foam, or thrown into the air in jots of spray, all combined, present an accumulation of sights and sounds sufficient to fill a less superstitious beholder than the Indian with mysterious awe.

The astronomical and meteorological ideas of the Makahs are wrapped in vague [12 December, 1869] [90] and mythological tales. Of the revolutions of the heavenly bodies they know nothing more than that the sun in summer is higher in the heavens than during the winter, and that its receding or approach causes the difference of cold and heat of the seasons. The stars are believed to be the spirits of Indians and repre sentatives of every animal that has existed on earth, whether beast, bird, or fish. Their notions, however, are very confused, for as they think that all who die go immediately to the centre of the earth, they find it difficult to explain how they get

Makah

from there to become luminaries in the sky.[16] Most, if not all the constellations have names, such as the whale, halibut, skate, shark, etc., but I have never had any of them pointed out to me; they seemed to have a superstitious repugnance to doing so, and although they will at times talk about the stars, they generally prefer cloudy weather for such conversations. The moon they believe is composed of a jelly-like substance, such as fishes eat. They think that eclipses are occasioned by a fish like the "cultus" cod, or *toosh-kow*, which attempts to eat the sun or moon, and which they strive to drive away by shouting, firing guns, and pounding with sticks upon the tops of their houses. On the 5th of December, 1862, I witnessed the total eclipse of the moon, and had an opportunity of observing their operations. There was a large party gathered that evening at the house of a chief who was giving a feast. I had informed some of the Indians during the day that there would be an eclipse that evening, but they paid no regard to what I said, and kept on with their feasting and dancing till nearly ten o'clock, at which time the eclipse had commenced. Some of them coming out of the lodge at the time, observed it and set up a howl, which soon called out all the rest, who commenced a fearful din. They told me that the *toosh-kow* were eating the moon, and if we did not drive them away they Avould eat it all up, and we should have no more. As the moon became more and more obscure, they increased their clamor, and finally, when totally obscured, they were in great excite ment and fear. Thinking to give them some relief, I got out a small swivel, and with the assistance of one of the employes of the reservation, fired a couple of rounds. The noise, which was so much louder than any they could make, seemed to appease them, and as we shortly saw the silvery edge of the moon make its appearance after its obscuration, they were convinced that the swivel had driven off the toosh-kow before they had swallowed the last mouthful. I tried to explain the cause of the eclipse, but could gain no converts to the new belief, except one or two who had heard me explain and predict the eclipse during the previous day, and who thought as I could foretell so correctly what was going to take place, I could also account for the cause.

Their idea of the aurora borealis I have already explained. Comets and meteors are supposed to be spirits of departed chiefs. Rainbows are supposed to be of a malignant nature, having some connection with the *T'hlookloots*, or Thunder Bird, [91] and to be armed at each end with powerful claws with which to grasp any unhappy person who may come within their reach.

Of time they keep but little record. They have names for the different months or moons, twelve of which constitute with them two periods, the warm and cold. They can remember and speak of a few days or a few months, but of years, according to our computation, they know nothing. Their "year" consists of six months or moons, and is termed *tsark-wark it-chie*. The first of these periods commences in December, when the days begin to lengthen, and continues until June. Then, as the sun recedes and the days shorten, another commences and lasts till the shortest days. It is owing to the fact of these periods being only six months in duration, that it is so difficult for them to tell their ages according to our estimate, for as their knowledge of counting is very limited, they cannot be made to understand our reckoning. I have never known them to remember the proper age of a child of over two years. Sometimes they give the age of an individual by connecting his birth with some remarkable event, as, for instance, the year of

---

[16] I believe that this may be explained: the stars are the spirits of the pre-human and not of the existing race. Almost all nations have given the names of animals to certain constellations; thus the Eskimo call the Great Bear the Cariboo, the Puget Sound Indians call it the Elk, etc. GG

Makah

the smallpox, or when a white man came to reside among them, or that when a vessel was wrecked.

The seasons are recognized by them as they are by ourselves, namely, spring, by the name of *klairk-shiltl*; summer, by that of *kla-pairtch*; autumn, by *kwi-atch*; and winter, by *wake-puett*.

The names of the months are as follows: December is called *se-hwow-as-put'hl*, or the moon in which the *se-whow*, or *chet-a-pook*, the California gray whale, makes its appearance. January is a-a-kwis-put hl, or the moon in which the whale has its young. February, *kluk-lo-chis-to-put'hl*, or the moon when the weather begins to grow better and the days are longer, and when the women begin to venture out in canoes after firewood without the men. March is named *o-o-lukh-put'hl*, or the moon when the finback whales arrive. April, *ko-kosc-kar-dis-put'hl*. The moon of sprouts and buds. May, *kar-kwush-put'hl*. Moon of the strawberry and "salmon berry". June, *hay-sairk-toke-put'hl*. The moon of the red huckleberry. July is *kar-ke-sup-he-put'hl*, or the moon of the wild currants, gooseberry, and sallal, *Gaultheria*. August is *wee-kookh*, or season of rest; no fish taken or berries picked, except occasionally by the children or idle persons; but it is considered by the tribe as a season of repose. September is *kars-put'hl*, when all kinds of work commence, particularly cutting wood, splitting out boards, and making canoes. October, or *kwar-te-put'hl*, is the moon for catching the *tsa-tar-wha*, a variety of rockfish, which is done by means of a trolling line with a bladder buoy at each end, and a number of hooks attached. November is called *cha-kairsh-put'hl*, or the season of winds and screaming birds. The terminal *put'hl* seems to be equivalent to our word "season," for although the words to which it is added signify but one moon, yet when speaking of a month's duration the word dah-kah is used, as *tsark-wark dah-kah*, one month. [92]

Daylight or daytime is expressed by the word *Kle-se-hark*, which also means sun; but in enumerating days the word *che-al'th* is used, denoting a day and night, or twenty-four hours; thus, *tsark-wark che-al'th*, one day, &c. The divisions of the day are sunrise, *yo-wie*; noon, *ta-kas-sie*; sunset, *art hl-ha-chitl*; evening, *ar-tuktl*; midnight, *up ht-ut-haie*.

Wind is called *wake-sie*; the north wind, *batl-et-tis*; the south, *kwart-see-die*; the east, *too-tooch-ah-kook*; the southeast, *too-chee*; the west, *wa-shel-lie*, and the northwest *yu-yoke-sis*. These are each the breath of a fabulous being who resides in the quarter whence the wind comes, and whose name it bears.

Kwartseedie, the south wind, brings rain,[17] and the cause of it is this: Once upon a time the Mouse, the Flounder, the Cuttlefish, the Skate, with several other fishes and some land animals, resolved to visit *Kwartseedie* and see how he lived. After a journey of many days they found him asleep in his house, and thought they would frighten him; so the Cuttlefish got under the bed, the Flounder and Skate lay flat on the floor, and the other visitors disposed themselves as they thought best. The Mouse then jumped on the bed and bit *Kwartseedie*'s nose, which suddenly awakened him; and as he stepped out of bed he slipped down by treading on the Flounder and Skate, while the Cuttlefish, twining round his legs, held him fast. This so enraged him that he began to blow with such force that the perspiration rolled down from his forehead in drops and formed rain. He finally blew all his tormentors home again; but he never has forgotten the insult, and comes at intervals to annoy his enemies, for the land animals at such times are

---

[17] It is the prevalent winter wind of the northwest coast. GG

very uncomfortable, and the fish are driven from their feeding grounds on the shoals by the great breakers, which also oftentimes throw vast numbers of them on shore to perish.

The legends respecting all the other winds are very similar, and their blowing is a sign of the displeasure of their imaginary beings.

The Indians are excellent judges of the weather, and can predict a storm or calm with almost the accuracy of a barometer. On a clear calm night, if the stars twinkle brightly they expect strong wind, but if there is but a slight scintillation they are certain of a light wind or a calm, and consequently will start at midnight for the fishing grounds, fifteen or twenty miles due westward from Cape Flattery, where they remain till the afternoon of the following day. Their skill is not sur prising when it is understood that their time is in great measure passed upon the water, on a most rugged coast; that their only means of travel is by canoes, and that from childhood up it is as natural for them to watch the weather as it is for a sailor on the ocean to note the sky.

MAKAH VOCABULARY[18]

A

Above; or over head, (when spoken of things in a house.)	hā-dás-suk.
Above; up high (expression used out of doors.)	hā-tárts-tl.
Aboard	hay-túks.
go on board	hay-túks-itl.
it is on board	hay-lúks-uk.
Across as to cross	
A stream	kwit-swar-tis.
Afraid	win natch.
After	wa-hark.
Agreeable or pleasant, to taste or smell	{cháb-bas or {chám-mas.
Again	klao.
give me again	klao-káh.
Another or other	klá-oukh.
Another; personal	do-wd-do.
Alive	tee-chee.
All	dobe.
Always	kay-uitl.
Angry	koh-sap'h.
Ankle	kul-lá-kul-lie.
Arrive at, to	wartrluk.
When did you arrive at Victoria?	
ardis chealth kwiksa wartluk Bictolia.	
When did you arrive home?	
ardis chealth kwiksa ut-sáie.	
Arms	wak-sas.
right arm	chah-bát-sas.
left arm	kart-sar.
Arrow	tsa-hút-chitl, or

---

[18] In the Makah, as in all the languages of this part of the Western Coast, the letters *r*, *f*, and *v* are wanting; as also th, whether hard or soft. Mr. Swan has employed the *r* following the vowel *a* to indicate the Italian sound, as in father, and after *ai*, &c., to represent the neuter vowel u, as in the English *but*, and the Freneh *je*. The letter v in pronouncing English words is changed to *b* or *m*. These last are convertible letters, as are also *d* and *n*. *Th*, when it occurs in the text or the vocabulary, is to be understood as an aspirated *t*, as in the French *thé* – GG

	tsa-hat-tie.
Arrow-head, of wood	tsā-tsuk-ta-kwilth.
of bone	hah-sháh-biss.
of iron	chee-chair-kwilth.
Autumn	kwiatch.
Axe	he-sée-ak.

B

Back, the	hey-túks-uthl.
Bad	klay-ass.
Bag or sack	klar-airsh.
Barberry (*berberis oregoniensis*)	klook-shítl-ko-bupt.
Barbs of harpoon	tsa-kwat.
Bark	tsar-kar-bis.
Barrel	bat-lap-tl.
Barnacle	kléep-é-hud.
Bat	thlo-thle-kwok-e-batl.
Battledore, or boy's bat	klā-hairk.
Basket	bo-whie.
little basket	pe-koe.
Beach	sís-sá-bits.
Beads	cluk-partl-shitl.
large cut beads	kar-kwap-pah.
Behind	o-uk'-atl.
Berries	hoats-ak-lup.
ripe berries	sa-kálch-tl.
to gather berries	chí-ark.
Birds (generic)	hooke-toop.
young birds	de-dak-tl.
sea ducks	ko-whaithl.
cormorant (*gracculus violaccus*)	klo-poise.
crane	kwar-less.
crow	char-kar-do.
butter duck	chish-kul-ly.
Birds	
mallard duck	dah-hah-tich.
surf duck	al-ló-hain.
harlequin duck	tsat -tsowl-chak.
scaup duck	ko-ho-ash.
eagle, bald	ar-kwár-tid.
eagle, golden	kwa-kwát-i-buks.
goose	hah-dikh.

Makah voc

guillemot	klo-klo-chuh-sooh.
gulls	kwá-lil.
grebe	ah-low-ah-háiu.
(*Podiceps occidentalis*)	
grouse	too-too-artsh.
heron	hah-to-bad-die.
humming-bird	kwe-tá-kootch.
jay	kwísh-kwish-ee.
kingfisher	chesh-kully.
pigeon, band-tailed	háij-aib.
raven	klook-shood.
woodpecker, red-headed	kla-kla-bethl-putch.
woodpecker, golden-winged	kle-haib.
sandpiper	ho-hope-sis.
oyster-catcher	kwe-kwe-aph.
Black	toop-kooh.
Blanket	hey-laid.
blue blanket	art-lartl.
red blanket	klā-har-thl.
white blanket	kle-sethl.
green blanket	kor-buk-athl.
Blood	klar-klar-wdrk-a-bus.
Blue	kwish -kwish-á-kartl.
Board	klo-ailth.
Body	chath-leet.

    Body, parts of

head	to-hote-sid.
hair, on head	app-sahp.
hair, on body	chee-pee.
face	hā-túk-witl.
face, handsome woman	kloolth-sooh hā-túk-witl.
face, handsome man	kloo-klo hā-túk-witl.
forehead	hā-tuk-ant.
ear	pay-paer.
eye	kóllay.
nose	choo-oáth-tl-tub.
mouth	hā-tarks-tl.
tongue	la-kairk.
teeth	chee-chee.
beard	hah-puks'-ub.
neck	tse-kwár-bits.
shoulder	hey-dah-kwitl.
arm	wah-sas.

Makah voc

elbow	hā-dah-park-tl.
wrists	he-he-dlár-kwe-dook.
Body, parts of	
hand	klar-klar-he-do-koob.
fingers	tsar-tsár-kwle-de-koob.
thumb	bă-bă-bits-ă-de-koob.
nails	chath-latcht.
breast or chest	héy-dus-hothl.
woman's bosom	a-dab.
back	ha-tuks-itl.
leg	klā-ish-chid.
ankle	kul-la-kully.
foot	klar-klar-tsoob.
toes	tsark-tsark-itl-sub.
bones	hah-shah-biss.
heart	chah-pah or kle-buks-tie.
blood	klar-klar-wd rk-a-bus.
liver	pil-lok.
fat or tallow	hā-biks.
kidney	alsh-pahb.
bladder	kal- láh-tah -chib.
stomach	koo-you.
belly	ko-só-ar-ty.
intestines	tse-keup.
skin	klā-hark'.
penis	che-war.
pudenda (female)	jude.
testes	kar-ko-bits.
swelled or enlarged testes	dā-uk-tl.
Boil, to	klo-báhkst.
Bone	hah-shah-biss.
Bore a hole, to	tséet-kā-tsit.
Both	dobe.
Bottle	chah-bát-sits.
Bow	bis-lat-tie.
Bowstring	tsee-tsíts-see-dub.
Boy	wik-we-ak.
Bracelets	klar-klár-do-whas.
Break or destroy	kokh-shill.
Breasts of woman	a- dab.
Bring, to	o-hóse.
Broad or wide	klo-ko.
Brother	
elder	tak-ke-ai.

Makah voc

younger	kar-thlatl-ik.
Bucket or box for carrying water	hoot-uts.
Buy, to	bar-kwátl.
Burying-ground	péets-uks-sie.
By and by	ar-déei.
Bread, soft	tlay-tlay-skook.
ship bread or hard biscuit	ar-hósh-kook.
Buttons	hoop-sooelth.
Butter	tlat-say. [95]

C

Canoe, Chienook pattern	chap-ats.
large size for whaling, to carry eight men	pah-dow-thl.
medium size, to carry six men	bó-kwis-tat.
small size, to carry two to four persons	ar-tlís-tat.
very small, to carry one person	ta-kaów-dah.

(The whaling canoes are divided by thwarts or stretchers into five compartments, which are named as follows, as are also the occupants: –)

the bow	hey-tuks-wad.
the next behind	kah-kai-woks.
centre of canoe	chah-thluk-do-as.
the next behind	hey-tuk-stas.
stern	klee-chah.
Candle, lamp, or torch	la-kar-joss.
Carry, to	hā-dáiks.
Carpenter, worker in wood	kar-sár-kuk-tl.
Calico for woman's dress	hah-dah-kwits.
Catch, to	tsoo-kwill.
Cattle	boos-a-boos or moos-a-moos (borrowed).
Cedar-bark	péet-sup.
Chair	ko-kōke-we-dook or ta-kwát-ses.
Chest or breast	héy-dus-ho-thl.
Chest or box	klā-he-dethl or ar-hwe-dooks.
Chisel for making canoes	klar-kar-yuk.
Chicken-pox	yah-bass.
Chief	cha-bátlh.
Child	yá-duk.
infant	ya-duk-kow-i-chee.
Chop, to	hē-sis.
Clams (generic)	cha-its.
qua-haug	cha-its.
large clams (Lutraria)	har-loe

Makah voc

blue striated	har-ar-thlup.
Clouds	kle-deek-a-bus.
Coat	sa-se-tuk-lee.
Cock	ahá-hah-cha-kope.
Cookie	kla-lab.
Codfish, true	kár-dartl.
Codfish (a variety called in the jargon cultus cod)	toosh-kow.
Codfish, black	be-shŏwe.
Cold, I am	che-leer-hus.
cold weather	bat-latld.
Colors	
white	kle-sook.
red	klay-hoke.
black	toop-kook.
blue, dark	toop-kook.
blue, light	bo-kobe.
green	kwar-buk-uk.
Comb	kle-pe-ak.
Common person	mis-che-mas or bis-che.
Come, to	ut-sai-ce.
I come	ut-sai-atl-shie.
you come	shoo-oógh.
Contempt, expression of	
to a male	kā-shook.
to a female	héy-hook.
Cook, on stones	tá-chope.
Copulate	koo-kook.
Corpse	kok-shitl.
Cougar	háy-aed.
Cough	wa'-wa-se-koss.
Cradle	ya-duk-spa-tie.
Crab (generic)	hol-lo-wah.
Cranberries	pap-pas.
Crane	kwar-less.
Crow	cha-kár-do.
Crooked	wake-iss-soo-its.
Cry, to	kay-hark.
Cup	tsiar-koob.
Cut	karl-sap.
Cuttlefish	tc-thlope.

D

Dance, to	hóth-look.
Darkness	wis-tá-huk.
Daughter (child)	har-dów-e-chuk.
Day	kle-sé-hark.

(This also means daylight. In enumerating days, the word *chealth* is used.)

Dead	kok-shal.
Deadland (country of the dead)	hay-tár-puthl.
Deep	har-chée.
Deer	bo-kwitch. [96]
Demons (the primal race)	che-che-wuptl.
devils	ché-war.
Dig, to	tsar-kwar-kethl.
Dirt	sar-kwák-ā-bus.
Do, to	bar-bóo-ak.
Dog	keh-deill.
Dogfish	yáh-chah.
Door	boo-shoo-i-sub.
Down, bird's	pó-hoke.
Down stream	ik-tar-wárk-liss.
Dream, to	o-oár-portl.
Drink, I	hoo-tuks-ill.
Drive, to	a-aiks or aáh-eks.
Drunk	a-whatl-youk.
Dry	klo-shówe.
Duck, mallard	dah-hah-tich.
Dull	wee-we-thuk-tl.
Dung	shab.
to dung	shab-bah.

E

Ear	pā-páer.
Earth	kwe-che-ar.
Eagle, bald	ar-kwár-tid.
Osprey	kwa-kwal-i-buks.
Eat	hah-ouk.
Echinus (sea-urchin)	
Large	toot-sup.
Small	koats-kappr.
Eggs	doo-chak.
Eight	ar-tles-sub.
Elbow	hā-dah-park-tl.
Elk	tóo-Kuk.
End (or point)	yu-chíl-tish.

Makah voc

Evening	ar-tuk-tl
Eye	kollay.
Exchange, to	hó-oe-yah.

F

Face	hā-tuk-witl.
Far	táh-ness.
Fat or fleshy, applied to persons	ă-kti-ko-shee.
Father	do-waks.
Grandfather	dar-dairks.
Fathom	ailtsh.
one fathom	tsark-we-ailtsh.
two fathoms	art-lailtsh.
three fathoms	wee-ailtsh.
four fathoms	bo-ailtsh, &c.
Feathers	shoo-hóobe.
quills	ki-thlā-id.
down	pó-koke.
Fence	klar-kub.
Fight, to	be-túk-we-dook.
Find, to	soo-kwartl.
Finish, I have finished work or eating	he-ártl.
File	tee-chair-uk.
Fingers	tsar-tsar-kwle-de-koob.
Finger-ring	kar-kar-buk-e-dóo-kvp.
Fir-tree	sah-bah-tah-ha-ko-bupt.
Fire	ah-dahk.
make fire	ah-dákk-sa.
get up and make a fire	koo-dook-shitl-ah-dahk-sa.
Firewood	ar-tik-sáh.
First or before	o-oltht.
Fish, to	o-oash-taytl.
Fish	

(There is no generic name for fish; but when going for fish, the species are designated; for instance, for halibut, *o-oash-taytl-sltoo-yoult*; for codfish, o-oash-taytl-kar-dartl, &c.)

brook trout	klar-klek-tso.
codfish, true	kar-dar-tl.
cod, false	toosh-kow.
cod, black	be-shŏwe.
red rockfish, or grouper	klā-háp-pahr.
black or mottled rockfish	tsā-bár-whar.
catfish (Porichthys notatus)	ā-o-wit.
dogfish	yah-chah.
flounder	klu-klu-bais.

flounder, large spotted	kar-láthl-choo.
halibut	shoo-yoult.
herring	kloo-soob.
salmon,	
spring or silver	tsoo-wit.
salmon, young	tsow-thl.
salmon, summer	háh-dib.
salmon, dog-tooth or fall	cheech-kó-wis.
salmon trout	hópe-id or ho-péd.
sapphire perch (*embiotoca perspicabilis*)	wa-á-kupt. -
sculpin, buffalo	kab-biss.
sculpin, large	tsa-dairtch. [97]
Fish	
Skate	bil-la-chie.
Shark	sah-bass.
Fish-club, for killing fish	tíne-thl.
Fish-gig	heche-tl-tah.
Fish-hook	koo-yak.
halibut-hook	che-bood
barb of halibut-hook	kóo-aub.
wood of halibut-hook	tsar-whár-to-wik. [97]
Fishing-line of kelp	sar-dat-tlh.
Fish-weir	boo-shóo-wah.
Five	sheutche.
Flea	bat-cha-seed.
Flesh	béet-sie.
Flounder, flatfish	klu-klu-bais.
Flour	tlik-tlay-skoop.
Fly, the insect	bats-kwad.
Food	har-ouk.
Foolish	a-whatl-tsuck.
drunk	a-whatl-youk.
Foot	kla-ish-ted or klar-dark-sub.
Forehead	há-tuks-aht.
Four	boh.
Formerly or a long time ago	hó-ai.
Freckled	joke-see.
Friend	yár-kwe-dook-uks.
Fry-pan	soo-uk-itl.
Full	tsar-bar

G

Gamble, to	húl-láh-ah.
to win at gambling	hā-tarp.

Makah voc

to lose at gambling	hā-tā-itl
Gambling-disks	la-hullum.
the wood from which the disks are made, a species of hazel	hul-iár-ko-bupt.
Get up, to	koo-dóok-shitl.
Get, to, or receive	tsóo-kwitl.
Girl	har-dów-e-chuk.
Give, to	klá-kase.
Go, to	klark-shitl.
I go	he-de-ár-saiks.
you go, spoken to one	he-de-ar-sitl-gie.
you go, spoken to a number	he-de-ar-sitl-chik.
one of you go	ar-dé-siche har-du-ass.
go quick	wá-háh-tle-gie ā-ā'-shie.
go along	wa-hah-tle-gie.
Go	
I go to the house	wáttle-shaiks.
I am going	wattle-sfie-áitl.
Good-bye	ā-kúth-lik-kar.
Good	kloo-klo or klo-shish.
very good	kwar-cés-sar.
Goose	hár-duk or há-dikh.
Grandfather	dá-dairks.
Grandmother	dá-dairks.
Grave, a	peets-uk-sie.
Grass	klar-kúpt.
Grain, growing	á-hósh-ko-bupt.
Grease	tlair-bass.
tallow	hā-biks.
oil	kár-look.
Grebe (*Podiceps*)	ă-low-ah-haiu.
Green	kwar-búk-uk.
Grind, to	teh-chár-shitl.
Grouse	too-loo-arlsh.
Guillemot	klo-klo-chúk-sook.
Gull	wha-líl or kwa-lil.
Gum or pitch	kluk-áit-a-bis.
Gun, double barrel	artl-dooh.
single barrel, with flint lock	poo-yah
single barrel, with percussion lock	hah-kul-la-kubtl

H

Hail	kart-see-die.
Hair	ahp-sahp.

Makah voc

Haikwa (the dentalium)	che-tā-dook.
Half	yóoh-tah-dit-lait-so.
Halibut	shoo-yoult.
halibut-hook	che-bood.
Hand	klar-klar-he-do-koob.
right	char-bat-aas.
left	kart-sar.
left-handed	kart-sook.
Hands	lo-la-pie.
Hard or tough	kar-lark.
Hare, rabbit	too-toop-jis.
Haul, to	cheatl.
haul canoe	cheatl-cha-pats.
portage for hauling canoes	cheatl-tar-shee.
Hawk	tast-át-wik.
Hat	se-ke-áh-poks.
Hay	klar-kupl.
He, when present	o-hok.
if absent	o-hoh.
Head	to-hōte-sid. [13 January, 1870. [98]
Head-dress of dentalium, worn by young girls	batl-kup-klā-o-koob.
Hear	dah-áhh.
Heart	cháh-páh.
Hen	ah-hah-ha hai-up.
Here, I am	yatli-tláy-ad.
Here	tee.
Heron	háh-to-bad-die.
Herring	kloo-sóob.
Hide, to	úptah.
Hit, I	há-porp.
Hole	kó-we-tar.
Holla	hō'hh-shitl.
Hog	klā-klā-kwar-tiltl.
How many	ár-dis.
Hoe	e-túks-darp.
House	ba-as.
Hundred	klă-hó-oke or sheutch-e-uk.
Hungry	hár-koh.
are you hungry	hár-koh-kuk.
I am hungry	hár-koh-huss.
Husband	chá-kope.
Hurry, make haste	ā-ā-shie.

Makah voc

I

I	sé-ir.
Ice	koo-hooh.
Indians, people	kleits-a-kwad-die.
Infant	ya-duk-kow-it-chie or ya-duk-kwa-ow-i-chuh.
Iron	klair-yuh.
Island	oper-jec-ta.

J

Jay	kwish-kwish-shée.
Just now	kluh.
Jest, to, or a jesting person	tlá-tla-wik.

K

Kamass (Scilla esculenta)	kwad-dis or kwa-niss.
Kettle or pot	o-páh-suk.
Key	tluk-tlairk.
Kill, to	kokh-saph.
Knee	ko-ko-ahák-le-áe-koob.
Knee-pan	klu-thluk-le-de-koob.
Knife, sheath	kar-kairk.
Pocket	kar-kairk.
Dagger	to-kwark.
for splitting halibut	ko-che-tin.
Know, I	kum-ber-tups se-ir.
I don t know, or perhaps, or implying a doubt	kwóws.

L

Lake	chā-uk-tsope.
Large, great	ā-ā'-ho.
Lately, just now	kluh.
Laugh, to	kle-war.
Lazy	wee-wa-i.
I am lazy	wee-wá-i thluk-ā-thlits.
you are lazy	wee-wa-i lhluk-a-thlus.
Leaf	klā-kupt.
Leap	á-úts-kutch.
Left, the	kart-sass.
left-handed	kart-sook.
Leg	klā-ish-chid.
Lice	kā-cheed.
nits or eggs of lice	karts-ar-kleed.
Lie, to; a falsehood	ká'-tah-bat-soot.
Light	dah-chówtl.

Makah voc

day-dawn	you-oui.
Lightning	kā-káirtch.
Like, similar	o-bobe-te.
Listen	dah-áhh.
Lively, spry	hāli-háhts-tzae.
Long	há-ă-tse.
long time	kail-chilli.
Look! to call the attention	kled-da.
Look for, to e	dā-dáh -chu-chish.
look her	har-dássie.
Love, to	yáh-ah-kups.
Low tide	klu-show-a-chish-ch uck.
high tide	tsu-bá-i-chish-chuk.
Lynx	??
Looking-glass	dah-chówtl.
Lose, to	eesh-sap.

[THE INDIANS OF CAPE FLATTERY 99]

M

Mallard duck	dah-hah-tih.
Mammals	
bat	thle-thle-kwok-e-battl.
bear, black	árt-leit-kwitl. [99]
beaver	de-hai-choo.
cougar	hā-aéd.
deer	bo-kwitch.
dog	keh-déitl.
elk (C. Canadensis)	too-suk.
hare, rabbit	too-toop-jis.
mink	kwár-tie.
mole	took-tooksh.
mouse	se-bit-sa-bee.
land-otter	kar-to-wee.
sea-otter	tee-juk.
sea-lion	ar-kar-wad-dish.
seal (hair)	kars-chowee.
seal (fur)	káith-la-dose.
skunk	e-aíl-ā-hai-use.
squirrel	se-bi-towie.
wolf	choo-choo-hu-wistl.
whale (generic)	chét-ā-pook.
sperm	koats-kay.
Right	yách-yobad-die.
fin-back	kow-wid.
blackfish	klos-ko-kopphr.

sulphur-bottom	kica-kwow-yak-thle.
killer	che-che-wid.
California gray	se-wliow or chet-a-pook.
porpoise	ár-ich-pethl.
puffing pig	tsailth-ko.
white-fin porpoise	kwar-kwartl.
Man	cha-kope.
young man	kla-hoka-shft-lhlar-sad.
old man	ai-choob-e-chul.
Many, how	ar-dis-ailth.
Masks used in ceremonies	hooh-ków-itl-ik.
Mat of cedar-bark	bak-lap.
large mat	kla-hairlt.
small mat	che-bat.
rush mat	to-dahh.
Meat, fresh	beel-sie.
Medicine	ko-ie or kow-ie.
Medicine man, magician, or doctor	oash-tā-kay.
Medicine performances	tsi-ark.
Medicine or tamana was ceremonies	du-kwally or klookwally.
Middle or mid-way	ah-pów-wad.
Milk	a-dab.
Mill	chit-chit.
Mind, the	
male	kla-buks-tie.
female	ha-dáh-dittl.
Mink	kwar-tie.
Miss	
a mark, to	wake-tuch-e-dook.
miss the road	wee-kuttl-shishlar-shee.
mistake in speech	kā-tárk-lish.
Molasses	chám-o-set.
Mole	took-took-sh.
Mollusks	
barnacle	kle-be-húd.
clams	
large (lutraria)	har-loe.
blue striated	har-ar-thlup.
cockle	klá-lab.
haikwa (*dentalium*)	che-téh-dook.
mussel	klo-chab.
oyster	kloh-kloh.
thorn oyster	ko-okh-sā-de-buts.
scallop, large	klá-er-kwa-tie.

Makah voc

small	wad-dish.
sea-egg	koats-kapphr. {urchin}
Month	dah-kah.

Months, names of

January	a-a-kwis-puthl.
February	klo-k'lo-chis-puthl.
March	o-o-tukh-puthl.
April	ko-kose-kar-dis-pullil.
May	kar-kwugh-puthl.
June	ha-sairk-toke-puth I.
July	kar-ke-supphr-puthl.
August	wee-kooth.
September	kars-puthl.
October	kwar-te-puthl.
November	chā-kairsh-puthl.
December	se-whow-ah-puthl.

(The year consists of six months, and is called tsar-wark-itchie.)

Moon	dah-kah.
More	tali-kah.
Morning	yoo-ie.
Mosquito	wah-háts-tl.
Mother, my	a-bairks.
Mountain	hai-airch.
Mouse	se-bit-sa-bee.
Mouth	hā-tarks-tl.
Moxa,	boo-chitl.

a small cone of combustible matter burnt slowly in contact with the skin, to produce an eschar (The inner bark of the white pine is used for the purpose.)

Music or bell-ringing	tsar-sik-sap. [100]
Mussel	klo-chab.
My house	seir-bass.
My sister	klo-chuk-sub.
My things	ko-kote-sa-kut-liks.
Mythology	ho-hó-e-up or ho-ho-e-up-béss.

(Names of two fabulous men of antiquity who changed men into animals, trees, and stones.)

N

Nails (finger)	chath-latch.
iron nails	klap-a-koob.

Naked (without clothing)

male	sho-she-dáhh.
female	she-she-dă-tartl.
Name	á-júk-kluk-kik.

Makah voc

Near	klar-weích-i-ka.
Neck	tse-kwar-bits.
Needle	kar-juk.
Nest (bird's)	par-huts.
Never	wake-kā-kwows.
New	soost-ko.
Night	ut-haie.
Nine	sar-kwas-sub.
No	wa-kee or wake-isse.
None	wake-kade.
Noon	takh-assie.
Nose	choo-oath-tl-tub.
Now	kluh-o-ko-wie or kluh. Numerals[19]

(In counting, it is usual to enumerate ten, and then commence at one, repeating in tens, and at the end of each call the number, thus: ten, *kluh*; two tens or twenty, *tsarkaits*; three tens or thirty, *karhook*, &c.)

1	tsark-wark or tsar-kwok.
2	attl or uttl.
3	wee.
4	boh.
5	sheutche.
6	cheh-partl.
7	at-tleph or attl-poh.
8	ar-tlés-sub.
9	sar-kwás-sub.
10	kluh.
11	tsark-woke.
12	ut-tlai-ouk.
13	wee-ouk.
14	boh-kwe-ouk.
15	sheutch-e-ouk.
16	cheh-pártl-ouk.
17	artl-pook.
18	ar-tles-sub-ouk.
19	sar-kwas-sub-tsar-kart-sit.
20	tsar-kaits.

---

[19] The method of counting on the fingers is as follows: they commence with the little finger of the left hand, closing each finger as it is counted; then pass from the left thumb, which counts five, to the right thumb, which counts six, and so on to the little finger of the right hand, which counts ten. I have sometimes seen Indians commence counting with the little finger of the right hand, but it is invariably the custom to commence with that finger instead of a thumb.

Makah voc

30 kar-hook.
40 art-leik.
50 art-lei-kish-kluh.
60 wee-oúk-ish.
70 wee-ouk-igh-kluh.
80 boh-kwe-uk.
90 boh-kwe-uk-ish-kluh.
100 sheutch-e-uk. (Any things round or oval, as pans, cups, plates, eggs, beads, &c., are counted with the following terminals to the simple numbers: –)

1 tsark-wark
2 attl-kuptl.
3 wee-a-kuptl.
4 boh-kuptl.
5 sheutche-a-kuptl.
6 cheh-partl-kuptl.
7 at-tleph-o-kuptl.
8 ar-tles-sub-o-kuptl.
9 sar-kwassub-o-kuptl.
10 kluh-o-kuptl.

(Articles having length, as rope, cloth, &c., have the terminal *ailsh*, which also means fathoms.)

1 tsark-wark-ailsh.
2 attl-ailsh
3 wee-ailsh
4 boh-ailsh.
5 sheutche-ailsh.
6 cheh-partl-ailsh.
7 at-tleph-ailsh.
8 ar-tlessub-ailsh.
9 sar-kwas-sub-ailsh.
10 kluh-ailsh. [101] (In counting fish, or measuring oil or potatoes, they make use of the terminal *ul*, which is an expression of assent. One person will call the number, which another will repeat, adding the terminal *ul*, meaning, as we would say, this is one, this is two, &c.)

1 tsark-wark.
2 attl-ul.
3 wee-ul.
4 boh-ul.
5 sheutche-ul.
6 cheh-partl-ul.
7 at-tleph-ul.
8 ar-lles-sub-ul.

9	sar-kwas-sub-ul.
10	kluh-ul.

O

Oar	e-sáib-e-suk.
Off shore	hai-árt-stat.
Oil	kár-took.
Oláen time or formerly	ho-ái-o-kwi.
Old man	ai-chope.
Old woman	ái-chub.
On or towards shore	klar-wárt-stat.
One	tsar-kwart or tsar-kwoks.
Open	kotle-tah.
Opposite or the other side	kwis-paink.
Otter	kar-tówe.
Ours, we, or us	do-wár-do.
Outdoors	uée-á-aiks or kwee-á-aiks.
Out of the canoe	oós-tah-setl.
Overturn	hoke-shitl.
Owl	took-te-kwad-die.
Oyster	kloh-kloh.
thorn oyster (Spondylus)	ko-ok'h-sa-aé-buts.

P

Paddle, a	kla-táh-juk.
Paddle, to	klé-huk.
Peas	tsóosk-shitl-
Penis	ché-war.
People	kleits-ā-kwad-die.
Pigeon	háy-aib.
Pipe	kŭsh-sets.
Pitch	kluk-áit-ā-bis.
Plank	kló-ailth.
Plants	
barberry	klook-shitl-ko-bupt.
berries	hóats-á-kupt.
fern	dit-se-bupt.
grass	klar-kupt.
kamass	kwad-dis.
rush	sal-láh-hutl.
sallal (*Gualtheria*)	sal-láh-ha-bupt.
salmon-berry	kar-ke-wai.
salmon-bush	kar-ke-weep.

salmon-sprouts	ko-kose-kárdlth.
strawberry	hár-de-tup.
thumb-berry (*Rubus odoratus*)	lo-lo-wits.
sprouts of the same	kothl-kowie.
cranberry	páp-pas.
red huckleberry	héy-se-ahd.
blue huckleberry	ko-ho-ák-tl.
gooseberry	shatch-káh-bupt.
currant	hă-pá-pá-bupt.
crab apple	dópt-ko-bupt.
white birch	klā-hap-partl.
alder	kwárk-sah-bupt.
spruce	do-hó-bupt.
hemlock	klar-kár-bupt.
cedar	klá-e-shook.
yew	klá-hairk-tle-bupt.
dogwood	kitl-che-bupt.
elder	sik-ke-ár-she-b upt.
liverwort	thle-thle-sús-sok-kowie.
bittersweet	bar-chíl-loh-kowie.
Liquorice fern (*Polypodium falcatum*)	hur-há-tee.
nettles	kau-lup-kay.
blind nettles	a-dab-a-biqrt.
arbutus uva ursi	klár-kupt.
vine evergreen	tsce-tsee-ess.
tobacco	kóo-shá.
Plenty	ar-ke-yúk.
Point, to	kope-shitl.
Point or end	yu-chíl-tish.
Poor	há-há-datl.
very poor, unfortunate	tlá-kwo.
Porpoise	tsáilth-ko.
Potatoes	kau-its.
Poultry	a-hă-há
cock	a-hă-hácha-kope.
hen	a-hă-hahai-up.
Pound, to	kláts-klai. [102]
Pour, to	klook-sáp-gie.
Powder	boot-sis-suk.
Pregnant	kleet-séet.
Presently	ar-déei.
Prongs of fish-gig	héche-ta-kethl-tub.

Makah voc

Pronouns
    I   seir.
    I work   ohó-bits-kwi-seir.
    I laugh   ohóse-ā-ā-wika.
    my   o-kwiks-te.
    thou   sú-er.
    he   ohó-te-da.
    we   ohode.
    ye   do-bits.
    they   ah-dithl-tits.

Proud   to-póh.
  I am proud   to-póots.
  he is proud   to-tó-bush.
  they are proud   tóp-kwitl.
Pudenda   jude.
Push, to   chák-shitl.

Q

Quick; come quick   ut-sai-shoo-oókh.
Quills   ki-thla-id.

R

Rain   beit-la or beitlal.
Rainbow   tsów-Ofiise.
Rake   kle-pé-ak.
Raven   klook-shóod.
Receive, to   tsoo-kwitl.
Red   klá-hoke.
Relations   ó-o-arts.
  father   dó-wiks or dó-aks.
  mother   ă-baiks.
  grandfather   da-dairks.
  grandmother   ko-iáks.
  son, my (child)   a-kúse-ch.
  son (grown up)   ó-sha-hode,
  daughter, my (child)   há-dów-e-chuk.
    (grown up)   ă-tuk-hu-áttl-bus.
  husband, my   chá-kope.
  wife, my   hái-up.
  brother, elder
    said by a male   tak-ke-ai.
    said by a female hah-chóop-siks.
  brother, younger   kar-thlátl-ik.

sister, elder	kloo-chuk-Kub.
younger	ba-bā-ik-sa.
half-sister	yu-kiva-uk-sa. [b]
Return	ho-wái.
by and by return	ar-deei-ho-wái.
Rifle	tsoo-tsark-witl.
Ring, finger	kă-ka-buk-e-dú-kup.
River	tsā-ark.
Road or trail	tar-shee.
Roast by the fire	kla-ah-pis.
Rope	ses-tópe.
Rotten, as wood	kwer-kwer-juk-tl.
as fruit	ko-it-ják.
Rum	lum-muks.
Run, I	ă-hárts-its.
Rush	sal-láh-hutl

S

Sallal berries	kár-ke-sup
Salmon	
spring or silver	tsóo-it.
young	tsow-thl.
Summer	háh-did.
dog-tooth	cheéch-kowis.
Trout	hó-pid.
Salmon roe	ách-pahb.
Salmon berries	kar-ke-wai.
Salt	too-páthl.
Salute on meeting a friend	
to a male	kwátch-im.
to a female	koáth-lub.
Sand	ses-sá-bits.
Sandpiper	ho-hópe-sis.
Saw	chee-te-ak.
Scallop	bo-whits-ae.
Sculpin	ka-biss.
Sea (salt water)	too-páthlcha-uk.
Sea-fowl	hooke-toop.
Sea-lion	ár-ká-wad-dish.
Seal, hair	kars-chówe.
fur	kaíth-la-doos.
Seal's bladder	kal-lá-ka-chub.
Seal's paunch	koo-yow.

Makah voc

Seal-skin buoy	du-koop-kuptl or do-ko-kuptl.

Seasons
Spring	klairk-shiltl.
Summer	klu-pairtch.
Autumn	kwi-atch.
Winter	wake-pentl.

Seat, the	wāk-its.
See, to	dartl-shitl.
I see	ohose-dartl-chatl.
I do not see	chár-dis. [103]
See; look; to call the attention	kled-da.
Seine	ché-iks.
Seven	attleph or attl-poh.
Sew, to	de-kā-dek.
thread	de-káib.
Shadow	ko-di-e-chid.
Shark	salt-bass.
Sharp	káek-shitl.
Shells	kai-ish-kud-dy.
Ship	bar-bethld.

(This is a Nootkan word, *mar-meth-ld* and signifies a house on the water. It is also applied to all white men, and signifies, when so applied, those who came in or who live in houses on the water.)

Shirt	kle-hairk-tl.
Shoes	klā-klā-kús-tobe,
Short	dé-its.
to snatch or take a thing forcibly	kap-shitl.
Shot	klā-klā-o-kwók-ut-shiltl
Shoulder	klā-ho-pa-tie.
Shovel	chat-kard.
Shut or close, to	boo-shú-it-tá.
Shuttlecock	o-kó-ey.
Sick	tá-ithl.
Sing	du-duke.
Sister	
elder	klu-chúk-sub.
younger	bar-bā-ik'-sa.
Sit, to	klă-dairk.
squat down	klă-deilth.
you sit down	ta-kwit-la-dáit-so or to-kwitl-suer.
I will sit down	ta-kwit-lik-seir.

Makah voc

all sit	ta-kwilsh.
Six	cheh-partl.
Skate (the fish)	bil-lá-chie.
Skin	klā-hark.
Skunk	ā-áil-a-hai-use.
Sky	e-lah-ártstl.
Slave	o-th lo.
common person	mis-che-mas *or* bis-che-bas.
Sleep	wée-atch.
Slow	klā-wá.
When applied to persons	wee-wich-kub-bik.
When applied to ships or canoes	wée-chook.
When applied to animals	wée-chu-kuptl.
Small	kwā-óe-chuk.
Smallpox	he-he-dahl.
Smell, to	bé-shitl. [b]
Smell	
unpleasant smell	u-bus-suk be-shitl.
agreeable smell	chab-bas be-shitl.
Smoke	kóo-sha.
Snake	tlay-ee.
Sneeze, to	too-toóp-uks.
Snow	koo-sié.
Sorrow	kwă-úk-wiks-seuk-iktl
Speak, to	ó-she-buts.
Spear	beelt-sie.
bird-spear	heich-il-tah.
Spear fish, to	hă-poorp.
Spill	hóke-sah.
Split	hey-sís.
Spoon	chat-káirk.
Spring	kláirk-shitl.
Squirrel	sib-be-tab-be.
Stand, to	klaerk-sh ill.
Star	tówie-sub-buts.
Steal, to	koathl.
Stone	teh-deh-chooh.
Stone pestle or maul for splitting wood	tă-kă-wă-dă-ăks.
Stop (imperatively)	e-yáhh.
remain	e-yáh-has-sie.
Stop; to finish	hé-art.
Story	kúm-itl-kups.
Straight	tar-kárpt.

Makah voc

Stranger	hó-o-war-te-duks.
Strawberries	háh-de-tup.
Strike, to	kok-sap.
Strong	dah-shook.
Stubborn	
male	wáy-a-buktl.
female	u-a-áib.
Summer	kloop-pairtch.
Sun	kle-sa-kairk.
Suppose (if)	kwá-kai.
Surf	sis-sa-káft -dá-kās.
Sweet, or pleasant to taste or smell	chab-bas or cham-mas.
Swim	soo-soóke.

T

Table	ko-aph.
Table with food	how-athl.
Tail	wah-huts.
Take, to	silk-will.
Talk, to	ó-ahe-biits.
Talk, trifling	hé-he-huy. [104]
Talk	
stop your talk, or you talk foolishly	uthl-kud.
Tallow	hā-biks.
Taste, to	he-dáouks-tl.
Tell the truth, you	tā-ko-bats-suer.
do not lie	wake-iss kā-tuk-tliss.
Ten	kluh.
Testicles	kar-kó-bits.
Thanks	ho-shee-árk-shis.
That	teé-dah.
There	téit-ser.
They	do-dóbe.
Thick	ár-look or utt-he.
Thin	wát-chid.
Thirsty	cha-éer-hus.
This	tée-kahor
Thou	suer.
Thunder	thleu-kloots.
Thus, or the same	kwar-ces-sie.
very good	kwar-ces-sar.
Thread	de-kábe.
Three	oui or wee.
Throw away, to	hésh-tsap.

Makah voc

Tide, high	tsu-bá-i-chish-chuk.
Tide, low	klu-show-a-chish-chuk.
Tie, to	bátl-shitl.
tie canoe	batl-sap.
Tired, weary, or exhausted	tahk-ke-á-you.
Tobacco	kush-á.
smoke	kush-á.
Tobacco-pipe	kush-sets.
to smoke a pipe	kush-she-áiks.
To-day	kle-sée-ă-kow-ă-ka-die.
Yesterday	kláo-cheelth.
Toes	tsark-tsárk-itl-sub.
Together	do-dó-buks.
To-morrow	ár-bei or ár-bi.
To-night	ut-hāi-u.
Tongue	lā-kairk.
Towards shore	klar-wárt-sat.
Trade, to	bar-kwátl.
Trail or road	tár-shee.
Trap	kap-páirk.
Tree	ah-hahts-ish.
Trencher or -wooden dish	klo-kwaks.
Trifling (jargon *cultus*)	wake-isse.
very trifling	hah-háh-datl-wake-isse.
Trout, brook	klá-klek-tso.
Trowsers	kla-ísh-ja-kuk.
True	klu-klo-oshe-buts.
Trunk or chest	ă-huy-dookst. [b]
Turn around	
a kettle	arts-kwe-dúk-sah.
a canoe	hóh-who-al.
or look here	ar-tis-kwe-dook.
Two	attl or uttl.

U

Under	há-tá-post-luk.
Understand	kúm-ber-lups.
Unpleasant, or offensive to taste or smell	u-bús-suk.

(For instance, the smell of a skunk, snuff, ammonia, pungent spices, carrion, &c; the taste of vinegar, spice, anything bitter, &c. Whatever is pleasant to taste or smell is termed *cháb-bas* or *chám-mas*.)

Untie	kluk-tl-sup.
Up	hi-ér-chi-ditl.
Up, to place anything	he-dás-ho.

Makah voc

to take anything up and place it on a table	he-dás-pe-tup.
to place anything from a table on the ground or floor	oas-tap-a-ter.
Upright, as to stand up or put up a post	klár-kisht.
to drive down a stake perpendicularly	klar-kisht-să-ho.
Upset	kook-aah.
Up stream	hā-dárd-tl.
down stream	ik-tark-wárk-kliss.
get up, applied to a child	sé-kah.

V

Vinegar	tse-há-puthl.

W

Wagon	tsark-tsárk-as.
Walk, to	tlā-uk.
Want, to	o-ote-sus.
Warm	kloo-partl.
Warrior	we-e-bukil.
Wash, to, the head	tso-ai-ouk.
the face	tso-kwów-itl.
the person	hah-táhd.
clothes	tso-kwitl-gee. [105]
Water	chă-ouk or chá-uk.
Waterfall	toó-withl.
Waves	whe-ups.
Weary; exhausted	tahk-ke-ā-you.
We	ohóde.
Wedge	klár-dit.
Weir for fish	boo-shóo-war.
Whale (generic)	chet-a-pook.
What	buk-kuk or art-juk.
what do you want	búk-ke-klair-sik.
what are you doing	búk-ke-da-har-pik.
what is your name	art-juk-kluk-ish.
what is his name	cha-ká-dah.
an expression of doubt when trying to think of a person's name	
Wheat	bar-ba-chéss-kook.
Where	wa-as.
where are you going	wa-ás-a-kleesh or wa-ás-a-kartl.
where do you come from	wa-ás-ă-te-kleesh.
where do you go	wa-ás-a-te-kleesh.
Whistle, to	Sā-sáhb.
White	kle-sóok.
White men	bar-bethld.

Makah voc

Who	art-juk.
Why	ba-ka-dah.
Wife	hai-up.
Wind	wake-sie.
north wind	batl-el-tis.
south wind	kwart-see-die [b]
Wind	
east wind	too-toóch-ah-kook.
west wind	wa-shél-lie.
southeast wind	too-chée.
northwest wind	yu-yoke-sis.
Wings	klap-ā-hub.
Winter	wake-parthl or bat-láthl.
Within or in	
canoe	e-túks-is.
house	bál-che-ailth.
Wolf	choo-choo-ustl.
Woman	har-dairk.
old woman	ai-chub.
Wood, dead	pathl-hukl.
Work	bar-boo-ak.
Worthless	pé-shak.
Wrist	he-he-diár-kwe-dook.
Write, to	char-tar-tle.
writing or drawing	char-tái-ouks.
writer or painter	chár-tik.

Y

Yard, measure	kart-sark.
Yawn, to	pas-táhk-shitl.
Yes	a-ah or háh.
Yesterday	clá-o-cheelth.
You	suer.
Young man	klā-hoke-shé-tlāi-sad.
Yours	su-wátch.

NOTE

The following words which appear in the text do not belong to the Makah, but are "Jargon" words, derived from other languages. GG

Cultus, Chinook *kal-tas* {*cultus*}, worthless; good for nothing; inferior.

Skookoom, Chihelis *sku-kum*, a ghost; an evil spirit or demon {'strong'}.

Tamanawas, Chinook {*tah-*} *i-ta-ma-na-was*, a guardian or familiar spirit; magic: luck; fortune; anything supernatural; conjuring.

Makah voc

LOCAL NOMENCLATURE OF THE MAKAH

Kwe-nait-che-chat. Tribal name.

Deeart or Deeah {di•ya•}. Neeah Bay and village.

Chardi {ča•di•}. Tatoosh Island. This is also termed Opa-jecta {hu•pačakt}, or the island.

Ho-selth {'u •se•ił}. Village at Flattery Rocks. {Ozette}

Tsoo-ess. Village on the Tsooyes River, near its mouth. {c'u•yas = water hole}

Tsow-iss. The rock at the mouth of the river, on its southwest side. [14 February, 1870]

Ba-ho-bo-hosh. The rocky point on the north side of the mouth of the river. {buxu•bu•xš = boiling up}

Tsoo-yescha-uk. The river flowing past the Tsooess village.

Wa-atch. Village at month of Wäatch Creek. {wa'ač' = cove}

Ar-kut-tle-kower. Point west of Wäatch village. {'aq'iλqa•wa• = cave going around point}

Kid-de-kub-but {q'idi•q'abit}. A village half-way between Tatoosh Island and Neeah Bay.

Ba-a-dah {bi'id'a}. The eastern point of Neeah Bay. [106]

Koit-ldh {q'ʷiλa•}. The western point of Neeah Bay.

Wa-ad-dah {wa'a'da}. Island between Ba-d-dah and Koitlah points.

Sah-da-ped-thl. Rocks west of Kiddekubbut village, on which H.B.M. steamer *Hecate* struck in 1861 (Aug. 19th).

Kee-sis-so. The rocks at the extreme point of Cape Flattery.

Tsar-tsar-dark. The conspicuous pillar rock at the northwest extremity of Cape Flattery.

To-kwdk-sose. A small stream running into the Straits of Fuca, two miles east of Neeah Bay.

Kaithl-ka-ject. Sail rock opposite the mouth of Tokwaksose River.

Sik-ke-u {sikyu• = sand bar}. A river east of the Tokwaksose.

Ho-ko {hoqu•}. A river six miles east of the Tokwaksose, a fork of the Sikkeu.

  (This river is incorrectly spelled Okeho. The Makahs strongly aspirate the first syllable, and pronounce as I have written it, Ho-ko.)

Kld-kld-wice {xigi•dit}. Clallam Bay.

Makah index
INDEX.

Acantbias Sucklcyi, 29
Adze, 34
Age of Makahs, 4
Ahchawat, 6
A-ikh-pet'hl, 30
A'-ka-wad-dish, 30
Anarrhichthys, 30
Arbutus uva ursi, 27
Arrows, 47
Arum, 31
A-tlis-tat, 21
Aurora, 87

Ba-bet-hl-ka-di, 14
Bah-die, 49
Bark, 18
Bark clothing, 44
Barter for wood, 4
Baskets, 42, 45, 4(i
Bastard cod, 24, 28
Beds, 5
Berberis, 46
Be-sh6-we, 28, 40
Bird-spears, 47, 48
Black skin, 22
Blankets, 32
Boards, 4
Bo-he-vi, 46
Bo-kwis -tat, 21
Bows, 47
Boxes, 42
Building, 5

Canoes, 35, 3fi, 37
Cape Indians, 1
Cha-batta Ha-tartstl, 61
Cha-t'hluk-dos, 21
Chá-tatl, 7
Cha-tai-uks, 7
Cha-tik, 7, 9, 10
Che-bud, 23
Che-che-wid, 19

Chet'-a-puk, 7, 19
Chiefs, 52
Childbirth, 82
Children's amusements, 14
Chisel, 34
Clallam mats, 5
Cleanliness, 19
Cod-hook, 41
Colors, 45
Cooking, 25
Cradle, 18

Dee-aht, 58
Deluge, 57
Diatomaceous earth, 44
Diseases, 79, 80
Disposition of property, 85
Dog-fish oil, 29, 31, 32
Dopt-ko-kuptl, 21
Do-t'hlub, 62, 75
Dreams, 76
Dress, 15, 16
Drying fish, 7
Duels, 15
Dukwally, 62, 66, 73, 75
Du-poi-ak, 21

Echinus, 24
Eclipses, 90
Esquimaux, 87 Feasts, 26

Feather and dog's hair blankets, 43
Flattening of the head, 3
Fish-club, 42
Fishing-lines, 40
Fish-spears, 47
Food, 19
Forts, 51
Fiicus gigantea, 2
Funeral ceremonies, 83

Gambling implements, 44
Games, 44
Gaultheria shallon, 27
Genealogy, 58
Government, 52
Great Spirit, 61 [c]

Ha-hek-lo-ak, 7, 8, 63
Halibut fishery, 22, 23
Halibut hook/41
Haliotis, 47
Hammers, 4, 35
Hardiness of Makahs, 4
Harpoons, 19, 20, 39
Hats, 45
He-stuk'-stas, 21
He-se-yu, 18
He-tuk-wad, 21
Hippo campus, 8
History, 55
Hosett, 6
Houses, 4
Hul-liak, 44
Hul-li-a-ko-bupt, 44

Interior of a lodge, 7

Kab-bis, 28
Kd-dutl, 28
Ka-kaitch, 8
Ka-kai-icoks, 21
Kak-te-wahd'-de, 42
Kas-chá-we, 30
Kat-hla-das, 30
Kau-wid, 19
Kelp, 40
Kid-de-kub-but, 6
Kla-hap-pa, 28
Klas-ko-kopp li, 1 9
Klas-xet, 1
Kli -Kca-kark-ll, 62
Klc-tait-lM, 21

Makah index

Kli-cha, 21
Khok-xliood, 65
Kltikxko, 21
Knives, 34
Kobetsi, 88
Ko-che-tin, 23
Kots-ke, 19
Kwa-kwau-yak-t'hle, 1 9
Kwak-watl, 30
Kwahtie, 64
Kwartseedie, 92
Kwe-kaptl 21 [108]
Kwe-net-sat'h, 1
Kwe-net-che-chat, 1
Kut-so-wit, 21

Labrets, 18
Ladles, 25, 27
La-hull, 44
La-hullum, 44

Magic, 76
Makah census, 2
Makah reservation, 1
Makah villages, 6
Mak-kdh, 1
Manufactures, 35
Manufacture of canoes, 4
Marriage, 11, 13
Marriageable age, 12
Masks, 69
Mats, 42, 45
Medicine, 76, 78
Mink, 64
Mixed blood among Makahs, 3
Months, 91
Moxas, 79
Mussels, 24
Mythology, 61

Natica, 81
Neeah, 6
Neeah Bay, agriculture, 2

Neeah Bay, animals at, 2
Nceah Bay, climate at, 2
Neeah Bay, soil at, 2
Nose ornaments, 17
Neshwats, 8

Octopus tuberculatus, 23
Onychotenthis, 24
Origin, 56
Ornaments, 45, 47
Otter, 27
Oysters, 24

Pa-dau-t'hl, 21
Paddles, 37
Paint, 17 [b]
Painting, 9, 10
Parapholas, 89
Pá-ko, 46
Physical characteristics of Makahs, 3
Picture writing, 7
Pillar rock, 86
Pipe clay, 44
Polypodium falcatum, 80
Polygamy, 13
Porpoises, 30
Potatoes, 23, 25
Pot-lat-ches, 13
Pottery, 48
Punishments, 53
Pyrola elliptica, 79

Rainbows, 90
Rattles, 77
Raven, 65
Roofs, 6
Ropes, 39
Rubus odoratus, 25
Rubus spectabilis, 25, 27

Scallops, 24
Scilla esculents, 25
Seals, 30

Seal-skin buoy, 20
Sea-otter, 30
Seasons, 91
Seclusion of girls, 12
Se-hwau, 19
Se-ka-jec-ta, 87
Shamanism, 76
Shogh, 5
Skoo-koom, 63
Slaves, 10
Smoking, 27
Sneezing, 61
Social life, 10
Songs, 49
South wind, 92
Spanish settlement, 55
Spears, 47
Spoons, 26
Squid, 24
Stature of Makahs, 3
Stone weapons, 49
Superstitions, 86

Tamanawas ceremonies, 9, 13, 61
Tatooche Island, 1, 6, CO
Tattooing, 18
Te-ka-au-da, 21
Thlu-kluts, 7, 8, 72
Thorn-oyster, 79
Thunder-bird, 7, 9
Tides, 66
Ti-juk, 30
Time, 91
Ti-ne-t'hl, 23
Tools, 33
Toosh-kow, 28, 90
Trade, 30, 31
Traditions, 55
Treatment of women, 11
Treaty of 1855, 1
Tsa-ba-hwa, 28
Tsa-daitch, 28
Tsailt'h-ko, 30

115

Makah index

Tsa-kwat, 21
Tsiark, 62, 72, 75
Tsis-ka-pul, 21
Tsuess, 6
Tush-kau, 28, 90
Tu-tutsh, 8
Twins, 82

U-butsk, 21

Vocabularies, 93

Wäatch, 6
Wäatch Creek, 2
Wäatch Marsh, 2
Warfare, 50
Whales, 7, 19
Whale oil, 22
Whales bones, 8
Whaling, 19

Whaling canoe, 21
Whaling gear, 39
Wooden utensils, 42, 43
Wrestling, 15

Ya-cha, 29
Yakh yo-bad-die, 19

https://archive.org/details/indianscapeflatt00swanrich/mode/2up

https://ia600309.us.archive.org/33/items/indianscapeflatt00swanrich/indianscapeflatt00swanrich_djvu.txt

Published by the Smithsonian Institution
Washington City, March, 1870.

Chemakum

Notes on the Chemakum Language
by Franz Boas

When George Gibbs wrote on the tribes of western Washington (Contributions to North American Ethnology, vol. 1, p. 177), the Chemakum still numbered 90 souls. When I visited Puget Sound in the summer of 1890 I learned of only three individuals who spoke the language – one woman, living near Port Townsend, and one man and his sister, who live at Port Gamble. As the Indians of Puget Sound are very restless in summer I had great difficulty in finding any of these individuals. After a protracted search I succeeded in meeting "Louise," who lives at Port Gamble, where she makes a living as a washerwoman. Although she speaks Chemakum occasionally with her brother, she uses mostly Clallam in conversing with the other Indians of the village, and the Chinook jargon in her intercourse with the whites. She has, therefore, undoubtedly forgotten part of her language. She stated that neither she nor her brother and the woman living near Port Townsend speak Chemakum fluently and properly. Besides, she was somewhat addicted to the use of liquor, and as she herself and the white man with whom she lived indulged alternately in their libations, the conditions for the collections of good linguistic material were not very favorable. Still, I was able to collect about 1,250 words, grammatical forms, and sentences, which were all corroborated by repeated questioning. From this material the following notes have been derived:

According to Gibbs the original country of the Chemakum, who call themselves *Aqoχulo*,[20]* embraced Port Townsend, Port Ludlow, and Port Gamble. According to the uniform testimony of Louise, a few Clallam and a Puyallup, they were restricted to the peninsula between Hood canal and Port Townsend.

Phonetics. – The vowels are not quite as variable and indistinct as in the neighboring Salishan dialects, but still obscure vowels are [38] very frequent. Diphthongs are rare. I am sure only of the occurrence of *ai* and *au*. The following consonants are found in my list of words:

h, k, ӄ, q, y, n; t; s, c, t$_c$, ts, tc, m, p, l, l'. The following sounds begin words:

ā, a, ē, e, ĕ, ī, ō. u is not found in my list as an initial sound. All consonants with the exception of *y* and *t$_c$* are found as initial sounds. Combinations of consonants in the beginning of words are very rare. I found only the following examples: tsӄ-, striking, sptcō'o, berry basket.

The following terminal consonants and combinations of consonants are found in my collection:
k, ӄ, q, n; t; s, ts, tc, m, p, l, l'.

ӄt   ks   ӄl'
lt   ӄs   tsl'
nt   ns
tst
tct

---

[20] * ӄ == deep guttural k.   e == e in flower.   t$_c$ == dento-alveolar t.   q == ch as in Scotch "loch."   l' = explosive posterior l.   ! following a letter indicates more than ordinary strength of articulation.

Chemakum

The Article. – It seems that nouns have two genders, masculine and feminine, which have separate articles.

    qō hē'na, my father   kō hē'na, my mother.
    qō ōt!tēts, thy house   kō hē'ēlotsēts, thy canoe.
    qō hā'maa, the tree.

The plural article is the same for both genders:

    hō tsitsqa'll'ē, my cousins.

In interrogative sentences other articles are used – *qa* for masculine, *tca* for feminine, *qā* for plural.

  χō'ōχ qa hē'nēets ? — Where is thy father ?
  χō'ōχ tca hē'nēets ? — Where is thy mother?
  χō'ōχ qa tĕtc'ukl'as ? — Where is my arrow?
  χō'ōχ tca hē'elōχul'ĕs ? — Where is my canoe?
  χō'ōχ qa taχōlχulĕs ? — Where is my axe ?
  χō'ōχ tea χuē'lĕs'ĕts ? — Where is thy knife?
  ātc'ĕs qa hā'acēttēts ? — What have you bought?
  χō'ōχ qā ō't!l'ē ?   — Where are my houses?
  χō'ōχ qā tsilō'leχl 'ĕs ? — Where are my canoes? [39]

The Noun. — It appears from the examples given above that the noun has two genders. It is of interest to note that pronominal gender, by means of which male and female are distinguished, is found in all Salishan dialects spoken west of the Cascade range and on the coast of British Columbia, while real gender occurs in all dialects of the Chinook.

The plural is, more properly speaking, a collective, but is frequently used in a way similar to our plural, namely, when the collective and plural ideas nearly coincide. The difference between the two is, however, brought out clearly in the following instance:

ē'sa-i (1) tc'ā'l'ai (2) tca'qul' (3) — many (1) stones are (2) on the beach (3).
l'ē'sai tc'ē'tc'al'a — a heap of stones.

The collective is formed in a variety of ways:

Chemakum

(1) By the prefix *ts* with the first vowel of the stem:

Singular	Collective	
ha'maa	tsa'hamaa	tree.
tsu'qot	tsitsu'qot	lake.
a'māas	tsaa'māas	grandparent.
hēlō'leʟ'	tsilōleʟ'	canoe.

(2) By reduplication:

hau'atska	hahaua'tska	deer.
quĕ'ltĕm	qaquē'ltĕm	European (borrowed from (Clallam).
ʟu'ēlĕs	ʟuʟuē'lĕs	knife.
tē'eriāas	tētēel'ā'as	husband.

(3) By diaeresis:

tcā'atcis'is	tcāatcā'is'is	my mother's sister.

(4) By amplification of the stem according to unknown rules; frequently with the infix *ts*:

koō'tlis	kutsi'tlʟaaa	my wife.
qā'aqāas	qatç'ēqāas	my sister's husband.
taʟō'olʟul'	tatsʟō'oʟul'	axe.
ĕtç 'ēʟaa	ōot!'ō'qʟaa	house.

(5) From distinct stems :

ts'ēʟatcil'	kō'la	dead. [40]

A few nominal suffixes (nouns as used, in compounds) form plurals:

-atcĕt, plural: -ts'ā'it, blanket; pĕca'tcĕt, white blanket; tlakuats'ā'it, two blankets.

-tē'ia, plural: -ta, day; kuētē'ia, one day ; mĕ'ēsta, four days.

-ʟtsĕl, plural: -aʟal, person in canoe.

Numerals. ──

Counting	Persons	Canoes	Fathoms	Dogs or horses	Persons in canoe
1 kuē'l'	koāl'	kuē'ekō	kē'l'ĕkō	kuē'ĕns	kuē'ʟtsĕl
2 l'a'kua	l'a'wuʟas	l'a'kuakŭ	l'a'kuēlō	l'a'kuāns	l'a'waʟaʟal
3 ʟoā'lē	ʟoa'l'tsō	ʟoa'lakŭ	ʟolē'lō	ʟoalā'ns	ʟoā'lētsaʟal
4 mĕ'ēs	mĕ'ēs	mĕ'ēskō	mĕ'ēsa'lō	mĕ'ēsĕns	mĕēs 'saʟal
5 tcā'aa	tcā'aa	tcā'aakŭ		tca'aans	

Chemakum

6 tsĕ'l'as	tsĕ'l'as	tsĕ'l'askŭ	tsĕ'l'āsĕns
7 ts!ҟō'olkoant		ts!ҟō'olkoantko	ts!ҟō'olkoantĕns
8 ҟ!'oa'yēkoant		ҟ!oa'yēkoantkō	
9 kuē'l'tsqal		kuē'tsqalkō	
10 tc!'ē'taa		tc!'ē'tā'akŭ	

11 tc!'ē'taa qsī kuēl'
20 koā'l'atstci
30 ҟoalā'koanlo
40 mĕ'ēskoanlō, (etc, up to)
100 tc!'ē'tkoanlō

The numerals seven, eight, and ten mean the first, second, and fourth fingers, respectively. Nine is derived from one, meaning, probably, ten less one, twenty is one man, thus indicating the vigesimal origin of the numerical system. It appears from the above list that numerals may be compounded with any of the innumerable nominal suffixes.

    kuē'ēsĕlō, once   l'a'kuasĕlō, twice.

Personal Pronouns. ——

lā'al', I   tsē'ia, thou   ō'ĕtcō, he
mā'al', we   tsē'tal', you   ？, they

Possessive Pronouns. ——

tā'ĕlaai — it is mine.
hēēlē'ets'ē — it is thine.   ma'al'ōoi — it is ours.
(hēēlē'ets'ai ō'otcō — that is his.)   hēēlēesti'tcē — it is yours.
(hēēlē'ets'ai ō'uksō — that is hers.)   hēēlēetcā'as — it is theirs. [41]

-ĕs, my.   -ĕts, thy.   -qĕs, his.   -tcuks, her.
-t̨uҟ, our.   -stĕtc, your.   -tcāas, their.

For instance : taҟō'lҟul'es — my axe.   hē'nēĕtcuks — her father.
       hē'nēt̨uҟ — our father.

Chemakum

Intransitive Verb. ──

	Singular.	Plural
1st person,	-la, lē	-ma
2d "	-ĕts	-ĕtsāl'
3d " masc.,	-tĕq, -ē	aē
3d " fem.,	-uks	aē

For instance; — from kuētsā'at, sick:

kuētsā'atĕla — I am sick.   kuētsā'atae — they are sick.

Tenses are formed by a series of affixes, which are placed following the stem of the verb and preceding the pronominal suffix. There are a great many of these suffixes, but I am sure of the meaning of the following only: *-kuē*, future; *-tsī*, perfect; *-lĕm*, imperfect (see following page, transitive verb).

ꝗōtcilekuē'la — I shall drink.
takuil'tsē'la (1) kuē'tsaatāis (2) — yesterday I have been (1) sick (2).

Interrogative:

kuētsā'atal'ē — am I sick?
kuētsā'atatts — art thou sick?   kuētsā'atatĕtsl' — are you sick?
kuētsa'at'e — is he sick?   kuētsā'at'aē — are they sick?

Negative:

	Singular.		Plural.
1st person,	kuā'alqa kuētsā'al'l'ē.	1st person,	kuā'alqa kuētsā'al'tĕt̞nꝗ.
2d "	kuā'alqa kuētsā'al'tĕts!	2d "	kua'alqa kuētsā'al'tĕstĕtc.
3d " masc.,	kuā'alqa kuētsā'al'tĕtca'as.	3d "	kua'alqa kuētsā'al''tĕtca'as.
3d " fem.,	kuā'alqa kuētsā'al''tē'etcuks.		

It appears that the endings of the negative coincide closely with the possessive pronouns, while those of the indicative agree with the personal pronoun. [42]

Transitive Verb. ──

I have only an imperfect record of the forms of the transitive verb with incorporated pronominal object. The most striking peculiarity of these forms is the separation of pronominal

Chemakum

subject and object by the temporal character. In the following table = signifies the stem of the verb, — the temporal character:

	me	thee	him	her
I		= q — la	= — laē	== — layuks
thou	== l — tsa		= — tsaaē	== — tsayuks
he	== — la	= ē — tsa		
we		= q — ma	= — maē	== mayuks

	us	you	them.
I		= q — lā'al'ōl'	== — layaē
thou	== lao — tsa		== — tsāēyaē
he	= ē — ma	= ē — tsā'al'ōl'	
we		= q — mā'al'ōl'	

For instance : — aĕltse'squkuē'la, I feed thee. tĕpātĕlaolĕ'mtsa, thou hast vanquished us. āĕltsēsqukuē'ma, we feed thee.

Suffixes which are used for forming derivations are placed in the same position in which the temporal characters are found. For instance, with -t!'ati, which forms the desiderative : — taχuksĕlot'a'tlĕma, he wants to strike us (from tāχ-, to strike).

The reflexive is formed by the suffix -itqa : — qoatst!atcitqala, I wash my hands (qoats-, washing; -t!atc, hand; -itqa, reflexive; -la, I).

When the verb is accompanied by an adverb, the latter is inflected, while the verb remains unchanged. A frequentative is formed by amplification of the verbal stem.

Formation of Words. ——

A great number of nouns are found in two forms, independent and dependent, the latter being used for the formation of compounds. When numerals, adjectives, verbs, or other nouns are connected with such nouns, the dependent form must be used. It seems that all these dependent forms are suffixed. For instance: -spa, fire; kuē'espa, one fire; mā'ttcaspa, a great fire; la'uspēela, to pour water into fire. [43]

It seems that in many cases there is no traceable connection between the dependent and independent forms of the noun.

	Independent	In compounds.	
back	χ!'ē'enōkoat	-χ!ĕnuk	t'ca'apχ!ĕnukoatqala, I warm , my back.
belly	χamātcit	-ētcē	kuaχē'tcē, scar on belly
breast	tamĕtsa'ml'it	-tsaml'o	t!'ĕtstsa'ml'ōt, half fathom, viz., middle of breast.
lanket	pe'ests'atc	-atcet	tcenā'nōχatcēt, dog-hair blanket.

122

Chemakum

canoe	hē'lōlaӽl'	-ko	mē'ēskō, four canoes.
day — sing.		-tē'ia	l'akuata, two days.
plur.		-ta	
dollar		-tcĕ'sit	l'akuatcĕ'sīt, two dollars.
domestic animal (dog and horse)		-ans	kutsā'patans, bitch, mare.
ear	sisl'alt	t! 'a	ӽuӽuyēt!l'ā'a, deaf.
face	kul'ōӽul'	-l'ō, -l	kuaӽl'ō, scar on face; qoatslitqala, I wash my face.
finger	___	-koanu	ӽ!l'au'ikoanut, finger-ring.
fire	nē'ia	-spa	mā'ttcaspa, a great fire.
foot	laakut	-anqō	kōolanqō, lame.
hand	t'atct	-t'atc	ӽ!'aut'atct, bracelet.
head	qa'nĕt	-t'ēӽ!	cā'act'ēӽ!, bald.
		-t!'ĕt	tō'pt!'ĕt, head-ring; = "tied around head."
house	ot!l'ē	-tĕ'tco	alĕutĕtcō'ola, I build a house.
language	___	-tӽulō	Bostontӽu'lō, English.
mind	___	ēqatc	l'!ō'omē'qatc, courageous = strong-minded.
moon	ts!ĕtsu'ӽl'a	-tl'el'ō'a	kuā'ӽt!'el'ō'a, half moon.
mouth	ӽō'otō	-ӽ!ō	tsāuqoāӽ!ō, mouth bleeds.
neck	ӽ!'amō'ӽs	-ӽ!ōs	pā'atĕӽōs, collar bone.
nose	sĕmō'sĕt	-ōs	l'ōӽ!ōsĕt, perforation of nose.
point	___	-t!'ēӽoa	luӽ!ut!ē'ӽoala, I cut off point.
river	ӽu'māa	-atsit	mā'ttcatsit, large river.
trail	mō'ӽlunt	-l'ĕmĕt	kuēĕl'ĕ'mĕt, one trail.
tree	hamaa	-tcat	kuē'etcat, one tree.
		-pat	ӽā'ĕltcitpat, maple ; = "paddle tree."
water	ts!ō'ua	-sĕna	tcitc'ē'sĕnāala, I jump into water.
to look	___	-al'sē	ts'ĕlĕkoā'l'sē, looking up.
made with	___	-tcil'	ta'ӽatstatcil', chips, "made with axe."
instrument	___	-ӽul'	koā'atӽul', whetstone; = "instrument for sharpening."

The American Anthropologist Vol. V: 37-44 Jan. 1892

Quinault texts

III
TRADITIONS OF THE QUINAULT INDIANS.
By LIVINGSTON FARRAND
Assisted by
W.S KAHNWEILER.

Contents.

	Page
INTRODUCTION	79
I. The Story of Misp'	81
II. The Adventures of Bluejay	85
III. Another Story of Bluejay	102
IV. How Bluejay brought the Dead Girl to Life	105
V. The Ascent to the Sky	107
VI. Raven's Visit to the Underworld	109
VII. How Eagle and Raven arranged Things in the Early Days	111
VIII. The Origin of the Quinault Salmon	111
IX. How Siserno won Thunder's Daughter	113
X. The Magic Flight	114
XI. The Adventures of the Spearman and his Friends	116
XII. The Young Wife who was abandoned in a Tree-top	121
XIII. The Girl who married Owl's Son	122
XIV. The Story of SEp'ak'a'	124
XV. Tsa'alo the Giant	125
XVI. Wren and Elk	126
XVII. Story of the Dog Children	127
ABSTRACTS	128 [77]

Introduction

The Quinault Indians, from whom the following collection was obtained by the writer in the summer of 1898, are found on the coast of Washington with their main seat at the mouth of the Quinault River. A reservation has been established, and small settlements beside the one mentioned are to be found at scattered points within its limits.

The tribe is of Salish stock, and up to a few years ago was of a decidedly low degree of culture.[21] There is evident of late years, however, a marked advance in the cultural development of the group. This improvement is due partly, of course, to the educational advantages afforded by the reservation school, but also, to a great extent, to the introduction of the so-called "Shaker" religion,[22] which has taken a firm hold upon the tribe. Whatever may be the absurdities of this

---

[21] See Indians of the Quinault Agency, Washington Territory, by C. Willoughby (Smithsonian Report for 1886, Part I, pp. 267ff).

[22] See The Ghost-Dance Religion, by James Mooney (Fourteenth Annual Report of the Bureau of Ethnology, pp. 746ff).

belief and practice, there can be no doubt that its general influence is salutary. Its prohibition of alcohol, the general sobriety and steadiness which it recommends, and the comparative faithfulness with which its precepts are observed, have done much to advance the welfare of its followers.

The conditions of life are so easy for the Quinault that strenuous effort Is not called for on their part. The climate is mild throughout the year, the supply of salmon is never failing, deer and elk are abundant and frequently killed by the more energetic hunters, and berries of various kinds are plentiful. It is not surprising that, under these circumstances, government efforts to foster agriculture among them have not met with encouraging results. In consequence of these conditions the majority of the people are indolent, but peaceable and comparatively prosperous.

The old customs of the tribe have practically disappeared under the influences mentioned above, except in the case of a few of the older men who have thus far refused to join the Shaker movement, and still cling to the old beliefs and "medicine" rites. This state of affairs made it both harder and easier than it would otherwise have been to obtain information as to earlier conditions. The members of the Shakers look upon the old beliefs as of evil origin, and prefer not to discuss them at all. At the same time, when one could be induced to describe them, the common, half-superstitious hesitancy so often found among Indians was absent. The majority of the people claimed to know nothing of, or to have forgotten, the old customs. Among the older unregenerates the writer was fortunate in finding one, Bob Pope, who proved to have a first-rate knowledge of the tribal traditions; and the following collection was obtained mainly from him. It has been enlarged and modified by other informants, but the bulk of the stories are Pope's. [80]

It will be noticed at once that the general character of the tales is that of the northwest coast modified by and merging into a more southerly type, of which the Chinook is the most familiar example. As collections of traditions from neighboring tribes become available, this gradual transition is more and more striking. We now have at our disposal a practically unbroken series of traditions from Alaska to California, there being no considerable gap in this continuity, except in Southern Oregon; and while the extreme northern traditions are quite different from the extreme southern, the change is gradual, with at no point a sudden break in type. It is probable that the most marked diversity will be found among the Athapascan tribes of Oregon, from whom as yet we have but meagre accounts; but it is not to be expected that the general principle of modification by contact, or the general continuity just mentioned, will be seriously affected even by them.

Of the Quinault tales which form the present collection, it will be seen that the Culture Hero or Transformer story[23] bears the usual distinguishing marks. There is the introduction, dealing with the hero's antecedents, birth, and youth, with adventures exhibiting his power and trickery, followed by the account of his journey through the country and along the coast, benefiting the people in various ways. The Bluejay stories[24] of the Quinault are particularly full and extensive, and are for the most part the same as those told of Raven by the tribes of the north. Tracing these tales from north to south, it is here that Bluejay first takes on the chief role as trickster and buffoon; the Quilleutes, the nearest neighbors of the Quinault on the north, still having Raven as their subject. It is interesting to note that Raven is not entirely discarded by the Quinault; but the stories of him are meagre and few, and quite evidently borrowed from northern

---

[23] See The Story of Misp', pp. 81ff.
[24] See pp. 85ff.

sources. The standard traditions of The Ascent to the Sky, Raven's Visit to the Underworld, The Magic Flight, etc., are all found here in characteristic form. The last story of the collection, that of The Dog Children, has probably been taken bodily from the north, where it is found everywhere.

The chief sources for comparison, to which frequent references are made in the notes, are the works of Boas,[25] Petitot,[26] Teit,[27] and Farrand.[28] There are also occasional references to Krause, Rand, and others, where analogies of wider import demand attention. [81]

I. — THE STORY of Misp‘[29]

There was once a young man who had a fishing camp up a certain creek, and there he lived alone during the salmon season. One night when he came in from fishing, he found that the salmon he had caught the day before, and had not had time to dress, were all split and cleaned ready for drying, and he wondered much who could have done it. The next evening he found the same thing, and so it went on until he determined to solve the mystery. So one day, instead of going to fish as usual, he hid himself and watched; and pretty soon a woman came into the camp from the woods and began to dress the fish. The young man watched her a while and then went in and spoke to her.

Now, the woman's name was *Kwŏtsxwō'ē*, and she had fallen in love with the man and thought in that way she could win him. So they lived together at the camp until the fishing season was over, and then they started back for the young man's village, the woman going with him as his wife. Just before they reached his home, *Kwŏtsxwo'e* let down her hair and covered her face, for she was ashamed. Thus for a long time she sat in her new home with her face covered, and never laughing or talking with the other people who gathered in the house.

Now Bluejay, who was a great talker and always meddling in other people's business, kept saying, "I wonder what is the matter with *Kwŏtsxwō'ē*, that she never laughs and never shows her face." At last *Kwŏtsxwō'ē* grew tired of Blue-Jay's chatter, and, calling her husband

---

[25] By Franz Boas: Chinook Texts, Washington, 1894; *Indianische Sagen von der Nord-Pacifischen Kuste Amerikas*, Berlin, 1895; The Mythology of the Bella Coola Indians (Memoirs American Museum of Natural History, Vol. II), New York, 1898; Traditions of the Tillamook Indians (Journal of American Folk-Lore, Vol. XI, pp. 23ff, 133ff); Traditions of the Ts'Ets'aut (Ibid, Vol. IX, pp. 257ff, Vol. X, pp. 35ff); Kathlamet Texts, Washington, 1901.

[26] By Emile Petitot, Traditions Indiennes du Canada Nord-Ouest, Paris, 1886.

[27] By James Teit, Traditions of the Thompson River Indians of British Columbia, Boston, 1898.

[28] By Livingston Farrand, Traditions of the Chilcotin Indians (Memoirs American Museum of Natural History, Vol. IV), New York, 1900.

[29] Cf. various Transformer myths, particularly Boas, Indianische Sagen, etc, pp. 1 (Shuswap), 16 (Thompson), 241, 263 (Bella Coola); Boas, Chinook Texts, pp. 17ff; Farrand, Traditions of the Chilcotin, Introduction, and pp. 7 ff; Teit, Traditions of the Thompson River Indians, pp. 42ff, 62ff; Morice in Transactions Canadian Institute, Vol. V, pp. 28ff; Petitot, Traditions Indiennes, etc, p. 311. The Chinook Transformer myth is almost identical with the following story of Misp‘. (The final letter of Misp‘ is aspirated, as indicated by the inverted comma.)

out, she took him back into the woods and said, " Now, you wait here for me, for I am going back to the house to laugh and show my face. " Then, going back to the house, she walked up to Bluejay, and, throwing back her hair, said, "Now you can see my face." And he looked, and her face was horrible, and her teeth were covered with hair from the people she had eaten; for the woman was a cannibal. Then *Kwŏtsxwō'ē* laughed, and the people began to fall down dead. Five times she laughed, and by the fifth time all the people in the village were dead. Then she ate them all up from one end of the village to the other, and started back to find her husband. But just outside their house she found him lying dead, for he had followed her to see what was going to happen, and, having heard her laugh, had fallen dead with the rest. Then she ate him too, but saved his privates and put them into a basket.

Now, *Kwŏtsxwō'ē* was pregnant, and soon gave birth to twins, Misp' and Kwĕmō'lēLĕn, of whom she took great care, and bathed them often, that they should grow strong and healthy. The boys grew rapidly, and learned many things, — how to hunt with bow and arrows, and how to fish; but people they had never seen. [82]

One day their mother said she was going to a prairie on the Chehalis River to get camass-roots, and would be gone all day. She told the boys that while she was away they might go to hunt, but that they must not go toward the north (for it was there that her husband's village lay), and also that they must not look into the basket that hung in the roof of the house. But the boys were curious, and, as soon as *Kwŏtsxwō'ē* had disappeared, they started toward the north and came upon a village where the ground was covered with bones; and when they came back to the house, they looked into the basket and saw the private parts of a man. Then Misp', who had magic powers, felt sure that the privates were those of their father, about whom he had often wondered, and that the bones were those of their relatives and friends whom their mother had killed and eaten. The boys talked it over, and decided to burn the house and run away before their mother could get back. So they set fire to the house and started.

Now *Kwŏtsxwō'ē*, while still at work on the prairie, saw smoke coming from the direction of her home, and ashes flying in the air, some of which she caught in her hand, and recognized the design of the basket which hung in the roof of the house. Then she knew at once what had happened, and started back in great anger, intending to kill and eat the boys. But on reaching the house she found they had gone. *Kwŏtsxwō'ē* followed the boys' tracks, and very soon they knew she was pursuing them, for they could feel the ground tremble as she ran; and when she had nearly overtaken them they climbed to the top of a tall fir-tree. The mother came to the tree, and, looking up, saw the boys. She spoke kindly to them, and told them to come down and all would be forgiven. Misp' laughed, and said, "All right; come close to the tree, and we will come down. " She came close, and he said, "Come closer yet." She came closer, and he said, "Clasp the tree in your arms, and we will come down." So she put her arms about the tree; then Misp' shook it, and all the bark came off, and fell upon her and crushed her. Then the boys came down and went on their way.

Soon they saw a woman, resembling their mother, playing with a lot of children. The woman would take a child by the feet, and, swinging him around her head, let him fly through the air to a great rock some distance off. Most of the children were dashed to death against the rock, and the woman ate them up. The boys hid themselves, and watched for some time. Then Misp' took the juice of a plant and rubbed it on Kwĕmō'lētLĕn's face to make it look pale and sickly, and they came out to the place where the woman and children were. Now, the woman

Quinault texts

was their mother's sister, and when she saw the boys, she asked at once after their mother. Mispʻ replied that she was coming on later; whereupon his aunt proposed that they should join the game, and said she would swing Kwĕmō'lēLĕn first. But Mispʻ replied, "You see my brother, how sick he is. Swing me instead." So the woman agreed. Now, the children had been taught to sing, "ō'xō mĕlsh shiō'ls, kwātsĭ'l jŭk" (" you will go and not come back again ") whenever a child was swung: so Mispʻ went over to them, and whispered to them to sing, " ē'sō mēlsh shīō'ls, kwatsĭ'l jŭk" (" you will go and come back again ") when [83] he was swung. Then his aunt took him by the ankles and swung him with great force; and he flew through the air, but landed on his feet on the rock, and came back laughing, for the children had sung as he told them. Then he said, "Now, my aunt, it is your turn to swing." But the woman said, "No, I am too heavy; you might let me fall." But Mispʻ promised to swing her easily, and she consented. Then, making a sign to the children to sing, "ō'xō mĕlsh shīō'ls," etc. , he gave his aunt a mighty swing, and she crashed against the rock and was killed; and in her belly were found the bones of hundreds of children whom she had killed and eaten. These he gathered together and washed in the river, and some he brought back to life, but some he could not revive. And that is the reason that some children die today.

After this the boys went on until they heard a great noise on the prairie near Humptulips, and looking from a distance, they saw a woman, who was another one of their aunts, swinging children by the feet in the same way as the first had done. They lay down to watch, and as they lay there, Mispʻ, to pass the time, split with his knife a young shoot that grew beside him; and it grew to be a great tree with five spreading branches, which can be seen to this day. Then they went up to their aunt, and Mispʻ treated her and the children just as he had treated the former woman, and they went on their way.

After a time they heard a noise, and, creeping up, they saw another woman. who was also their mother's sister, and with her were a lot of children. They were playing *xwŏ'tĕl*;[30] and whenever a child laughed before it reached the stick, the woman would kill and eat it. As soon as the boys came up, their aunt proposed that *Kwĕmō'lĕtLĕn* should try his hand at the game; but Mispʻ excused his brother on the ground that he was not well, and said that he himself would try instead. He did so, and succeeded in reaching the stick, and at once killed his aunt and freed the children.

Again the boys went on, and came upon another woman of the same kind, who was pretending to tattoo on the breast the children who were with her. But she would press the needle through their hearts, and then eat them. As soon as the woman saw the brothers, she asked Mispʻ to let her tattoo *Kwĕmō'lĕtLĕn*; but he excused his brother, as before, and offered himself instead. So he lay down, and his aunt pressed the needle against his breast; but it would not pierce the skin, though she pressed with all her strength. Mispʻ then declared that it was his turn to tattoo his aunt; but she was unwilling, being afraid that he would press too hard. However, upon his promising to press lightly, she consented, whereupon Mispʻ, placing the needle against her breast, threw all his weight upon it, drove it through her heart, and killed her.

---

[30] A game in which a person is required to walk slowly toward a stick around which are gathered other players, who jeer at him, and try to make him laugh. If he smiles or laughs before he reaches the stick, he loses. {see DVD Come Forth Laughing, Suquamish}

Quinault texts

Then he opened her and took out the bones of the children she had eaten. Some of them he brought to life, but some he could not.

From this place, Misp' and his brother travelled all about the country, and [84] finally came to Neah Bay, and there Misp' called to the people and they came out; but they were in the form of dogs. So Misp' turned them into men, and gave them whale-spears and canoes, and told them they would be whalers for all time. And he tried to teach them the Quinault language, but could not; and so the people of that place can only speak Makah.

Coming south from Neah Bay, the brothers reached the mouth of the Quilleute River; and Misp' called the people, and they came out as wolves. Misp' turned them into men, and gave them whaling outfits and salmon-spears and dip-nets for smelts, and he also tried to make them speak Quinault, but did not succeed; and so they speak Quilleute.

From here they went on to the Hoh River and called the people, and a very few came out, — miserable and weak, and with nothing but dip-nets. And Misp' helped them, treating them as he had the Quilleute, and went on his way.

A little farther south the brothers came to the Queets River; and Misp' called the people, but none answered. He called and called, but none came out. Then Misp' rubbed his arm with his hand, and from the little rolls of dirt and sweat under his fingers he made people, and he gave them nets and salmon-spears, and told them they should live there always; and they were the ancestors of the present people of the Queets. And that is the reason that the place is called Kwe'tsux ("something made of dirt").

Then they came down as far as Raft River; and Kwĕmō'lēLĕn saw the tail-feathers of an eagle floating in the river, and he swam out to get them, for he wanted them to wear in his hair. But when he reached the middle of the stream, he was caught by a whirlpool and carried under, and was swallowed by a monster *tsēēxē'ēma* or *k'āk'ā'tsk* ("the swallower"). Then Misp' built a fire and heated great bowlders, and threw them into the river until it began to boil. Then a *tsēēxē'ēma* drifted down, and Misp' speared and opened him; but his brother was not inside. Then another one came floating down, and him also Misp' killed and opened; but still Kwĕmō'lēLĕn was not there. Then a third one, the biggest of all, came down; and when he was caught and opened, there was Kwĕmō'lēLĕn, but he was already dead. So Misp' took him ashore and tried to restore him, but could not; for, every time he came to life, he turned into a duck. Again and again he tried; and finally he gave it up, and said, "You shall always be a duck, and people shall call you Kwĕmō'lēLĕn."[31]

From Raft River, Misp' went on alone; and when he reached Quinault and called the people, they came out, and they were already men with all kinds of implements and weapons. So Misp' did nothing for them, except to tell them that they should always be men.

He went on and came to the mountain (three miles below Quinault River), and there saw a man grinding shells for knives, and as he worked he sang, "I am making this for Misp', I am making this for Misp'." Misp' approached, and asked him what he was doing. The man, whose name was Lł!ē ("deer"), [85] replied, "I am making this for Misp', to kill him when he comes." Misp' asked to see the shell, and the man handed him three; whereupon Misp' clapped one on each side of his head for ears, and, putting him down on all-fours, turned him around, and

---

[31] Kwĕmō'lēLĕn is the present Quinault name for a variety of duck plentiful at certain seasons. {old sqwauk, pintail, formerly 'old squaw'; see following section}

fastened the third on behind as a tail. Then Misp' ordered Lł!e to jump about, and to run a little way and look back. And Lł!e did so. Then Misp' told him to run toward the woods, but to look back before he disappeared. And Lł!e did as he was told. "Hereafter," said Misp', "you shall always act like that when people see you." And that is why deer behave in that way to-day.

After that he went on and reached Copalis Rock, and there he saw a man moving toward the ocean across the beach. The man was upside down, walking on his hands, grunting and groaning, and apparently going against his will. Misp' asked him what the trouble was, and he said his head was full of lice, and they were dragging him into the sea. So Misp' took the knot of a tree and made a comb of it, and combed out the man's hair; and he turned him right side up, and gave him the comb, and told him to use it thereafter and he would be safe.[32]

Misp' next came to Copalis River and called the people; and they came out upside down, with nothing but small flounder-spears and short sticks for digging clams. And he told them that such should be their work; and after turning them right side up he left them. And the people of Copalis River have lived on small fish and clams ever since.

Thence he went on to Oyhut and called the people; and they came out, walking upside down, with short clam-sticks, and using their heads as hammers for splitting wood, and grunting and groaning with the pain of it. Then Misp' turned them right side up, and gave them stone hammers, and left them.

From Oyhut he went south along the beach, stopping at different places, and changing the people, until he reached the Chinook at the mouth of the Columbia River, and there he turned into a rock that can be seen to this day.

II. — THE ADVENTURES OF BLUEJAY[33]

People used to live on the Quinault River from the mountains down to the mouth. All the birds and animals were people then, and Bluejay lived near the upper end, in the last house upstream. He had a lot of children, and they were out of food and hungry; for Bluejay never hunted or fished, but just sat around doing nothing.

One morning just before daylight, Bluejay said to his wife, whose name was Jui, "Let us go down and visit my cousin Magpie this morning, and see if we can get some food." Jui agreed: so they started early and came to Magpie's, and found him alone. Bluejay looked all around the house, but could see nothing [86] to eat. Pretty soon Magpie made a fire and heated the stones. When they were hot, he set the pot by the fire and threw in the stones, and the water began to boil. Then Magpie let down his hair and took out one salmon-egg which he had in his hair, and, throwing it into the pot, began to stir it about. He stirred and stirred, and the water grew thicker and thicker until the pot was full to the brim of salmon-eggs. Bluejay set to work, and ate and ate until he could hardly move, but still there was plenty left: so he prepared to take the rest home to his children. His wife went out first; but she heard Bluejay saying to Magpie, "You come up to my house to-morrow, and you shall have a feast." When Bluejay came out to the

---

[32] The Indians of Copalis Rock were notorious for vermin.

[33] Cf. Boas, The Mythology of the Bella Coola Indians, p. 93; Boas, Indianische Sagen, etc, pp. 76, 106, 177, 245, etc; Boas, Chinook Texts, p. 172; Farrand, Traditions of the Chilcolin, p. 18; Teit, Traditions, etc, pp. 40 ff; Rand, Legends of the Micmacs, p. 300.

Quinault texts

canoe, Jui scolded him for inviting Magpie when he knew they had nothing in the house to eat. Bluejay excused himself, and said he was Just thanking his cousin, that it was only polite to ask him to visit them, and that he knew how he could get food.

Night came; and next morning, just before daylight, Bluejay made a big fire and went out. Soon he came back, all wet from bathing. He lay down by the fire for a while, and then went out and sat on the roof of the house, thinking hard all the time. Pretty soon he called out that he saw Magpie coming up the river, he could tell him by his hat. His wife began to scald again, but it did no good; and soon Magpie arrived. Bluejay was happy, and took the pot in which he had brought the eggs from Magpie's, filled it, and heated the water with stones, just as Magpie had done. He had already hidden in his hair one of the eggs he had brought from Magpie's, and as soon as the water was boiling he fingered around in his hair until he found the egg. Then he threw it in and began to stir. He stirred an. d stirred until the water was cold; but there was nothing there but the one salmon-egg bobbing up and down in the pot. At last he gave it up and sat there much ashamed. Magpie waited, but Bluejay could give him nothing. Finally Magpie grew tired, took the stones and heated them, and put them into the pot. Then, taking one egg from his hair, he threw it in, and in a few minutes the pot was full. Magpie refused to eat, however, and, leaving all for Bluejay, went home in disgust.

Next morning Bluejay said to his wife. "Let us go down to see our neighbor Sawbill Duck to-day, and try to get something to eat." So they started downstream, and soon came to Sawbill's house. Going in, they saw a large fire, and on both sides of the fire were salmon-heads cooking.[34] When Bluejay and his wife came in, Sawbill told them to help themselves; and Bluejay did so, and ate until he could hold no more. Sawbill then told his sons to go out and get fresh salmon for their grandfather. The boys went, and soon came back with five steelheads, and cooked them all for Bluejay. When they were done, Bluejay was so full that he could just sit and look at them. So, when they were ready to go home, Sawbill packed up the salmon for Bluejay to carry to his house. Jui tried to make Bluejay go out first, but he refused, and she overheard him saying to Sawbill, "Cousin, come up to my house to-morrow and [87] have a feast." Jui was angry, and scolded Bluejay after he came out; but it did no good. So they reached home with the salmon, and gave them to the children.

Next morning, before daylight, Bluejay made a fire, bathed in the river, lay down by the fire, went out and sat on the roof, and waited. At sunrise he called to his wife, "Some one is coming up the river, and I can tell by his hat that it is Sawbill." And so it was, — Sawbill and his whole family, his wife and five sons. They came in, and Bluejay was happy. They sat talking for a little while, and then Bluejay told two of his children to go out and catch salmon. When they came back they were nearly drowned and frozen, and had no salmon; and Bluejay sat there silent and ashamed. Sawbill's family were quiet for a while, but at last grew tired; and Sawbill told his sons to go out and get some fresh salmon. They went, and in a few minutes came back with five big steelheads, but they left them for Bluejay, and all went away home without eating.

Night came; and before daylight Bluejay said to his wife, "To-day we will go down to our third neighbor, Bear, and get food." They started; and when they arrived at Bear's house they found him and his wife, but there was no food. They were sitting with their backs to the fire, and Bear's wife was making a basket. Bear built a big fire and made Bluejay welcome. His wife said

---

[34] In the old days, salmon-heads were cooked by placing hot stones in the mouths.

nothing, but worked on. Still Bluejay could see no food. Bear put the pot by the fire, then, taking his knife, he slashed the sole of his foot up and down, and held it up by the fire, so that the fat ran out and soon filled the pot. Then, going over to his wife, he cut a big piece of meat out of her back, while she sat still and apparently never felt it at all. He cooked the meat and they ate it with the fat, Bluejay ate until he could hardly move, and thought it was fine, especially the fat. Bluejay urged his wife to eat, but she would not, and they stood there scolding and quarrelling. At last Jui went out to the canoe; and Bluejay said to Bear, "Now, you come up to my house tomorrow morning and you shall have a feast." Bear said he would, and Bluejay went out and joined his wife, taking the rest of the meat with him, and when they reached home they gave it to the children, and all were happy.

Next morning he did as he had done before, sat on the roof, and at sunrise called to his wife that he could see Bear's hat coming up the river. Then Jui was angry and frightened, for she suspected what Bluejay had in mind. Soon Bluejay came down from the roof and told his wife to get to work just as Bear's wife had been, with her back to the fire. She refused at first, but finally gave in and sat down as she was told. Bear and his wife arrived, and Bluejay bustled about, built a great fire, and began to prepare for a big feast. He put on the pot and started to cut the sole of his foot; but he was nervous, and every time the knife touched him he squealed with pain. At last he made a quick cut; but nothing but black blood came out, while he yelled and screamed with the pain. Then he went for his wife, to cut meat from her back; but she resisted, and they fought and struggled together. He got in one cut; but she screamed so, and made [88] such a time, that at last he quit in despair, and they both sat there bleeding and sore. And there was no food to give to Bear. At last Bear told Bluejay to build up a big fire; this done, he cut his other foot, and filled the pot with fat, cut the other side off his wife's back, and, leaving it all for Bluejay, took his wife and went home without eating.

If all this had not happened, there would still be plenty of fat on the bear's feet, and much meat on its back; as it is, there is very little.

Early one morning after the bear-meat was eaten up, Bluejay proposed that they go down to Land Otter's to get food. They went, and found the whole family in the house. After a while Land Otter sent his sons out to get fresh salmon for Bluejay, and in a few minutes they came back with five big steel-heads. Bluejay ate all he could hold. When they were ready to go home, Bluejay sent his wife out ahead, and then told Land Otter to come up to see him the next day. All the same things happened, and before daylight Bluejay was on the roof watching. At sunrise he called to his wife that he could see Land Otter's hat in a canoe coming upstream.

Land Otter arrived with his whole family, and Bluejay lighted a big fire to welcome them. Pretty soon Bluejay told his children to go out and catch fresh salmon. After a long time they came back, wet and cold and nearly dead, but brought no salmon. At last Land Otter grew tired of waiting, and sent his own sons out, who came back in a few minutes with five steelheads. But they left them all for Bluejay, and went home without eating.

After some days, early one morning, Bluejay said to his wife, "Come, let us go down to Beaver's to-day, and get something to eat." They went, but when they arrived, found no house at all, but saw the young Beavers playing around in the water. The young ones dived down and told their father that Bluejay was there, and he sent the children up to invite him in. Bluejay could not see how he was to get in, so two young Beavers took him, one by each arm, to dive down with him. Bluejay was afraid, and struggled so that they gave him up, and took his wife;

and after a while they got her into the house, but she was nearly strangled. Then they tried Bluejay again, and at last got him in, but he was nearly dead too. When he had recovered and looked around, Bluejay saw that the house was all right, and was on dry land: so he felt contented again. Beaver built a fire and said to his wife, "Take the children and go get salmon-berry-sprouts for our friends." They went, and soon came back with salmon-berry bush instead of sprouts. Bluejay tried to eat it, but found he could not, for it was hard wood. The Beavers, however, ate it easily, and liked it. Bluejay gave it up: so Beaver sent his family out to get some elderberries, and soon they came back with baskets full of black mud, which they said was preserved elderberries. While they were preparing this, Bluejay looked at it and made a face, and said, "I can't eat that black mud; I don't eat mud." But the Beavers ate it all and said it was fine, while Bluejay and his wife went hungry. After a while the Beavers took them up to the surface of the water, and Bluejay invited [89] Beaver to visit him next morning. This time Bluejay and his wife did not quarrel, for they knew it was easy enough to get mud and salmonberry-bush.

Next morning Bluejay did as before, and called from the roof that he saw some one coming, and he thought it was Beaver. Beaver's family came in, and Bluejay told his children to go out and gather salmonberry-sprouts for their guests. They came back soon with nearly a houseful of salmonberry-bushes, but in a few minutes the Beavers had eaten them all up. Bluejay then sent his children out to get black mud, and they came back with all they could carry; but in a very short time the Beavers had eaten that all up too, and said they liked it. So Beaver and his family had all they could eat before they started home.

Next morning Bluejay waked his wife and said they would go down to visit *Kwēt*[35] and get something to eat. So at daylight they went down, and found *Kwēt* and his wife and five daughters at home; but, though he looked all around, Bluejay could see no food in the house. After a little while, *Kwēt* said to his wife and daughters, "Go back into the woods and get some salmonberries for your grandfather." So they took six big baskets and went out, and soon came back with all they could carry. *Kwēt* filled a dish and set it before Bluejay, who ate until he could not move, but he had not finished the dish by a good deal. When they were ready to go, Bluejay took the six baskets of berries along with him, and invited *Kwēt* to bring his family to visit him next morning.

Early next day, Bluejay did everything as before, and *Kwēt* and his family came in. Bluejay told his children to go out and get berries, and they went, but did not return until toward evening, and they had found no berries. *Kwēt*'s family had been sitting around all day with nothing to eat: so, when Bluejay's children came home and brought nothing, *Kwēt* said to his daughters, "You go out and get berries for Bluejay. "They went, and in a little while came back with their baskets full. But they left them all there, and went home without waiting to eat.

One morning soon after this, Bluejay waked his wife, and proposed going down to Kingfisher's for food. They went, and found Kingfisher and his five children all at home. Kingfisher sent the children out for fresh salmon, and they soon came back with five big ones. Bluejay ate as much as he could, and then started for home, first inviting Kingfisher to visit him next morning. When he arrived at the house, he ate the remaining salmon with his children.

Next morning the same things happened as before. Bluejay saw Kingfisher coming, and sent his children out for salmon. They did not succeed in getting any, and, after waiting some

---

[35] A small warbler.

time, Kingfisher sent his own children out, who soon came back with five big salmon. But they left them there, and went home without eating.

Next day Bluejay and his wife went down to Shadow's. On their way they saw a canoe loaded with wood, but with no one in it. "Let's hurry," said Bluejay, "and we may be able to get that canoe." They tried, but could not [90] catch it; and pretty soon it stopped in front of a house and the wood disappeared. Still Bluejay could see no man with it. They reached the village and went into the biggest house, but saw no one. They could see furniture and clothing and plenty of dried salmon, but not a single person. There was a dress lying on one of the beds, and in the upper part a pearl nose-ring. BlueJay also noticed that every now and then one of the salmon would come down from the drying-pole and go on the fire, of its own accord, Bluejay would take it off again, fearing that the people would think he had done it. Now it was really the Shadow people trying to cook salmon for Bluejay. Along in the afternoon, Bluejay said to his wife, "There is nobody here, and that dress there on the bed is good looking, and will be all right for you. I'll steal it." Going over to the bed, he took hold of the dress and pulled it; but something spoke from out of the dress, "Look out there, Bluejay, you'll tear my dress!" and he jumped back, startled and frightened. After a little he tried the same thing with the pearl nose-ring, but it spoke too; so he gave it up and sat still. There they were, tired and hungry, and toward night they started for home, having had nothing to eat, and they went to bed exhausted as soon as they reached the house.

Next morning he called to his wife, "Wake up and we will go down to the mouth of the river, to Hair-seal's, and see if he will give us something to eat." They went, and found Hair-seal and his wife and five children. Hair-seal built a fire, and sent his wife and children to bathe in the river, and told them while there to lie clown on a certain sand-bar and wait. They did as he said, and the youngest lay at the end of the row. Hair-seal waited until he saw them lying on the sandbar, then, taking his stone hammer, he went out, while Bluejay watched him. He went over to the sand-bar, and struck the youngest child on the forehead and killed him. Then he told the rest to go into the water, which they did, and in a moment re-appeared, and there were still five children. Hair-seal took up the dead one to carry it home, but it was so fat he could hardly get it along. When he finally got it to the house, and the children had come in, he put the dead seal on the fire to singe the hair off. Then he dressed the meat, and Bluejay watched, and saw that it was covered with fat. Hair-seal boiled the meat, and gave it to Bluejay and Jui; and Bluejay ate so much that he just lay back where he was and couldn't move. When they were ready to go home, Bluejay, as usual, asked Hair-seal to come up and visit him next morning. At that his wife was frightened, for she felt sure Bluejay would try the same trick that he had seen Hair-seal do, and she cried most of the way home.

Next morning Bluejay did everything as before, and called from the roof that Hair-seal was coming. His wife was furious, and scolded and scolded until Hair-seal and his family arrived and came in. Bluejay made a big fire, and told his children to swim in the river, and then to lie down on the point of a certain sand-bar, and keep their eyes shut. He watched them, and when they were on the bar he went over and hit the youngest on the forehead with his hammer, and smashed in his head. Then he cried to the other children, "Dive down, quick, [91] quick, quick!" But the others were so frightened that they couldn't get under water, and just lay there crying and whimpering, and there were only four of them left. Bluejay's wife was nearly crazy with grief over the death of her youngest child, and furious with Bluejay, and there was a great uproar. Then Hair-seal told his boys to bathe and lie on the sand-bar; and when they did so, he

Quinault texts

clubbed the youngest, and the four jumped into the river and came out five, as before. Then they carried the dead seal to the house, and left the meat for Bluejay, and all went home.

Now Bluejay and his family were filled with grief for the child, and cut the hair from their heads, all but a tuft at the top, and paid no more visits.

And some one told Squirrel and Black Diver what had happened, and they made fun of Bluejay because he had killed his own child.

So Bluejay said to his wife, "We will go down and find those fellows, and tie them up and bring them home." They went, and came to the house, and from the outside they could hear the men laughing, and making fun of Bluejay. Then Bluejay went over and kicked on the door, and said, "Is it true that you are mocking me because I killed my child?" And they said, "Yes, it's true: see what you have got on your head for doing it," pointing to the crest of hair on his head. Then Bluejay and his wife went in, and took the men and dragged them out, and, after tying their hands and feet, threw them into the canoe and started for home. But every time Squirrel or Black Diver moved in the bottom of the canoe, the ropes broke. Then Bluejay asked them, '*What kind of rope is the best to hold men like you?" And Black Diver answered, "Weeds are the best." Bluejay said to his wife, "I know where there are some weeds. In that big slough over there: let's go and get them." So they went and picked some long weeds, and tied the men's hands and feet once more. Then, when they lay there grunting and crying. Bluejay said, "It serves you right: if you had not made . fun of me, I would not have done this to you." Suddenly, when they were about halfway home, Diver jumped up, and, breaking the weeds, dived over the edge of the canoe. Bluejay poked his pole after him in the mud and cried, " Now I've got you!" But Diver came up on the other side of the river, and laughed, and made fun of Bluejay, and then went ashore. Now Bluejay had only Squirrel left, and when they got farther up the river, he asked Squirrel where would be a good place to put a man like him. Squirrel answered that the best place for him would be a brush-pile. So they ran close in to some brush overhanging the water, and Squirrel jumped up and ran ashore, and laughed, and poked fun at Bluejay.[36] When Bluejay and his wife arrived home, they decided they would go somewhere else to live, they felt so badly about their dead child.

So they started down the river, and when they came to the beach they saw a crowd gathered, and went up to see what it was all about. There they found [92] xwōnē' xwōnē' and Snail having a contest of eyesight, each claiming that he could see better than the other. Snail said, "I can see the smoke of that village out there over the ocean." And xwōnē' xwōnē' answered. "I can beat you, I can see that woman carrying wood." Snail did not believe xwōnē' xwōnē': so he said, "Let's trade eyes for a few minutes. I would like to see how good your eyes really are. "xwōnē' xwōnē' agreed, and took out his eyes and gave them to Snail, who put them in and looked, but could see nothing. They were just ordinary, common eyes. But xwōnē' xwōnē' with Snail's eyes could see the smoke as clearly as possible. Then they traded back, and all went south along the beach, Bluejay with the rest.[37]

Now Snail had come up to Quinault from Wreck Creek to get Crow for his wife. Crow was a fine girl, but blind. He took Crow back with him, and she gave a name to every place between Quinault and Wreck Creek. As they went along, Crow sang, and every time she

---

[36] Cf. Boas, Chinook Texts, p. 121.
[37] Cf. p 108.

Quinault texts

finished her song, she would ask, "How far are we now?" Snail would tell her, and she would give the place a name. When they reached home, Snail took out one of his eyes and gave it to his wife, and they each had one eye. Every morning Crow used to go out digging clams, and every evening, when she came back, she used to say, "It looks queer to see each of us with only one eye: one of us ought to have the pair." So at last, to keep her quiet, Snail gave his wife his other eye, and so she had two and he had none; and he had to sit in the house all the time, for he was blind.

Crow was white in those days, but became black. This is how it happened: one day, when she went out to dig clams, she told Snail to go and get wood. He groped about, and finally came to the house-post, and, taking It for a tree, cut it down; and the house fell in on the fire and was burnt up, and Crow's white dress was there, and was burnt black in the fire. Crow saw the smoke and came hurrying home, but she was too late, the dress was already burnt; and since that time she has always been black.

Bluejay left his wife at Wreck Creek and went on south with xwōnē' xwōnē', and had many adventures.[38]

When they came to Oyhut they parted, for Bluejay found his master living there in a large house, and with him his two daughters. So there he staid, and one day a beautiful duck appeared in the bay, so bright and shining, that, whenever he came up from diving, a light spread about him.[39] All the people wished to get him, and tried continually to shoot him with their bows and arrows. This went on until the whole bay was lined with canoes chasing the duck. They followed him day after day, but could never get him. Sometimes, when an arrow struck very near him, it would ring out as though it had struck metal. [93]

Bluejay was angry because his master had nothing but daughters, for if they had been boys, they would have been out hunting the wonderful duck. As it was, they were no good at all. "It's a shame," Bluejay kept saying, "to have nothing but girls!"

Now, the girls used to get up at daylight, and, taking their root-diggers with them, would go out and be gone all day. In the evening they would come back with only a handful of roots, and Bluejay would begin to scold again. And all the time the people were hunting the wonderful duck. Now, what the girls really did was to take their canoe up a creek between Oyhut and Humptulips. There they had found good yew-wood, and had made two fine bows, and five arrows for each; and they had practised every day until they were good shots at long range. Then they decided to go out for the wonderful bird. They had made their bows and arrows different from any others in use, and one night they hid them close to the canoe so that they could get them in the morning without any one knowing it. When they came in to go to bed, Bluejay, as usual, scolded and scolded, and was so angry he couldn't eat the roots they had brought in.

---

[38] A number of stories of Xwone' xwone', all of a gross character, were interpolated here; but, as they were obviously borrowed from southern sources, they have been omitted. See Boas, Zur Mytliologie der Indianer von Washington und Oregon (Globus, Vol. LXIII, Nos. 10, 11, 12); also Boas, Traditions of the Tillamook Indians (Journal of American Folk-Lore, Vol. XI, 1898, p. 140).

[39] Cf. Boas, Kathlamet Texts, p. 39.

Quinault texts

Next morning at sunrise, the girls rose, and said they were going for roots, as usual; but, instead of doing so, they went down to their canoe, took off their women's clothes and put on men's, painted their faces and tied their hair up in knots on the backs of their heads. When this was done, any one would have taken them for strangers. They started out in the canoe, the older girl in the bow and the younger in the stern. They found the bay crowded with canoes, but they started after the duck just the same, keeping apart from the rest, and watching where he usually rose. When they were near enough, the older girl shot. It was a long shot, but it almost hit the duck, and the sound it made rang all over the bay. She shot four times and the fourth shot just touched the duck, and it made such a beautiful sound that it nearly sent all the hunters to sleep. The girls did not pick up the arrows they had shot, but left them; and the people, finding them, saw that they were different from their own, and began to talk, and wonder where the strangers came from;. but, whenever they came near, the girls paddled away. The fifth arrow of the older girl wounded the wing slightly, and the duck began to make short dives. Now it was the younger girl's turn to shoot, so they turned the canoe around. The first shot nearly hit the duck, and the second hit him right in the head, and he floated on the water, dead. They paddled up as fast as they could, and, as soon as they had him in the canoe, went off to the creek before the others could come up to them. The other canoes had collected all the arrows; and the people were chattering and talking, and saying, "Now we shall soon find out who it is that has killed the duck. Probably they are from some distant place."

Bluejay and his master were out on the shore looking on when the duck was shot. Bluejay was nagging at his master, as usual, because he had only girls and no boys; but his master said never a word. Along toward evening the girls came home dressed as usual, and looking just as they always had before. That night [94] they all went to bed as usual, the girls sleeping in the upper bunk, in front of which was a *high* board. But they were too excited to sleep, and lay there talking and whispering. Their father heard them, and wondered what they were talking about. Now they had the duck with them in a sack, but nobody knew it.

At daylight the girls called to Bluejay, "Get up, Bluejay, and open the door." But Bluejay sneered at them, and said, "Why should I get up so early? You are no good. If you had been boys, you might have got the duck." The girls said, "You had better get up and open the door before it gets too light." At last he got up slowly, grumbling all the while, climbed the ladder, and opened the door.[40] Just then the girls opened the sack below, and there was such a bright light that Bluejay was knocked over, and fell off the roof. He was hurt and bruised, but he climbed up again to fix the door. The girls lay in bed laughing, and when he got up there, they opened the sack again, and he rolled down to the ground. Five times he tried, and each time he fell over at the flash of light, and lay there bruised and sore. Then the younger girl said, "Now, sister, that's enough: we don't want to kill him." So the sixth time he got the door open, so that the daylight came in; and they all got up.

That morning the girls cooked lots of roots, and told Bluejay to go around and gather in all the people to a big potlatch. Everybody came, and in a short time the place was crowded. Four days and four nights they danced, and on the fifth day the girls told their father to get out his best mat, and spread it where his bed was. He did so, and the girls took the duck and laid him

---

[40] This indicates a former use of the underground house, of which there are no traces among the Quinault to-day.

on the mat, and the people were surprised, and knew for the first time who it was that had killed the duck. The duck had a plumage of all kinds of beautiful colors, and the girls gave a little to each one; and that is how the birds got all their bright feathers, their crests, and their patches. And some, who were chiefs, got more than others; and they are the brightest birds to-day. After they had given some to each of the guests, they took Bluejay and rolled him around in the feathers that were left, and he got covered all over with blue, and is so to this day. After this, by the advice of the girls, all the people moved to Damon's Point and lived there.

The people used to go out on the ocean to hunt ducks, and the best hunters among them were a young man and his sister. The young man would sit in the bow of the canoe and do the shooting, and the girl sat in the stern and did the paddling; and every evening they came back with a canoe-load of ducks, and gave to all the people in the village. Whenever they went out, it happened that a fog came up, – a fog so thick that they could not see each other in the canoe, – and they could get close up on the ducks so that the young man could shoot them, and so get as many as he wished. Now, the girl always wore a pearl nose-ring; and the moisture of the fog would gather in a drop on the bottom of the ring, and she used to lick it off with her tongue.[41] [95]

Soon it became evident that the girl was pregnant; and as there was no stranger around, nor any one else who could have been the cause of it, the people began to think it must be her brother. Now, it was really the fog who was the father of her child, but no one dreamed of that. And the people were ashamed of her, and talked of going away and deserting her. However, the brother and sister continued to go out as usual every day, and this went on until near the time of her confinement. Then the people tore down the houses, and all went across the bay, leaving the two there alone. They also put out all the fires; but Crow, who was the girl's grandmother, took pity on them, and placed a live coal between two clam-shells, and hid it in the ground. The two were out hunting when all this happened, and when they came home, that night and found no one, they began to weep. The boy had no idea why the people had left, for he did not know that they suspected him. The girl began searching about where their house had stood, and at last, just where Crow's bed had been, she found the clam-shells with the coal still burning.[42] She built a fire, and told her brother to go out and look for wood. He found plenty of driftwood, and very soon they had a house to live in. Then he began to find sea-otter, two or three every day, then whales, lots of them, lying on the beach; and they had more than they wanted to eat. About this time the girl gave birth to a boy baby, and then for the first time the brother suspected why the people had left. Now, the girl used to sleep on the other side of the house from her brother, and at night he would hear her and some man talking together; but there was never any one there in the morning. And the whales became so plentiful, and they had so much, that the young man gave up trying to save the meat, and just let them lie there and rot.

One morning the brother waked early and saw a man gliding away from his sister's bed, – a tall man with a long blanket. After that for several mornings he saw him, and at last the man staid in the house all day, but he was a stranger, and the young man did not know who he was. Once the man

---

[41] Cf. Boas, Chinook Texts, p. 51.
[42] Cf. p. 127; also Boas, Indianische Sagen, etc, pp. 10, 20, 52, 93, 114, 132, 180, etc; Boas, Chinook Texts, p. 51; Farrand, Traditions of the Chilcotin, p. 8; Teit, Traditions, etc, p. 52; Rand, Legends of the Micmacs, p. 46.

went outside for something, and the boy asked his sister who he was and where he came from, and she told him his name was *xlĕō'lxtcū*,[43] and that he came from far out of the West.

Now, the people who had moved across the bay had seen smoke rising from the site of the old village; and one night Crow made up her mind to go over and see what was doing. She went, but, when she came to the beach, could not get ashore for some time, on account of the great quantity of whale-meat that was lying there. Finally she got ashore, and, going up to the house, looked in and saw two men and a child, besides the young woman, her granddaughter. She watched for a while, and then called out, "Let me in! I am Crow. I have come over to see you," – "Are you alone?" they [96] asked. "Yes," answered Crow. "Is no one with you?" – "No one," said Crow. Then they let her in, and gave her all the whale-meat she could eat, and, when she was ready to go, gave her some to take back with her, but told her not to tell the other people. Crow went home and gave the meat to her children, but said nothing about it to any one else. Now there was a famine there, and the people had nothing to eat. Next night Crow decided to go over again, and did so, and had whale-meat to eat, and was given plenty to take back to her children. Next morning, while the children were eating the meat their mother had brought, one of them choked on a piece of it. Bluejay, who happened to be there, slapped the child on the back and the piece of meat flew out on the ground. Bluejay saw that it was whale-meat, and told the rest of the people.[44] They came to Crow and asked her where she had got it, but she denied having any at all. The people hunted about, and at last found a basket half full of whale-meat. Then they questioned her until finally she confessed; but she only told them that the girl was living on the other side of the bay with her husband and brother and a small boy, but that the people had better find out for themselves before they did anything. So toward evening they decided to send three young men to look over the ground. After some trouble, on account of the whales on the shore, the young men got over the beach, and, going up to the house, looked through a crack, and saw the strange man sitting there by the fire. They called, and asked them to open the door, saying that they had come over to see how they were. But the girl answered, "No! You people were ashamed of us, and you can't come in. You had better stay away." So the young men went back without having got in, and told the girl's parents that there was a strange man there and also a small boy, besides the girl and her brother. So the father and mother decided to go over the next day, and the rest of the people said they would go along too. They went; but, as they were approaching the shore, the girl and the men saw them coming, and they took the little boy out and bathed him, and there sprang up a strong north wind which beat the people back. When the wind died down, the people tried to land again; but they bathed the child as before, and the wind sprang up and blew the canoes back. All day the people tried to land, but could not on account of the wind, which came up every time the boy was bathed. After the fifth time, the girl said, "Well, we might as well let them come. They can build their houses where they like. They can't get into our house, and they can't hurt us. " So they let them come, and the people got ashore. When the girl's father and mother wished to come into her house, she closed the door and would not open it. And they gave nothing to the people to eat, except the refuse that was lying about on the ground and on the beach.

---

[43] A well-known *tamanous* or supernatural helper for whale-hunters among the Quinault.

[44] Cf. Boas, Indianische Sagen, etc pp. 264ff; Farrand, Traditions of the Chilcolin, p. 10; Teit, Traditions' etc, p. 26.

Quinault texts

Next morning when they got up, there was a big whale lying on the beach [97] with his tail at the drift-logs and his head pointing out to sea. The girl made everything ready, and then she and her husband and small boy went down to the beach. They told a young man there to cut places in the whale's back for them to sit in; and when they had taken their seats, they told him to kick the whale. He did so, and the whale started westward through the ocean, and disappeared in the distance; and all the people on shore stared and wondered.

Now, the girl's brother had staid in the house, and when his sister left him he lay down on his bed and covered his face. Five days he lay with his face covered, but on the sixth he got up, and, calling all the people together, he divided among them the oil and meat he had in the house. Then said he to the people, "Let us go out into the west, where my sister has gone." And the people agreed. Now, Bluejay was bustling about, and more anxious to get off than all the others; and that night his sister told him he had better hide in the brush in the bottom of the canoe, that he would have less work to do. So Bluejay hid himself beforehand under the brush, and was not in the crowd that went aboard at daybreak. There were a lot of canoes, and at first they raced together; then, when they were tired, they rested. It was at this time that the young man first missed Bluejay. "Where's Bluejay?" he cried. "He must have been left behind." Then they raced again, and one of the paddlers braced his feet against Bluejay, and he began to squeal and groan. They all wondered what it was that was making such a noise under their feet; and on lifting up the brush, and looking, there was Bluejay, lying on his back, sore and grunting. They took him out and put him to work, and paddled on to the westward. Five days and five nights they paddled, and on the sixth day saw land. There was a big village there, and many people, so they stopped the canoes close to the shore to look over the ground. But Bluejay got impatient, and said, "Why do we stop here? Are we to starve to death?" and with that he jumped out on to the beach. But the beach was slippery as ice, and he slipped and fell, and banged his head, and slid off into the water, while all the people on shore laughed, and made fun of him. Then Bluejay got mad, and turned on Pelican, who was mocking him, and made fun of his long nose; but Pelican only laughed at him. Bluejay climbed into the canoe, but soon jumped overboard again, and slipped back under the canoe. Five times he tried and failed, and at last gave it up, finding that he could not get a footing. Then the people on shore called to the young man, and asked him what kind of blankets he would like; and he said he wanted sea-otter blankets, two pairs, each made of four skins. Then they asked each man in turn, and each said what he wanted, and all got what they asked. When they asked Bluejay, he said he wanted surf-duck blankets: so he got a lot of surf-duck skins.

After this they went ashore, the young man walking carefully ahead and the others behind him walking in his tracks. And they came up to a big house in which they found the girl living with her husband and child; and on either side of the door was an immense sea-lion. Now, these were her dogs. So they all went in, except Bluejay, who had not been able to get up there yet, it was so slippery, [98] and he was so lame and sore from his falls. At last he reached the house, and started to go in; but the sea-lions roared, and Bluejay was frightened and ran squealing away. Finally the girl came out, and, picking up the sea-lions as if they had been little dogs, threw them aside and let Bluejay in. Then the people brought whale-meat for them to eat and a very small bowl of whale-oil. Bluejay thought, "There isn't nearly enough for all, so I'll just get in first." So he took a piece of meat and dropped it in the oil, expecting to take it all; but after he had swallowed it, there was just as much oil left as there had been at first. So Bluejay went on gobbling down the meat until he was so full he just had to lie down; but still there was as much oil as ever.[45] Later, when they had all done eating, the people told them that the little bowl held as much as a sea-lion's stomach. When they were all ready to go home, each one got a piece of pearl; the chiefs got big pieces and the common people smaller pieces. Bluejay wanted to know where the pearl came from, and one of the people told him. So Bluejay made up his mind that later he would get his master to come back with him, and go to that place for pearl.

They all reached home safely after five days, and not long after, Bluejay began to urge his master to go after pearl with him. His master asked him if he knew where the stranger people had got it, and Bluejay told him that he knew all about it. So his master agreed that they would make a trip and try to get some.[46]

Now, Bluejay's master had five wives, and one of the wives had a small boy; and the next day Bluejay went up the beach and brought his own wife down to his master's house. Then he dragged his canoe up on shore, and burned and scraped the bottom to make it go faster. Before evening they had everything ready, and just before daybreak next morning they started west. They paddled for three days, and on the third day came to a place which Bluejay recognized, from what the man had said, as the place from which the pearl came. The man had also warned him that one person must stay with the canoe, or else the tide might rise and carry it out. So Bluejay staid with the canoe while his master went after the pearl. Late in the evening his master came back with all he could carry, and they started homeward, getting in after three days. They laid out the pearl where they could look at it, and Bluejay wondered if his master would give him half. Finally his master put all the big pieces on one side, and all the little, no-account pieces on the other, and gave the latter to Bluejay. Bluejay felt very sore at this, but said nothing.

Some time after this, his master said, "Bluejay, let's go and get some more pearl." Bluejay agreed, and made ready the canoe, and they started. After paddling three days and three nights, they reached the place, and Bluejay thought, "Perhaps this time my master will give me a chance to get the pearl, and will stop and watch the canoe himself." But his master would not, and made Bluejay wait with the canoe. In the evening he came back as before, with all the pearl he could [99] carry. After three days they got back, and . next morning took the meat from the shells and ate it; and all the poor shells his master gave to Bluejay, and kept the good ones for himself. Bluejay felt worse than before, but said nothing.

A few weeks later they went again, and everything happened as before. After they reached home, and Bluejay's share, as usual, was made up of little, broken shells, he did not even take the trouble to pack them up, but left them lying about, and went moping around, and evidently had something on his mind.

A fourth time they went, and everything turned out as before; and Bluejay felt worse than ever, and wondered how he could yet even.

Not long after, they made a fifth trip; and after they reached the place, and his master had started for the shells and was out of sight, Bluejay shoved off the canoe and paddled away. At nightfall his master came back to the place, and, finding Bluejay gone, he called and shouted, but heard nothing. At last he realized that he had been deserted.

---

[45] Cf. Boas, Indianische Sagen, p. 360; Kathlamet Texts, pp. 103ff.
[46] Cf. Boas, Chinook Texts, pp. 130ff.

Quinault texts

It took Bluejay four days to get back; and when the women came out to meet him, Bluejay was weeping, and told them his master had been drowned before his eyes. Of course they believed him. Bluejay went into the house and picked out the best four of the wives, and said, "Now, you are to be my wives after this," and with that he sent his own wife, and his master's fifth wife and her little boy, out of the house, and told them to build a hut for themselves, and live in it. Bluejay thought he was going to be a chief, and he opened his master's boxes and took out the sea-otter blanket, and began to play the part of a big chief. Every morning he would call the two women and the boy to draw water and clean the house; but he and the four wives did no work at all. And at night Bluejay used one woman for a pillow and one for a footboard. About this time Bluejay began to sing *tamanous* songs, and he sang, "I was out getting pearl, and I deserted my master." Bluejay never left the house, but just sat and sang; and his four wives sat about, and helped him with his tamanous.

Now, ever since Bluejay deserted him, his master had been on the pearl island, weeping. Every little while porpoises passed, and he would ask them to carry him to the mainland; but they all made excuses of different kinds. Then he asked the birds, but they said their canoes were too small. The whales said they staid under water too long, and he would drown. Finally the biggest whale in the ocean passed, and when he asked him to carry him to the land, the whale said, "All right, I'll carry you. Maybe you can stand it when I sound, for I only go just under the surface, and your head will still be out of water." They started about sunset, and the man sat just behind the dorsal fin, and held on tight. The whale sounded to see if everything was all right, and the man found that his head was still out of water and he could breathe: so they went ahead. They went so fast, that just after dark they reached the shore in front of the man's house. The whale told the man to cut five pieces of meat from his back, and put them above high-water mark. The man did so. Then the whale told the man to kick him so that he could go. The man did so, and the whale started off. [110]

Then the master went up to his house, and as he came near, he heard Bluejay singing his *tamanous* song. So he waited at the spring where they got their water, and soon saw some one coming with a torch, and it turned out to be his little son, and he had his hair all cut off in mourning for his father. Just as the boy was about to draw the water, he saw his father's reflection in the spring.[47] He was frightened, and ran back to his mother and told her what he had seen; but she scolded him for being foolish, and sent him back. He saw the reflection a second time, and then went and told his mother that if she didn't believe him she could come and see for herself. So the mother went with him and saw the reflection, and then her husband showed himself. The woman then told her husband all that Bluejay had done and how he had acted; and her husband told her to say nothing, but to go in and get Bluejay's wife, and then to bring up the whale-meat he had left on the beach.

Meanwhile Bluejay was just lying there doing nothing but eating, and defecating where he lay. He was too lazy to move. Pretty soon he called to the boy to come in and clean him. The boy's father asked him if Bluejay always made him do this, and the boy told him he did. Then he told his son to get a stone long and sharp, and they put it in the fire and made it hot. Then Bluejay called from the house a second time, and said, "Why don't you come? Has your father come back?" mocking the boy. The boy wrapped the handle of the stone so that he could

---

[47] Cf. p. 123; also Boas, Indianische Sagen, etc, pp. 66, 114, 168, 253. '

hold it, and, keeping it under his blanket, went in and told Bluejay to bend over so that he could see plainly. Bluejay bent over, and the boy jammed the stone in with all his might, Bluejay danced and screamed with pain, while the boy ran out laughing. Then Bluejay felt sure that his master must have come back, or the boy would never have dared to do it; and he told his wives to pack the good blankets away again. His master, however, did not come in. Next morning Bluejay put on his old blanket, and looked as poor and common as ever. That day his master came in, and beat Bluejay, and sent him and the four faithless wives outside to live as best they might, while he, Bluejay's wife, and the boy and his mother, lived comfortably in the house.

After a time Bluejay grew tired of this sort of treatment, and began to think of going away somewhere else to live. So one day he called his wife, Jui, and together they went away. Not long after this, Bluejay told Jui to go down to the Underworld and get another husband.[48] She went, and Bluejay wandered about alone from place to place; but he soon wished he had Jui back again, and decided to go and look for her. Now, there were two trails that led to the Underworld, and one of them was by way of a burning prairie. Jui had taken this trail, and died; and when she came to the Underworld she was just like the people there, and they seemed to her as if they were still living, and she married the chief of the place. Bluejay went by the other trail; and when he reached [101] the Underworld he was still living, and just as he had been in this world. He came to a river on the other side of which was a village, and he could see a fish-trap there, and lots of canoes. Bluejay called to Jui to come and take him across; and pretty soon Jui came out, and came over in a canoe to fetch Bluejay. Bluejay jumped in, but he saw a lot of holes in the canoe and a skeleton in the bow, and he was frightened and jumped out again. Jui asked him the reason, and he said it was a grave canoe and that there was a dead person in the bow, and that she should go fetch another canoe. She did so; but when Bluejay Jumped in he saw it was full of holes like the other, and tried to get out; but Jui held him, and finally got him safely across. Bluejay went into the house and saw skeletons all about, and Jui sitting beside a big one. Every now and then the skeletons would move about and make a noise Just like screech-owls, and Bluejay was nearly frightened to death. After a while he grew more used to it, and Jut told him to go out and fish. He started to go down to the river, and saw a small skeleton following him. He tried to kick it, but it cried out, and talked at him just like a screech-owl; and he was more frightened than ever. Bluejay reached the fish-trap and soon felt a fish; but when he got it up, it was nothing but the knot of a tree, so he threw it back. He caught a lot of knots, but threw them all back, except two large ones, which he saved for firewood. When he came in and told Jui what he had done. she scolded him, and told him that the small knots were blueback salmon, and that the two big ones he had saved were steelheads. But Bluejay would not believe her. Not long after, Jui told him a whale had come ashore, and when he went down to the beach, he saw a great tree-trunk lying there, and all the skeletons dancing around, and cutting at the log. Bluejay only took a few big chunks for firewood.

Finally Bluejay grew tired of the Underworld, and decided to go back home. Jui had told him of the trail by the burning prairie, so he made ready eight buckets of water to put out the fire. Jui set him across the river and said, "Now, when you come to the crossing of the trails, don't take the one toward the sunrise, for that leads toward the burning prairie, but take the trail to the right and you will be safe."

---

[48] Cf. pp. 109 ff; also Boas, Chinook Texts, pp. 167ff.

Quinault texts

Bluejay left her and went on until he came to the cross-roads, and then took the trail to the left, toward the sunrise, for it looked the better trail. Not long after, he came to a big prairie covered with red flowers; and Bluejay supposed it was fire, and began to use his water, and sing his *tamanous* song. He had used up most of the water before he discovered that he had made a mistake. Then he passed the prairie and through a wood, and soon heard the roaring of a fire ahead of him. Now, this turned out to be the burning prairie: so he began to sing his song, and use what little water he had leftm soon that was all gone, and he used the buckets to beat out the fire until they were all burnt and broken. Then he used his little bear-blanket until that was burnt up and he had nothing left; and the fire caught him, and he was burned, and died, and came back to the village he had left. He found now that he talked the [102] same as the people of the Underworld. Jui was angry when she saw him, for she knew he was dead; but she came over and set him across, and this time the canoe looked all right to Bluejay. And when he saw the village it looked fine, and he said to Jui, "You have a fine place here now." But Jut answered, "You are dead, and now you see as we do." But Bluejay said, "I'm not dead. You don't catch me dying as easily as that. "He went into the house, and this time the skeletons looked like regular people, and he saw Jui's husband and cliildren for the first time. Then Bluejay wanted to do everything, and they had a hard time to keep him out of danger.

At the far end of the village was a place they called *Gwēlshā'lātōměn* ("further dead"), and there the people were dancing constantly. The dancers were upside down, and some of them had danced so long that they had worn deep holes in the ground, so that nothing but their feet showed above the surface. Now, whoever went to *Gwēlshā'lātōměn* had to stay there ever afterward; but, in spite of that, Bluejay tried to go and join the dancers, but each time Jui would catch him, and bring him back. Finally she got tired of watching him all the time, so she told him to go back to earth again, and showed him a short trail that would take him there. Bluejay consented to go. and, following Jut's directions, he arrived at the surface of the earth, and after that he seemed satisfied, and lived there quietly.[49]

III. — ANOTHER STORY OF Bluejay[50]

Bluejay and his chief, with Land Otter, Beaver, and another man, used to go out seal-hunting together. In the same house with them, but at the other end, lived Grouse, who was a widower with a lot of children, and he spent most of his time in the woods building a canoe. Every trip that the five men made, they caught five seals, very fat ones; but they gave nothing but the poor, lean parts to Grouse. Bluejay was at the bottom of this, and kept saying that fat was too good for Grouse; and he poked fun at him and sneered at him whenever he was about. Grouse never said a word, but took what was given him without complaining.

One day Grouse made a wooden seal, carving it out of cedar, and burning it until. it was black. Then he talked to the seal, and told it what it was to do; and it dived down into the water and went out to sea.

---

[49] A variation of this story makes Bluejay steal away and join the dancers at *Gwēlshā'lātōměn*, and thus remain dead forever.

[50] Cf. Boas, Indianische Sagen, pp. 119, 191, 203.

Quinault texts

Next day before daylight, the five men started out, and about sunrise came upon a big seal, and speared it. The seal dived, and swam to the westward, dragging the canoe after it until they were out of sight of land. The spearman tried to get rid of it, but could not; and when night came they were still rushing westward, and when they waked in the morning they were still going, but not so fast. Not long afterward the line slackened, and they heard something butting against the canoe. Bluejay looked over, and saw a wooden seal with the [103] harpoon sticking into it just behind the flipper. Then his chief began to scold Bluejay, and said, "I know this is Grouse's work. He is angry because we gave him no fat, and because you talked to him so much." Bluejay could only hang his head and say nothing.

They cut the line and began to paddle back, but had no idea where they were going. Three days and two nights they paddled, and the third night they all fell asleep from exhaustion. When they waked in the morning, the canoe was stuck fast and they thought they were ashore, and one of them, the fifth man, jumped out, but he sank and was drowned; and then they saw that they were not ashore, but that the seaweed was so thick that they had stuck fast in it. So now there were only four of them. and they paddled on. On the fourth night they did not feel like sleeping, for they thought they could see the hills back of Quinault. In the morning they could discern the coast plainly, and after paddling all day they reached the shore, and landed at a place quite strange to them. Next morning they went on again in what they thought was a southerly direction, and suddenly, as they rounded a point, came upon a village. Several canoes came out through the surf and helped them ashore, and they were taken up to the village.

In the centre of the village was a tall smooth pole which the people said was Squirrel's pole, which he used for climbing; and they said that Squirrel would like to have a climbing-match with Bluejay.[51] Bluejay's master said to him, "Now, don't get frightened, but go in and do your best. You know you can climb well, and if you are beaten we may all be killed." Then both Squirrel and Bluejay took sharp bones, so that if one got ahead he could hit the one behind on the head; and they started to climb. All the people crowded around to see the contest, for the pole was high and the two were well matched. At last the people saw them reach the top, and saw one of them strike the other on the head so that he came tumbling down; and all the people shouted, for they thought it was Bluejay. But when he reached the ground, they found it was Squirrel who had lost. So now, since Bluejay had beaten their best climber, they let him and his companions go.

They paddled on down the coast, and after some time they rounded a point, and came upon another village, much like the first. Here Hair-seal challenged Bluejay to a diving-match, and Bluejay found himself in a difficult position, for he was no diver at all.[52] But his master turned the canoe over and washed it out, leaving the brush from the bottom floating about it on the water. Then he told Bluejay to accept the challenge and dive, but to come up under the brush and lie there concealed, and not to show himself. So both Bluejay and Hair-seal dived; and Bluejay came up immediately under the brush, and floated there where no one could see him. He waited until he shivered so with the cold that the brush moved with his shaking, and his master began to be afraid the people would notice it: so he rocked the canoe and made waves to conceal the motion of the brush, [104] and no one suspected that Bluejay was hidden there. Now,

---

[51] Cf. Boas, Indianische Sagen, etc, p. 2; Boas, Chinook Texts, p. 57.
[52] Cf. Boas, Indianische Sagen, etc, p. 79; Boas, Chinook Texts, p. 57; Rand, Legends of the Micmacs, p. 324.

they had agreed, that, when the sun had passed from one tree to another not far off, each was to have the right to hit the other in the head with a sharp bone. So, when Bluejay saw that the sun had reached the second tree, he dived down, and found Hair-seal lying with his head down close to the bottom. Bluejay jabbed him with the bone before Hair-seal knew what was happening, and Hair-seal came floating up to the surface. All the people shouted, "Bluejay's up!" But it turned out to be Hair-seal, while Bluejay went back under the brush without showing himself. There he waited about half an hour longer, and then came out shouting and laughing, and saying that he felt splendidly and not tired at all. In that way Hair-seal was beaten, and the people let Bluejay and his party go on again.

They paddled on as before until they came to another village, and there the people challenged the four wanderers to go into a sweat-house with four of their people and see which could stand the most heat.[53] So four of the village people went into one corner of the sweat-house, and the four travellers into the other. Then the door was closed so that it was pitch dark, and soon it became very hot. But Beaver and Land Otter began to dig, and in a very short time they had tunnelled to the river. Then all four got into the water and were as comfortable as could be, while the four men from the village were nearly baked. When the time was up, Bluejay and his friends came back into the sweat-house, and when the door was opened they all jumped out. Bluejay and his friends were as fresh as possible, while the four men from the village were nearly cooked, and their eyes were all white from the heat. So, having beaten the people at their own game, they were allowed to go on, and, paddling as hard as they could, before they knew it they had rounded another point, and come upon a village as before. They ran the canoe clear up on the beach and tied it, and, taking their paddles, went into one of the houses.

The people immediately challenged the new arrivals to sit up five days and five nights without sleeping, against four of their own number. The friends were afraid not to accept, so they started the match. One party sat on one side of the house and the other on the other. The men from the village had spears, and when any one of them was falling asleep, they would prod him with a spear and wake him. They kept calling out to each other all night, "Are you awake? Are you still awake?" And they reviled each other constantly. Bluejay did all the talking for his side, and was hardly quiet a minute. All the next day they jeered at each other, and so they did the next night. Bluejay and the spokesman of the other side kept talking back and forth the whole time. The next day they did the same thing, and so on the third night; and the fourth day and the fourth night it was still the same. On that night the men from the village nearly went to sleep; but Bluejay's men were all right as yet. Bluejay himself was almost done up; but his master would pull his ears and keep him [105] awake, for Bluejay's master was the best man of them all. The fifth night the men of the village went to sleep, and Bluejay's master told Land Otter and Beaver to dig so that they could get out. They did so, and fetched four pieces of old wood with phosphorescent spots on them; and they placed the pieces where they had been sitting, one piece for each man; and the spots looked like eyes. Then, while the other crowd was still sleeping, they got out, and, taking everything they could lay their hands on, they stole away in the canoe. Just before daylight one of the other four waked, and called Bluejay several times, but got no answer. So he waked the others, and, taking their spears, they speared what they

---

[53] Cf. Boas, Chinook Texts, p. 58; Boas, The Mythology of the Bella Coola Indians, p. 79; Farrand, Traditions of the Chilcotin, p. 25.

thought were their rivals. But when daylight came, they saw that they had been fooled, and that their spears were sticking into wood.[54]

There was great excitement, and the people decided to give chase, and, making ready their canoes, they started after the fugitives. Along in the afternoon, Bluejay's master said, "I feel sure some one is following us," and, looking back, they saw a lot of canoes in pursuit. Then they paddled with all their might; and Bluejay's master paddled so hard that at every stroke he broke a paddle, until he had broken all they had, and they floated helpless. Then the others turned to Bluejay and said, "You are always talking about your tamanous. Make use of him now, if you have one, for we are in a bad fix." But Bluejay could only hang his head, for he had no tamanous. Then Land Otter called on his tamanous, and a little wind arose. Then Beaver called upon his, and the wind became a little stronger; but all the time the other canoes were drawing closer. Then Bluejay's master called upon his tamanous, and there swept down a great storm and a fog. The storm lasted only a short time, and when it had passed, they looked about them and saw hundreds of capsized canoes, but not a man living; for all the people had been drowned. They went around and gathered up all the paddles they wanted, and went on, and at last reached the Quinault country, and were among good people. The people who had pursued them were probably Makahs, for they are a bad lot. Finally they reached their home near Damon's Point, and after that, whenever they came in from sealing, they were careful to give Grouse the biggest and fattest seal.

IV. — HOW BLUEJAY BROUGHT THE DEAD GIRL TO LIFE[55]

Once Bluejay was very anxious to have a certain girl for his wife. Her father was a chief in the country under the water, and neither he nor his daughter favored Bluejay's suit. But Bluejay kept urging her, and at last threatened to kill her if she would not come with him. The girl still refused, however, and told Bluejay to do his worst, that she would not have him; and both her parents backed her up, and said, "Don't take him! He's no good at all."

Not long after this the girl fell sick, and though many medicine-men tried to cure her, none of them could do anything, and she died. Her people mourned [106] for her, and placed her body on a scaffolding. Bluejay heard that the girl was dead, and after five days had passed he said, "I will go and see what I can do for her." So he came and saw where she lay on the scaffolding, wrapped in blankets and mats, and with great quantities of blankets and goods of all sorts around the grave; for her father was a very rich man.

At night Bluejay came to the grave and called to the girl, "Get up! Get up!" He heard the body move slightly on the scaffolding, and then he knew he could bring her to life, and was glad. So he took off the blankets and mats in which the body was wrapped, and pulled it out, and it only smelled a little. He carried her to his canoe and started up the river. Whenever he came to a rapid, he stopped and sang his *tamanous* song, and washed the body, and then went on upstream. By the time he had done this the third time, the body hardly smelled at all. At the fourth rapid the girl began to get warm. When they reached the fifth rapid, Bluejay shook the canoe, and said to the girl, "Get up! Get up! We are almost home." And the girl sat up. Then

---

[54] Cf. Boas, Kathlamet Texts, p. 115.
[55] Cf. Boas, Chinook Texts, p. 159.

Quinault texts

Bluejay fixed her eyes and her breath, and told her to stand up and walk; and she did so. "Well, are you awake now? Do you know me?" said Bluejay. "As soon as we pass these rapids, we shall be at my house, I am your lover, and don't you ever try to run away from me now, for if you do, you will die."

The girl did not know that she had been dead, she thought she had been asleep. When they reached Bluejay's house, the girl was glad to get there, for she was tired. And Bluejay took her in and said, "Now, if your father or mother come to take you away, don't go with them, for you will surely die if you do."

Not long after, some one did happen in at Bluejay's house, and when he saw the girl, he wondered, and asked if Bluejay had brought her to life. Bluejay said he had. The girl heard then for the. first time that she had been dead, and asked Bluejay if it were true, and he answered, "Yes. I took you from the grave. "

When the news reached her home, the girl's father would not believe it until he went to the grave and saw that it had been disturbed, and that the body was gone. Then the people gathered, and talked It all over and said, "Let us go to Bluejay's and get her back." So they went up to Bluejay's house, and found the girl in bed. Her father said to her, "Come, my daughter, get up and come with us." Bluejay sat still, and never said a word. The girl got up and asked her father, "Did I really die?" – "Yes," he told her. "And now I want you to come back with me." – "But," said the girl," if I go back with you, I shall die again." – "Never mind," replied her father, "come with me." All this time Bluejay never said a word. So they started for the canoes, the girl leading the way out of the house, while Bluejay followed last. As they pushed off, Bluejay called after her, "Now be sure you get a good man this time, for your father says I am no use."

When they got the girl home, they gave her food, but she could not eat. They put her in her old bed, and she immediately went to sleep. Next morning her mother called her to get up and wash, and get something to eat; but the girl [107] did not answer, and when they went over to her, they saw that she was dead. Then her family felt worse than ever, and wept and mourned. Some of the people were angry at the way her father had acted, and told him he ought to go up and see Bluejay again, and get him to cure her.

So he sent a message to Bluejay, saying, "We want you to come and doctor my daughter, for she is dead again; and this time, if you cure her, you can have her for your wife. "But Bluejay said to the messengers, "No. Tell them to get her a good man. I'm no good, you know; and I won't go." The messengers went back and told the girl's father what Bluejay had said, and some one proposed." Let's offer him lots of blankets and the girl too, if he will cure her." So they went up again with lots of blankets. But Bluejay said, "No. I won't cure her again. I am no good. I don't want your blankets. If any medicine-man hereafter should do as I did, the people would act the same way. After this the medicine-men can doctor the sick, but not the dead. If people are once dead, they shall remain so forever." And he refused to do anything.

If her father had let the girl stay as Bluejay's wife, all medicine-men could bring the dead to life again to-day. As it is, they can do nothing.

Quinault texts

V. — THE ASCENT TO THE SKY[56]

Once Raven's two daughters went out on the prairie to dig roots, and night came on before they knew it, so that they had to camp out where they were. And as they lay talking under the open sky, they came to speak of the stars; and the younger girl said, "I wish I were up there with that big bright star!" and the older said, "I wish I were there with that little star!" Soon they fell asleep, and when they waked they found they were up in the sky country, where the stars are; and the younger girl found that her star was a feeble old man, while the elder sister's star was a young man.[57]

The younger girl was afraid of the old man, and after a short time she ran away and came to an old woman named Spider (*Kōkwā'nē*), who had a great fat belly, and was sitting making rope, which she put into a basket. In answer to the girl's question, Spider said she was making the rope to use when going down to the earth. Then the girl begged the old woman to let her use the rope to help her get back to earth; for she was unhappy with her old man, for he was sick, and his eyes were sore and running, and he used her hair to wipe them with, and altogether she was homesick and miserable. Spider told her she would let her use the rope, but not until the basket was filled: so the girl went back to the old man to wait.

Every day she would go over to Spider and ask for the rope; and each time Spider would tell her to wait until the basket was filled, for then there would be [108] Just enough rope to reach the earth, and if she went sooner there would not be enough and she would certainly be killed. The girl kept insisting until at last Spider gave way and told her she could use it, though she felt sure it would take another day's work to make it reach. However, the girl said she would risk it. So Spider tied the rope under her arms and started to let her down gradually.[58] Down and down she came until, when she was almost down to the earth, the rope came to an end. Now, she had come down just over her father's home; and all the people, when they looked up, wondered what that thing was, hanging in the air. So there she hung day after day, until she died. Then her clothes began to drop down about her father's house, and then her bones, until one day Bluejay picked some up, and, looking at them, said he thought they belonged to Raven's daughter. So he called Raven, and they both decided it was so; and they gathered together all the fragments, and then called upon all the people, and all the animals, and all the birds and fishes, to gather and make an attack upon the Sky People to recover the other sister.

They all gathered together, and a small bird cried out, "*Hape'ts, hape'ts, silx tata'nux!*" ("Come down, come down, O sky!") And the sky came down closer. Each time the bird called, the sky came closer; but finally it stopped while still a long way off. Then they consulted as to how to reach the sky, and at last decided to shoot at it. So they prepared a bow of the trunk of a white-cedar and an arrow of a limb of a tree. Then Grisly Bear stepped up to string the bow, and tried and tried, but could not bend it; after him, Elk and all the large animals, but all failed.

---

[56] Cf. various traditions of ascents to the sky, and particularly Boas, in Introduction to Teit, Traditions, etc, pp. 12, 13; Boas, Kathlamet Texts, pp, 67ff; also Farrand, Traditions of the Chilcotin, pp. 24ff.

[57] Cf. Boas, Indianische Sagen, etc, p. 62; Riggs, Dakota Grammar, p. 83; Rand, Legends of the Micmacs, pp. 160, 308; Farrand, Traditions of the Chilcotin, p. 31 and Note.

[58] Cf. Boas, Kathlamet Texts, p. 17; Farrand, Traditions of the Chilcotin, p. 29.

Quinault texts

Finally Wren, the smallest of birds, hopped up, and all the people laughed; but Wren bent it and strung It easily. Then all the large animals tried to shoot an arrow at the sky, but none could bend the bow. After all others had failed, Wren pulled the arrow back to the head and let fly, and it disappeared in the air. All tried to follow it with their eyes, but could not until Snail cried out, "I see it sticking there in the sky." He tried to show it to the other people, but they could not see it; so the next time Snail aimed the arrow while Wren pulled it, and it new and struck the first in the notch, and stuck there. Then they shot arrow after arrow, and each stuck in the notch of the one preceding, and made a chain reaching down to the earth. As soon as the chain of arrows reached the ground, the people prepared to ascend; and while they were gathering around. Fish Hawk said he didn't believe Snail's eyes were as good as he said they were, and asked him to lend them to him to try. Snail took out his eyes and gave them to Fish Hawk, who tried them, and, finding them so good, flew off with them, saying that he needed them, while Snail did not: so he would keep them. And ever since that time Fish Hawk has had wonderful eyes, while Snail has been blind.[59]

Then Raven began to poke fun at Skate, and told him he ought to stay behind, for he was so broad that the Sky People would put a hole through him as soon as he got up there. Skate replied that he was all right, and bet Raven he [109] couldn't spear him. So Raven threw a spear at him; but as it neared him Skate turned sideways and the spear missed him. Then Skate threw a spear at Raven and it struck him in the nose, and that is why, ever since then, all ravens have had holes in their beaks. After this they all started up the arrow-chain, and on arriving in the sky country found it was winter there and very cold; and all the people shivered and shook with the cold. So they sent Robin to the Sky People to try to steal a firebrand. Robin came to a house of the Sky People, and went in and sat down by the fire to warm himself; and it was so comfortable that he sat and sat and forgot all about going back with the coals, and he sat so long that his breast was burnt with the heat and has been red ever since.[60] When Robin failed to appear, Dog was sent, and when he arrived at the house, the Sky People took him in and gave him camass to eat: so he staid and did not return. After Dog, Wildcat was sent, and was treated the same way: so he, too, sat down by the fire and did not go back. At last Beaver was sent and started to swim up the river. Soon he ran into a large net, but as the Sky People pulled in the net, Beaver broke through and swam on. The owner of the net called to the man next above him that he had just missed something he had never seen before, and that man called to the next, and so on up to the last net, and there Beaver was caught. He pretended to be dead, so that they would not club him; and they carried him up to the house, and all gathered around to examine him, for they had never seen anything like Beaver before, and did not know what this strange animal was. But the girl, Raven's daughter, was there in the house and recognized all her friends, but sat still in a corner and said nothing. When the people got their knives, and were all ready to skin Beaver, he sprang up suddenly, seized a firebrand in each hand, and, rushing out, jumped into the river and swam down to his people, holding the firebrands above his head. After they had the fire well started, they sent all the rats and mice among the Sky People to cut all the bowstrings of the men and the girdles of the women, and all fastenings of any kind which they could find.

---

[59] Cf. p. 92.
[60] Cf. Boas, Indianische Sagen. etc, p. 100; Boas, Kathlamet Texts, p. 67.

So, when all was ready, the Earth People attacked. The sky men tried to use their bows, but the bowstrings were cut. The sky women tried to put on their clothes to run away, but could not fasten them and had to stay. So the Earth People went from house to house and killed great numbers of the Sky People. At last the men of the Sky People rallied, and began to beat back the people from the earth. So, taking the girl with them, they retreated down the arrow-chain, and they had nearly all got safely down when the chain broke, so that some were left hanging in the sky and can be seen there now in the stars.

VI. — RAVEN'S VISIT TO The Underworld[61]

Once Raven decided to make a visit to the underground world where the dead people live, and as Raven was a very powerful man in those days he got [110] down there very quickly. The people saw him coming, and cried, "Here comes a man from the earth; let's give him something to eat!" Now, the people of that place had fish-traps, and in them they caught what looked to Raven like knots of driftwood. Raven looked at them, and declared he could not eat the knots; but the people told him if he would stay with them he would learn to like them by and by. Raven agreed to stay if he could get a wife: so they gave him a woman to wife.

One day, after he had been there with them for some time, a man came running into the village, and said there was a whale on the beach, and told all the people to come. They all took their knives, and went to the place where the whale lay, to cut him up. When Raven reached the spot, he saw nothing but a long cottonwood-log lying on the beach, and asked, "Is that what you call a whale?" – "Of course it's a whale," they told him. Then he saw the people cutting the bark from the tree in little pieces, and he asked a woman to lend him her knife. He took it and cut off long strips of the bark, so that the people wondered at his great strength which enabled him to pull off such huge pieces of whale-skin. Raven then stripped off all the bark, to the astonishment of the people. Raven's wife then told him to cut the meat up into smaller pieces, so as to make it easier to carry; but he answered, "No, I'll carry it down this way and cut it up afterward." So he carried the whole whale down to the canoes in such big pieces that the people again wondered at his strength. When the whale was all cut up, the people told Raven to go down and fish at the traps. He did so, and caught a great number of knots of wood. They felt like salmon until he pulled them up, and then they always turned out to be knots. He fished all night, and in the morning went back to the house and said, "I've caught nothing but a lot of knots all burnt on one end." – "That's all right," replied the people. "Those are Quinault salmon."

Raven staid there a long time, and finally learned to see them as fish and to eat them. He fished every night, and caught so many salmon that he did not know what to do with them all. So one night he took a few scales and put them under his wings and knees and also in his nose, for he wished to go back home and put some of these salmon in the river on earth. Then he went up to the house, and, finding the people still asleep, he crossed the river on the fish-trap, and started for the upper world.

About noon the next day the people missed him, and, suspecting what he had done, they followed him. Before long they caught up with him and said, "Raven, give us back those fish-scales you are taking away with you." Then they made him take off his blanket, and they found

---

[61] Cf. pp. 100ff; also Boas, Chinook Texts, pp. 167ff.

scales under his wings and knees; and they took away all he had except one in his nose, which they did not find. Then they let him go, saying, if he had only asked for the scales he might have had them, but since he had stolen them they would take them all back. So Raven got away with the one fish-scale, and came out on the earth at the Quinault River. Then he took the scale from his nose and threw it into the river, and [111] said, "If there are to be salmon here, then jump, and do not be angry if people catch you." And the salmon Jumped; and ever since then Quinault salmon have been plentiful in the Quinault River.[62]

VII. — HOW EAGLE and RAVEN Arranged THINGS in the EARLY DAYS

Eagle once proposed that Quinault Lake should be a prairie with the river running through the middle; but Raven objected, and said, "No, that would be too easy for the people; they ought to work if they want anything. If they want camass-root, they should be compelled to go through the woods and find the prairies, and pack the camass out." And so the lake has remained as it is.

Then Eagle said to Raven, "One side of the river ought to flow up, and one side down." But Raven said to Eagle, "That would be too easy for the people. When they wish to go upstream, they ought to have to pole up." And that is why all streams flow down; and the eddies are the only results of Eagle's words.

Another time Eagle said, "The 'eggs'[63] in the male salmon ought to be fat, so that the people can use them to cook the fish in." But Raven said, "No, the fish would be too good for the people that way. The 'eggs' shall be worthless and be thrown away: otherwise the fish would be too good."

Not long after this, Eagle's child died, and he went to Raven and said that it would be better if people who died should come back to life again. But Raven replied, that it was better that they remain dead, and not come back. And it was arranged that way.

Now, Eagle used to catch lots of salmon, and Raven asked him to tell him how he did it. Then Eagle explained how he used his little son for bait. He lowered him into deep water, and the boy would catch the fish and string them on a cedar rope which he took down with him. As soon as he had the rope filled, he gave a signal on the line, and Eagle pulled him up. So Raven went out to try, and took his daughter with him. He fastened her to a line, as Eagle had told him, and let her down into deep water. He waited and waited for the signal, but it did not come: so at last he pulled her up and found her drowned. He brought the body home in his canoe, and asked Eagle if he did not think it was better, after all, that the dead should come to life again. But Eagle answered that he had become convinced that it was better as it was, – that the dead should remain dead. And so he got even with Raven.

If it had not been for Raven in the first place, people would still come to life again.

---

[62] See p. 112.
[63] That is, the milt.

Quinault texts

VIII. — THE ORIGIN OF THE QUINAULT SALMON[64]

Once two brothers went out to spear porpoises, and they saw one without a dorsal fin, and, though it came close to them several times, they were afraid to [112] spear it. They continued to see it for several days, and at last they did spear it; but it seemed as if they had not struck it, but as if the creature had grabbed the spear in its hand. In any case, whatever it was, it dived and swam out to sea to the westward. The boys tried to throw over the rope, but could not; they tried to cut it, but could not make any impression. They were caught fast, and were in despair. At last they neared the horizon, which proved to be a wall of rock, and they wondered what would happen when they reached it. But as they approached it, the rock opened and they passed through, and the rock closed again after them.

Just in front of them they saw the smoke of a large village, and as they neared it saw that the smoke was of different colors, and that from the middle of the village rose a great column of reddish smoke, and they steered for this. When they reached the shore, they saw for the first time what it was they had speared; for a young girl rose from the water and started up the beach. In a moment, however, she turned back, and taking them by the hand, led them up to the house with the red smoke, which proved to be her father's house; and there the two brothers were made welcome. And the place turned out to be the home of the salmon. And all kinds of salmon lived there, and each kind of salmon had a different smoke. And the reddish smoke belonged to the bluebacks.

Then one of the girl's brothers took two of the village boys and threw them into the water, and they turned into salmon; and these the young man brought in and cooked for the visitors. When they were done and placed before them, the brother brought an extra dish, and told the boys to save every bone when eating the fish, and to put them into that dish. They did as they were told; and when they had finished eating, the girl's brothers took the dish, and, going out on the beach, threw the bones into the water. And almost immediately the two salmon boys could be seen swimming in their former shape; and they came ashore and went up to the house as if nothing had happened.[65]

After this one of the strangers married the girl and they staid on until she was pregnant. When it was nearly time for her to be delivered, she said, "Come, let us go back to your father's house." They started, and while they were on the way her pains came on, and they thought she would give birth to the child in the canoe. But they finally reached the shore at the Quinault River; and there her baby was born, and the mother said, "There shall always be plenty of bluebacks in this river." And so it has been ever since, and that was the origin of the Quinault salmon.[66]

When they reached home, the boys found that their family had cut their hair in grief for their death, but now they rejoiced to have them back again. [113]

---

[64] Cf. Boas, Indianische Sagen, etc, pp. 43, 159, 175, 191, 203, 210, 242, 246.
[65] Cf. Boas, Indianische Sagen, etc, pp. 27, 104, 210, 266; Boas, Mythology of the Bella Coola Indians, p. 76; Farrand, Traditions of the Chilcotin, p. 24.
[66] Cf. different explanations, pp. 110, 111.

Quinault texts

IX. — HOW SISEMO WON THUNDER'S DAUGHTER[67].'

Thunder had a daughter who married a man named Sisemo, at which Thunder was greatly displeased; for he thought the young man was worthless and that his family was too common. So he decided to set Sisemo certain tasks, and told him to go up into the mountains and get snow from five mountain-tops. The young man went, and returned with only a handful, which he gave to his father-in-law. The latter was furious when he saw how little there was, and scolded Sisemo for not bringing more; but the young man only said. "Eat it and see. You will find there is plenty." So Thunder ate and ate, but there was still as much as ever. Then he was angry because his son-in-law had got the better of him, and he threw the snow outdoors in a rage. And the handful of snow spread, and covered the house and trees. And Thunder was in despair again, and begged Sisemo to take it and carry it back whence it came. So the young man gathered it up, and there was only a handful, and he took it back to the mountains where he had found it.

When he came home again, Thunder told him to go and get him two mountain lions, that he wished them for pets. Sisemo went back into the woods, and soon re-appeared with two mountain lions tied together, which he gave to his father-in-law. But as soon as Thunder took them, they began to fight, and frightened him. He tried to play with them, but they tore and bit him until he was nearly dead; and he begged Sisemo to take them back to the mountains again, which he did.

When he returned and Thunder was well again, he told the young man to go and get him two bears to play with. Sisemo went off, and soon came back with two bears tied together; but when Thunder tried to play with them they rose on their hind-legs and made for him, and Thunder was frightened, and told Sisemo to take them back again. And he did so.

After that, Thunder told him to come with him to split a big cedar log. Thunder split one end of the log and put in wedges. Then he told Sisemo to get into the cleft and hold the sides apart. As soon as he was in the cleft, Thunder knocked out the wedges, and Sisemo was caught. Then Thunder laughed at him, and boasted over him, and at last left him there and went home. But he had hardly entered the house when he heard some one come to the door, and throw down something heavy. When he opened the door there was Sisemo with the great log, which he had brought in from the woods.[68] At that, Thunder was very much surprised, and hardly knew what to tell him to do next.

At last he told him to go down to the Underworld, and there he would find a ball of light which the Underworld people rolled about to make lightning and to play with. And he told Sisemo to get the ball and bring it to him. Sisemo went down; but the people there saw him, and guarded the ball. Then he [114] changed himself into *fog,* but still they could see him; then into smoke, but still they knew him. He turned into all sorts of things; but each time the people recognized him, and would not let him near the ball. At last he changed himself into something", no one knows what, that they could not see; and the people thought he had disappeared, and began to play with the ball again. Sisemo waited his chance between the two crowds that were rolling the ball; and when at last it came near him, he caught it and dashed away with it on the

---

[67] Cf. Boas, Indianische Sagen, etc, pp. 39, 68, 70; Boas, Chinook Texts, p. 33; Farrand, Traditions of the Chilcotin, pp. 26ff; Rand, Legends of the Micmacs, p. 12.

[68] Cf. Boas, Indianische Sagen, etc, pp. 118, 136, 198; Krause, Die Tlinkit Indianer, p. 256.

trail to the upper world. And as he ran off with the ball, it began to grow dark in the lower world and the people could not see. So they gathered pitchwood for torches, and pursued Sisemo by the light of their torches. They were beginning to overtake him; but Thunder and his friends were on the watch, and they got water and poured from above and it made rain in the lower world, which put out the torches. So the people gave up the chase and went back, while Sisemo came on and reached home with the ball.

Then Thunder was very glad, and he told Sisemo he could have his daughter, and he would not harass him any more. And of the ball of light he gave some to the humming-bird for its throat, and some to the woodpeckers for their crests, and to all the birds and animals which have red for a color; but the most of it he put under his armpits. And now, whenever Thunder is angry, he raises his wings,[69] and lightning is seen, and his talk is the thunder which we hear today.

X. — THE MAGIC FLIGHT[70]

There were once five brothers who lived on the north side of Greys Harbor, just below James Rock. The four older brothers were elk-hunters; but the youngest, who was the Wildcat, used to stay at home. Each day when the hunters would leave, they would tell their young brother to look out and not let the fire go out, and he would agree. But as soon as they were gone he would start out to hunt snipe, and in the afternoon, when he came in, he would find the fire nearly gone, and would have to build it up again. He did this four times, and the fifth time when he came in he found the fire entirely out, and no wood to build it up with. So he went across the bay to Damon's Point to see a woman, a sister of *Kwŏtsxwō'ē*,[71] who lived there, and to try to get wood for the fire.

Wildcat found her sitting before the fire, weaving a basket, and with five pieces of wood on each side of the fire. Wildcat changed himself into many forms, trying to steal a log of fire-wood; but each time the woman recognized him and stopped him. Finally he turned himself into smoke, and, bending over the fire, picked up a piece of wood without being seen, and started for home.

All this time the woman had been at work on her basket, and now, as she turned around to get something, she saw that one of the pieces of fire-wood was gone. As soon as she saw this, she took five belts and started after Wildcat. [115]

When she reached the water, she laid down one of the belts and it made a sandbar, on which she walked. When she reached its end, there was Wildcat just ahead of her. Then she laid another belt; and in the same way, when she reached the end of it, Wildcat was still ahead of her. With the third belt, in the same way she nearly caught him, but not quite; and so with the fourth and the fifth. But the last belt reached clear to the other side of the bay, and she followed Wildcat to the house.

The four older brothers had come home in the mean time. And as soon as Wildcat reached the house, he kicked one side of it and it turned to stone, and the same with all four sides and the door. And the door became a heavy rock, balanced just ready to fall if any one should

---

[69] The Quinault have the common conception of thunder as a large bird.
[70] Cf. Boas, Indianische Sagen, pp. 99, 164, 224, 240, 268; Boas, Chinook Texts, p. 78; Boas, Ts'ᴇts'a'ut, p. 260.
[71] Cf. The Story of Misp‘, pp. 81 ff.

push it. When the woman reached the door, she spoke kindly to them, and said she only wanted her log of wood. Wildcat invited her to come in and eat; but she said she was too big, and the door too small for her to get inside. So they offered her elk-fat. And she put in her head as far as her shoulders to get the fat, and they threw it to her as they would to a dog. Then Wildcat said, "My door, fall on her." And the rock fell, and cut the woman's head off and smashed it to pieces.

But the brothers were afraid she might come to life again, so they moved upstream to a prairie not far from Humptulips, and there they made their home. One day soon after this, they went upstream as far as what is now the falls, to hunt elk; and they placed their five canoe-poles against the rock, and Wildcat said, "In the future, people shall call this place 'Kāxā'lōmĭ'tcəmən.'"[72] And so it is, and the poles can be seen to this day as solid rock.

The brothers left their canoes here, and walked upstream until they came to another stream, *Tsāxwō'nĕlx*, emptying into the main river where the bottom is solid rock; and there they made their camp. The four elder brothers went out as before to hunt elk, and left the youngest, Wildcat, in camp to watch the fire. Five days they went out hunting and killed many elk, and on the fifth day, when they left, they told Wildcat to go get hemlock-bark for the cooking-pot. The boy went as he was bid, and, as he left camp, sang a song wishing that some one who could eat a lot would come and help them eat their elk-meat.[73] While he was peeling the bark, he felt the ground shaking as of some monster walking, and he started for home. As he came into camp he met his brothers, who told him he had done wrong to sing that song, for they felt sure there was some monster coming who would kill them all, and that they had better fly. And they kept scolding the boy as they made ready to escape.

When they started to go, Wildcat took with him five pieces of the belly-fat of an elk. They all ran; but before they had gone far the monster woman who had come to life, for it was she whom they had heard, caught up with them, and, seizing the eldest brother, swallowed him at one gulp. Then she seized the next oldest and swallowed him, and after him the third, and then the fourth. Now Wildcat, the youngest, was ahead of the others and had a dog with him, and, just [116] as the woman had almost caught him, he told the dog to stand crosswise behind him across the trail. And the dog did so, and changed into a mountain, which the old woman had to climb, while the boy had time to get ahead. When she had passed, the mountain changed back into a dog, and ran on with the boy. Again she nearly caught him; but he used the same trick and got ahead again, but that time the mountain was smaller. A third time it happened, and the mountain was smaller still, the fourth time still smaller, and the fifth it was nothing but a little hill. After that the old woman caught the dog and swallowed him, and Wildcat ran on alone. By this time he had reached a place where there were trees, and he asked them to let him climb up into them; but all the trees said "No." Then he asked the cedar to open and let him in, and the cedar did; and the boy took five big rocks and crawled inside the cedar. Once inside, he made a fire and heated the rocks, and waited. When the woman came up, she spoke kindly to the boy and told him to come out; but he declined. When the rocks were red-hot, he wrapped one of them in elk-fat and said, "Grandmother, open your mouth and I will give you something to eat."[74] The old woman opened her mouth and he threw in the rock wrapped in fat. Then he did

---

[72] That is, "the place where they set their poles."
[73] Cf. Boas, Chinook Texts, p. 31.
[74] Cf. Boas, Kathlamet Texts, p. 146.

the same thing with a larger one, and so on with all five rocks, each one larger than the last. When he had done, he said, "Now, grandmother, you take a big drink of water and I will come out." So she did as he told her, and went down to the stream and drank. Very soon she began to feel sick, and she vomited and died; for the fat and water boiled inside her and killed her. And Wildcat came out of the cedar and went on his way in safety.

And to this day the woman may be seen as a great black rock, and her vomit as a smaller white one, at that place.

XI. — THE ADVENTURES OF THE SPEARMAN AND HIS FRIENDS

One season in the old days there were three men who always went out sealing together. They hunted nearly every day and always had good weather, and this continued to the end of the season.

The next year they did the same thing. They used to go far out to sea where there was an island, and if ever a storm came up they could land there and be safe. One day while they were out, a storm arose and they were unable to find the island, and so drifted about aimlessly for several days. One morning they sighted a black speck like a cloud, which they took for land and paddled toward it. As they approached, it grew larger and larger. The spearman thought it was a strange place; but the helmsman insisted that it was the mouth of Greys Harbor. The land stretched away to the north as far as they could see, and they paddled straight for it as hard as they could, for they were entirely out of food and water, having been away from home five days and five nights. Toward sunset, after paddling all day, they reached the shore. They were worn out with [117] fatigue, and turned the canoe over where it lay and went to sleep under it; for the land was strange to them and there were no signs of people.

Next morning early they heard some one walking around the canoe, saying to himself, "I wonder where these men come from. " He turned the canoe over, and exposed the men lying there under it. They saw a short, chunky, strong-looking man, who asked them where they came from and what they wanted. The spearman told him that they were lost, that they had come from far away and did not know where they were. And then in turn he asked, "Are you a real man, or who and what are you?" The stranger answered "Yes. I come from the mainland, and am out on a trip. I am a man like you, and my name is White Owl." – "What place on the mainland do you come from?" said the spearman. "I am from *Kwĭnō'ltcō'sīūx-nĭ'tL*,"[75] answered White Owl. "We don't come over this way very often, for there are bad people here who eat men, and I advise you to get away as soon as possible." Then he left them. Now, these bad people were the Chicken Hawks.

The three men discussed the situation, and one of them said, "I think I'll go and see what kind of people they are." The spearman tried to dissuade him; but he insisted on going, and started. He walked until he saw a number of people in the distance, and as he came nearer he saw a man coming to meet him. It turned out to be White Owl, who thought, "How foolish these men are to come here!" and he went out to warn them again. The man paid no attention to White Owl, but went on; and, as soon as he reached the village, the people jumped on him, killed him, and ate him up. When the man failed to return, the two who were left decided to start for home; for they felt sure their companion had been killed.

---

[75] A creek of Greys Harbor, near Humptulips.

Quinault texts

Early next morning the spearman said to the helmsman, "Let's leave the canoe here and start on foot, no matter where we go." The other agreed: so they started and walked all day, and met no one at all. It was good country for travelling, and they went on the following morning. Toward evening of the second day they saw a house, and when they came up to it they looked in through a crack and saw a woman sitting there alone. They went in and the woman made a fire, but there was no sign of food. Soon they heard some one throw something heavy down at the door, and a big man came in. He was very tired, but he made the visitors welcome. The man prepared a great pot and heated the water with stones, and then brought in his sack, which was so heavy he could hardly lift it. The men heard a great noise in the sack, and when it was opened it proved to be full of toads and snakes and all kinds of reptiles. The two men thought this looked like very poor food, so they got up and went out into the woods to watt for the dinner to be cooked. There they gathered two stalks of *wā'kā*[76] and put them under their blankets. Soon the reptiles were cooked; and the big man spoke kindly to the strangers, and called them his grandchildren. And he filled a large dish and set it before them. Now, they had their own food [118] under their blankets: so they only pretended to eat the reptiles, but really dropped them down through the tubes of the *wā'kā*-stalks, and ate their own food instead. When they had finished the dish, the big man was much pleased and spoke kindly to them; but they slipped outside, and, digging a hole in the ground, buried the stuff they had dropped through the tubes.[77] In the evening the man went out and came back with a huge log several feet thick, which he brought for the fire for the night. He built up the fire and lay down with his feet to the flames, and told the men to lie on the other side of the log with their heads to the fire. The men were timid, and hesitated, and finally asked the big man what sort of a person he was. He told them he was strong, very strong, stronger than any one where they had come from; for they could not carry such big logs. Then he laughed and said, "Don't you know me? People call me East Wind." Then the men knew they were a long way from home, and they decided to keep a sharp watch on East Wind. They lay down, but kept awake; and several times they saw him lift one foot as if to kick the fire. Then they would make a noise, and he would think them awake and put his foot down again. Toward morning, East Wind went soundly to sleep and lay snoring. Then the two men slipped out, and, taking two logs of wood, painted faces on them, and put them in their places by the fire. They waited outside and watched through a crack, and soon saw East Wind wake and look over to where they had been lying. Then he raised his foot and gave the fire a great kick, so that it fell over on the two logs of wood. But when he rose and went over, he saw that, instead of men, they were two logs of wood, and that he had been fooled.

In the mean time the two men escaped. They walked on all that day, but met no one at all. The next morning they went on again, and toward evening came upon a house, and on looking through a crack saw a woman sitting inside alone. They went in and found it the same kind of a house they had stopped at two nights before. Soon they heard a heavy pack thrown down outside, and the door opened, and a man, bigger than any they had yet seen, came in. He immediately built a fire and made ready a huge pot. Then, bringing in his great sack full of reptiles, he poured them into the pot, and cooked and ate them. He gave the two men great dishes of the food; but they had saved their *wā'kā*-stalks, and disposed of the reptiles as they had

---

[76] A plant with a hollow stalk. No specimen was seen.
[77] Cf. Boas, Indianische Sagen, etc, p. 120; also Chinook Texts, p. 56.

Quinault texts

done before. When they asked the man who and what he was, he told them he was West Wind. At night he brought in a big log for the fire, and placed the men as they had been in the other house. After a time the helmsman fell asleep; but, just as West Wind raised his foot to kick the log, the spearman saw him, and jumped and saved himself. The helmsman was caught by the burning log and killed, but the spearman escaped.

So the spearman went on alone, and camped for the rest of the night in the woods. The next afternoon he came to a house like the other two. It turned out to belong to South Wind, and everything happened just as it had before. [119]

But the spearman made up his mind he would not be caught like his friend, so he slipped out while South Wind was asleep, and, watching through a crack, saw him wake, and kick the log. Then the spearman ran as hard as he could. When South Wind found that he had been fooled, he was terribly angry, and vowed he would follow the man wherever he went until he caught him. So South Wind took his belt and started on the trail. Both the man and South Wind after him ran as hard as they could. All that day and through the night they ran, all the next day and the next night they kept it up. On the third day the man came to a big body of water. It was the corner of the ocean where the whales run up like salmon; and on the other side of the river, which flowed in there, he saw a man working at his net beside his house.[78] The man called, "Grandfather, come and take me across." The man said nothing, but went on mending his net. Then the spearman shouted, "Uncle, come, set me across; some one is pursuing and trying to kill me." But the man went on minding his own business, and said never a word. Then he cried, "Brother, come, take me across. "But he got no answer. He called in every way he could think of; but the man paid no attention to him. At last he called, "Father-in-law, come, set me across." Then the man laughed and said, "All right. Now I will come and bring you over." With that he came down to the shore and stretched out his leg, and it reached to where the spearman was standing: so he walked across on the leg, and reached the other bank in safety. He went up to the house and found the man's wife and daughter there, and they gave him food. Not long after, he looked through a crack of the house, and saw South Wind come down to the shore on the other side of the river. He stopped, and called to the man who was mending his net, "Cousin, set me across the river, and I will give you my belt." But the man replied, "Oh, no! I have lots of belts. I don't need yours." Then South Wind offered his hat, but the man said he had plenty of hats. Then he offered cord for his nets, but the man said he had all the cord he wanted. He offered his stick and many other things, but the man refused them all. At last he said, "Cousin, if you will set me over, I will give you my little canoe." At that the man agreed, and said, "All right. Just turn around, and I will set you across." South Wind turned around and the man stretched out his leg. When South Wind saw the leg stretching across the river, he laughed and said, "What! Haven't you got a canoe?" – "No," answered the man, "that's why I want the canoe with which you are going to pay me." Then he told his leg to get small at the shin and at the ankle, so that it would be hard to walk on. When South Wind was halfway up the shin, he began to lose his balance and nearly fell, and he began to use his canoe to steady himself. "Don't put your canoe down!" cried the man. "You hurt me!" But South Wind steadied himself with the canoe just the same. Then the man cried out again, "Don't do that! Why don't you mind what I

---

[78] Cf. Boas, Indianische Sagen, etc, p. 32; Boas, Chinook Texts, p. 32; Rand, Legends of the Micmacs, pp. 164, 312; Petitot, Traditions Indiennes, etc, p. 409.

Quinault texts

say?" And with that he jerked his leg away, and [120] South Wind fell off into the river, which was very rapid, and drifted downstream, sinking and rising, until at last he sank and was seen no more. And his hat drifted up on the beach with a sound like the pounding of the surf.

Now, the man who made the bridge with his leg was Thunder, and he only came to this place at certain times of the year to get whales. So the spearman staid on, and married Thunder's daughter. Whenever Thunder went out to his traps for whales, the girl told her husband not to watch him; for it would make him lose the whale, and he would be angry. Nevertheless the spearman did look sometimes, and each time the whale got away. Then Thunder would be angry, and would take his bear blanket and shake it. And the wind would come, and the rain, and there would be a great storm. But whenever he caught a whale, he would pick it up in a baling-dipper, and bring it home and lay it down on the mat, and then it would get back to its original size. They staid on at this place week after week and month after month, until one day the spearman asked Thunder when they would go back home, for he wanted to get back to his own country. Thunder told him they would go back in the spring. And so it was, for when spring came they packed up and started for the mainland, and reached it in safety.

When the spearman arrived at his old home with his wife, the people were astonished, and could not believe that it was the man who had been lost the year before. So they called all the people together to make sure. And they gathered in a big house to test him, for, if he could do the same things as the man who was lost, then they would know it was the same man. First he told his story, – told of the winds and his adventures and escapes from them; how he had met White Owl, who lives half the year here and half the year there; and at last how he had lived with Thunder, and married his daughter. Now, the man who had been lost had been the strongest man of all the people. He could take an elk-horn and strip off the branches, and break the horn into small pieces in his hands. So they tried him with this, and he did it easily. Then they were all convinced, and welcomed him back. And later, when White Owl came back, they asked him, and he told the same story as the spearman, and told how one of the men had been eaten by the Chicken Hawks while he was there.[79]

After this the man started to travel with his wife, and five Wolves followed him to kill him. Before they had gone very far, the Wolves saw their chance, and attacked the man and killed him, and took the woman along with them; and the eldest Wolf brother made her his wife.

But after the Wolves had torn the man in pieces, he came to life again and chased them, and tracked them to a prairie where they were living. When he reached the house, he looked in through a crack and saw his wife sitting there alone. So he went in and took her again, and she told him how the Wolves did, and that they always came home at night. So he turned himself into an old man, and told his wife to tell the Wolves that he was her father. When the first Wolf [121] came home, she did so; but he suspected, from smelling him, who it was, and nearly killed him again. But the woman protected him. When the next Wolf came in, the same thing happened, and so with all five; but they were very suspicious. The youngest Wolf had brought in a deer, but the other four had each brought an elk.

The man staid on and made ten arrows, giving one to each Wolf; but five arrows and a bow he kept for himself, and hid them. Then the Wolves began to believe he was the woman's father, and they bothered him no more. Whenever the Wolves would go out. he would change

---

[79] The remainder of the tale appears like another story arbitrarily added by the narrator.

back to his own form and be young again. At last the time came when he was ready to try to kill the Wolves, so he made his plans. When the Wolves came in from hunting, the first thing they did was to go down to the spring and drink, and this was the time he had chosen to kill them. So he went out and hid near the spring, and soon saw the eldest Wolf coming in from hunting. He smelled all about, and then went into the house and dropped his pack, after which he came down to the spring to drink. He sniffed about as he came, and almost discovered the man, but at last knelt down to drink; and then the man shot and killed him, and carried the body back into the woods and buried it. Soon the next Wolf came, and he did the same to him; and so with all five. Then, having set the house on fire, he took his wife and went home, and lived quietly for the rest of his life.

XII. — THE YOUNG WIFE WHO WAS ABANDONED IN A TREE-TOP[80]

There was once a young girl who had been forced to marry an old man against her will, and she was very unhappy, and spent most of her time sitting in the house and weeping. Nor would she let the old man touch her. At last he became tired of this treatment, and one day told his wife to follow him, that they would go to get cedar-bark at a good place he knew of. They soon arrived at the place and picked out a tree, and he then told her that he always peeled a tree from the top downward. So they climbed to the top, and there he seized her, and, placing her in a crotch, tied her hair to the branches, and left her helpless. He then descended, peeling the bark as he went, and leaving the trunk so smooth and slippery that she could not have followed him, even if she had got loose. The old man then went home to his house.

Now, the young woman had three brothers who often came to see their sister. And when they came that day and asked the old man where she was, he told them that she had gone out that morning for bark, and had not yet come back. Five times they came to see her, and each time got the same answer, until they began to grow suspicious.

Now, it was the custom at that season, for all the young men of the place to go out to sea every morning to fish. And from her place in the top of the tree the young woman could see her brothers among the rest, and she used to call out [122] to them, "My brothers, you ought not to be out fishing while your sister is tied here and needs you." One morning while they were out in the canoe, the youngest brother heard a sound as of some one calling from a distance, and said, "I think I hear some one calling. Listen!" They stopped and listened, and sure enough there came their sister's voice calling faintly. They paddled straight to the shore, and, following up the sound, came to the tree where she was, and she told them all that had happened. They tried to rescue her, but could not get up the tree, it was so slippery. So they went back and gathered together all the people and brought them to the place. Under the tree were a lot of red berries, and these were her tears, which had turned to berries as soon as they fell. As soon as Bluejay reached the place, he began to eat the berries as fast as he could, until the girl objected, and stopped him. When all the people had reached the place. Bear and Squirrel tried hard to get up the tree, but could not. Bear especially made a great attempt, but he slipped back each time from the peeled trunk. Finally, after many failures, the youngest brother, Woodpecker, succeeded in reaching the top, and, untying her hair, brought his sister down on his back.

---

[80] Cf. Boas, Indianische Sagen, etc, pp. 22, 89, 96, 123, 129.

Quinault texts

The girl went home with her brothers, and when she was safe in the house, they went to see the old man, her husband. The youngest brother asked him to come out with them to gather shellfish from a certain rock in the sea. The old man made many excuses, – that he had no mat, nor paddle, nor any of the things necessary, – but they told him they had all those things in the canoe, and at last he consented and went out with them to the rock. They all climbed out and started to hunt for shellfish, and they put the old man to work on the farther side of the rock, where they told him the shellfish were large and plentiful; while the brothers worked on the side where the canoe was. They told him to call out now and then. And he did so, and they answered. But pretty soon, at a favorable opportunity, they all slipped away in the canoe and left the old man alone; and when he finally climbed to the top of the rock, he saw the canoe far away and nearing shore. And there he was forced to stay. And as the tide rose, the rock was covered and the old man drowned.

XIII. — THE GIRL WHO MARRIED OWL'S SON

There were once five brothers who were great elk-hunters, and they were sons of the great Owl who lives in the mountains. And there was also another man, named *Tksē'lĭsōmĭsh*,[81] who had a daughter, and, as he was very fond of elk-meat, he thought it would be a good plan for her to marry one of Owl's sons. He proposed the scheme to his daughter, and she agreed and said she would go and marry one of them. So her father showed her the trail she was to take, and said that farther on the trail would fork and the branch which led to the right would be covered with large white feathers; and that was the one for her to [123] follow, and not the one which led to the left, which would be marked by small ragged feathers, for that led to the house of little *Hohohos*, the Screech Owl, who was no good.

When the girl reached the branching trails, she took the left-hand one by mistake, and soon came to a house; but there was no one at home. She went in and sat down, and wondered if she were in the right place. Pretty soon she heard some one coming who threw a pack down outside the door, saying, "Dear me! but I am tired carrying that heavy bear." Then the door opened, and in came a man panting and blowing; and it was *Hohohos*, who, as soon as he saw the girl sitting there, said, "My wife, go and bring in that bear that I have left lying outside." The girl went out and looked all around for the bear, but the only thing she could find was a little field-mouse. So she picked it up and brought it in, and threw it down by the fire, and said, "This is all I could find." Hohohos looked at her in wonder, and said, "How strong you are, my wife! But be careful and don't burn that bear up when you cook it." Then the girl began to think she must be lost and in the place to which her father had told her not to come. When night came, Hohohos tried to sleep with her; but she would not let him, and kept pushing him away. Next day she began to plan to run away, and when Hohohos went out to hunt for more bear, she went back by the trail she had come. Hohohos soon discovered that she had gone, and followed her; and when she heard him coming, she climbed a tree leaning over the river, and hid in the branches. Pretty soon *Hohohos* came along the trail, calling out for his wife, and when he came to the river, spied her reflection in the water, and called out to it, "Come, my wife, come with me." The girl burst out laughing at this. When Hohohos saw the reflection laughing, he took off

---

[81] A sea-monster who was also a powerful *tamanous*.

his clothes, and jumped in to get her; but there was nothing there.[82] When he came out and looked again, there was the girl still smiling at him. *Hohohos* staid on watching the reflection, and shivering with cold until he was nearly frozen, and at last gave it up and went back home.

Then the girl came down from the tree, followed the path back to the forks, and taking the other trail came to the right house. Old Owl and two of his younger sons were at home, and when she had told her story, the old man said, "There is my oldest son's bed, take that. He is out hunting, but will be back soon." So she waited until the other sons came in from hunting, bringing great packs of elk-meat with them. They told the girl to cook some of the meat, and while she was preparing it the old man told the younger boys to go invite their uncle *Hohohos* to the feast. They soon came back bringing *Hohohos*, and as soon as he saw the girl he began singing, "My wife is sitting on the other side of the pot." He sang and sang until the girl was ashamed, and she dropped the hot stones into the water so that it splashed upon *Hohohos*, and scalded him until he squealed with pain. The girl's husband said to her, "Oh, let him be! It's only old *Hohohos*; don't mind him." And though she explained to [124] *Hohohos* that she had only come to his house by mistake, he kept coming for her again and again, and each time he made her angry. When he came the fifth time and began to sing, she grabbed him and mauled him, and, her husband coming to her aid, they tore him in pieces.

XIV. — THE STORY OF SƏ'P'ĀK'Ā'

There was once a young girl who had five brothers, and one day she went out to look for roots, and having found them she staid at the place for five days and five nights. Each night she dreamed of a strong man, Sə'p'āk'ā', and each morning she saw by her side a person who had the shape of the man of her dreams, but who never said a word. When she finally decided to go home and started, she found Sə'p'ak'a' always at her elbow, but still silent. Not long after she found herself near a house on the river which she had never seen before, and the first thing she knew she was inside and looking around, and the most noticeable thing was a number of fungi hanging from the beams of the house. And when Sə'p'ak'a' spoke, as he did now for the first time, all these fungi seemed to answer like an echo. Sə'p'ak'a' told the girl that these fungi were his wives, but now that he had her, he did not need them any more: so he pulled them all down, and threw them outdoors.

When he came in and sat down, he spat five times on the girl's belly. That night he did not attempt to sleep with her, but remained in a far corner of the house by himself. Notwithstanding this, the girl became pregnant, and very soon gave birth to a boy baby with two heads. This boy grew very rapidly; and before very long she gave birth to another child, a girl.

Now Sə'p'ak'a' used to go fishing every day, and one day while he was away, the girl's oldest brother, who had been looking for her a long time, came into the house and found her. She told him her story, and very soon he left her and started for home. A little later Sə'p'ak'a' came in, and, though his wife kept silent, the two-headed boy told his father that his uncle had been there. Sə'p'ak'a' sprang up and started after him, saying he would bring him back. But he soon returned, and said he had not been able to overtake him. But the woman was frightened, and thought to herself, "Perhaps he has killed my brother."

---

[82] Cf. p. 100; also Boas, Indianische Sagen, etc, pp. 66, 114, 168, 253.

Quinault texts

Next day came the second brother, who told her they had been looking for her everywhere, and he asked her if she had seen his oldest brother, for he, too, was missing. Then the woman told him what had happened the day before, and he started for home at once; but first they both told the two-headed boy to say nothing to his father of the visit. Nevertheless, when Sə'p'ak'a' came in, the boy told him, and he immediately started after him as he had done the day before, but returned, as he said, without overtaking him. The next day the third brother came and asked for his brothers; and his sister told him all, and urged him to go straight back. He did so; but Sə'p'ak'a' followed him, and everything happened as before. And so it was with the fourth and the fifth; and the woman felt sure [125] they were all killed, and taking her little girl she went out and wept for her brothers. While she was weeping, she found a piece of hard black rock (flint ?) which she threw into the fire; and when it became hot it popped, and flew into the body of the little girl, who was sitting by the fire, and immediately she gave birth to a boy.

This all happened while Sə'p'ak'a' was from home and the two-headed boy was out shooting with his bow and arrows. And when her husband came in, his wife told him she had given birth to another baby, and she said nothing of the little girl. This boy baby grew up very fast, and soon was full grown. Then his grandmother told him about her five brothers and all that had happened to them, and, showing him the trail along which they had come, she asked him to search it. This she did without the two-headed boy knowing anything about it. The young man went and found all the bodies of the five brothers split in two, one half lying on one side of the trail and the other half on the other. And when the young man looked on the bodies, he felt sad, and he placed his hand on the face of one of the dead men and then on his own, and found he had the features of the dead man. When he came back and told his grandmother what he had found, she told him to go back and come in again later, as though he were one of her brothers. He did so and the two-headed boy saw him. When Sə'p'ak'a' came in, the boy told him his uncle had been there, and Sə'p'ak'a' at once jumped up and followed him. When Sə'p'ak'a' overtook the young man, he seized him by the shoulders and tried to pull him apart, but could not. Then the young man laughed, and said, "Let us go back together." And as they turned, he seized Sə'p'ak'a' and tore him apart, and threw one piece on each side of the trail, just as Sə'p'ak'a' had done to the brothers. In the mean time the woman told the two-headed boy to go and look for his father, and he went along the trail until he met the young man, who seized him, one head in each hand, and tore him in two. Then the young man returned to the house, and taking his little mother in his arms they all went back to the old home.

XV. — TSA'ALO THE GIANT

Five brothers and a sister were in the habit of going up a small stream near the mouth of the Quinault River, because they knew there were many silver-side salmon there. One day the eldest brother started up the stream to get some of the fish, and saw many of them floating down, torn and bleeding. Not long after, he saw a sort of cloud approaching, and when it came nearer there emerged a giant, *Tsā'ālō'*. His toe-nails were huge icicles, and he wore a great belt and a big hat, bell-shaped and made of roots. *Tsā'ālō'* speared the young man and killed him, and hid away the body. The next day the second brother went to look for the elder, and met *Tsa'alo'*, and was killed in the same way. Likewise the third and the fourth; and Tsa'alo hid all the bodies under the bed in his house. [126]

Then the sister went to look, and, as she searched, came upon the house while *Tsā'ālō'* was away, and, making sure that no one was there, she went in, and at last found her brothers' bodies under the bed. The young woman had with her a girl baby, and the baby began to cry for some salmon-eggs which were hanging in the house. So the mother broke off a little piece, and while she was feeding the child, *Tsā'ālō'* came in. He noticed at once that some of his salmon-eggs were missing, and, seizing the child by the feet, he held and shook her over the fire until the egg's she had eaten dropped out of her mouth. Then *Tsā'ālō'* set five salmon to cook by the fire, and when one side of each of them was done, he ate, and went to sleep. While he slept, the girl escaped, and returning to her home she told her youngest brother how and where she had found the bodies of the other brothers. At that the boy declared that he would go up the river and find Tsa'alo, and fight him. So he made ready, and sharpened his harpoons, and started. He soon met Tsa'alo, who advanced to kill him. The boy placed himself near a stump, and when *Tsā'ālō'* threw his spear, he dodged, and it missed him. Then *Tsa'alo* tried to kick him with the icicles on his feet, and run him through; but when he raised his foot to kick, the boy jumped behind the stump, and the icicles were driven into the wood, and stuck fast. As soon as the boy saw that Tsa'alo was firmly held, he speared and killed him. He tried to take off the giant's hat, but could not move it; but the belt he took, and went back to the village.

Not long after they heard some one coming, and it turned out to be *Kwŏtsxwō'ē*,[83] the giant's sister. The earth shook as she moved along, and as she came nearer she cried out that she came for *Tsā'ālō*'s belt. Then the people were frightened, and hung the belt outside; and *Kwŏtsxwō'ē* took it and disappeared.

XVI. — WREN AND ELK[84]

One day during the salmon-run, Wren went fishing in the creek. He met Elk coining downstream, who asked him where he was going, to which Wren answered that he was just going upstream to get a few salmon, "You go back," said Elk, "and give me your spear." And with that he seized it, and took it away from him. Wren was helpless: so he went home without saying anything, and made himself a new spear. When it was finished he went out again, and again met Elk, who took the spear away from him as before. Wren was very angry, but went home and started a third one, and as he worked on it, he sang, "I wish to go straight into the nose of Elk. I wish to go straight into the nose of Elk. " When he had finished it, he started for the creek, and again met Elk, who asked him what he had come for. "To get salmon," answered Wren, and he sang his song. Elk took the spear away from him [127] and turned back; but Wren followed him and fought him. And as they fought, Wren jumped, and flew straight into Elk's nose, and there he scratched and scratched with his feet as hard as he could. Elk tried his best to get him out, but couldn't. He sneezed and sneezed, but Wren held fast; and at last the blood ran from his nose so fast that Elk fell down from exhaustion, and died. Then Wren came out, and taking his spears, went back home.

---

[83] See pp. 81 ff; also p. 114.
[84] Cf. Boas, Chinook Texts, p. 119; Farrand, Traditions of the Chilcotin, p. 10.

Quinault texts

XVII. — STORY OF THE DOG CHILDREN[85]

A long time ago, in a certain village there lived a young girl who had a dog of which she was very fond. She took the dog with her wherever she went; and at night, as was a common custom at that time with young girls, the dog slept at the foot of the bed. Every night he would change into human form and lie with the girl, and in the morning, before it was light, would turn back again into his dog shape: so no one knew anything about it. After a time she became pregnant; and when her parents found it out and knew that the dog was the cause, they were greatly ashamed, and calling the people together they tore down the house, put out all the fires, and moved away from the place, leaving the girl to die.

But Crow had pity on her, and, taking some coals, she placed them between two clam-shells, and told the girl secretly that after a time she would hear a crackling, and to go to the spot and she would find fire. So the girl was left alone, for the people had all gone a long way across the water. She sat still for a long time, listening for the crackling, and when she finally heard it she went to the place and found the fire as Crow had said.

Not long after this she gave birth to five dog pups, but as her father had killed the dog, her lover, she had to look after them by herself, and the only way she could live and care for them was to gather clams and other shellfish on the beach. There were four male pups and one female, and with the care their mother gave them, they grew very fast. Soon she noticed that whenever she went out, she heard a noise of singing and dancing, which seemed to come from the house, and she wondered greatly. Four times she heard the noise and wondered, and when, on going out again, she heard it for the fifth time, she took her clam-digger and stuck it in the sand, and put her clothes on it to make it look as if she were busy gathering clams. Then she stole back by a roundabout way, and creeping close to the house peeped in through a crack to see what the noise might be. There she saw four boys dancing and singing, and a little girl watching the place where the mother was supposed to be digging clams. The mother waited a moment and watched, and then coming in she caught them in human form, and scolded them, saying that they ought to have had that form in the first [128] place, for on their account she had been brought to shame before the people. At this the children sat down and were ashamed. And the mother tore down the dog blankets which were hanging about, and threw them into the fire.

So they remained in human form after this; and as soon as they were old enough she made little bows and arrows for the boys, and taught them how to shoot birds, beginning with the wren, and working up to the largest. Then she taught them to make large bows and arrows, and how to shoot fur animals, and then larger game, up to the elk. And she made them bathe every day to try to get tamanous for catching whales, and after that they hunted the hair-seal to make floats of its skin. And the mother made harpoons for them of elk-bone, and lines of twisted sinews and cedar, and at the end of the lines she fastened the sealskin floats. And when

---

[85] Cf. Boas, Indianische Sagen, etc, pp. 25, 93, 114, 132, 263; Boas, Chinook Texts, p. 17; Boas, Ts'Ets'a'ut Traditions, p. 37; Boas, Kathlamet Texts, p. 155; Krause, Die Tlinkit Indianer, p. 261); Petitot, Traditions Indiennes, etc, p. 311; Farrand, Traditions of the Chilcotin, p. 7; Teit, Traditions, etc, p. 62; Kroeber, Cheyenne Tales (Journal of American Folk-Lore, Vol. XIII, p. 181).

everything was ready, the boys went out whaling and were very successful, and brought in so many whales that the whole beach stank with them.

Now, Crow noticed one day, from far across the water, a great smoke rising from where the old village had stood, and that night she came over secretly to see what it all meant. And before she neared the beach, she smelted the dead whales, and when she came up she saw the carcasses lying all about, and there were so many that some of them had not yet been cut up. When she reached the house, she found the children grown up; and they welcomed her and gave her food, all she could eat, but gave her nothing to take back, telling her to come over again if she wanted more.

When Crow started back, the girl told her that when she reached home, she was to weep so that the people would believe they were dead. But Crow, on getting home, instead of doing as she was told, described how the beach was covered with sea gulls feeding on the whales that had been killed by the boys. Now, Crow had brought with her secretly a piece of whale-meat for her children, and after putting out the light she fed it to them; and one of them ate so fast that she choked, and coughed a piece of the meat out on the ground. And some of the people saw it, and then believed what Crow had told them, as they had not done before. Then the people talked it all over, and decided to go back; and they loaded their canoes and moved to the old village. And the boys became the chiefs of the village, and always kept the people supplied with whales.

Abstracts

I. — THE STORY OF MISP'

Young man marries monster woman named *Kwŏtsxwō'ē*. Takes her to his home, where she refuses to speak or show her face. Bluejay teases her, and at last she uncovers her head and laughs; and all the people drop dead, her husband included. *Kwŏtsxwō'ē* gives birth to twins, of whom Misp' is the elder. Children discover their mother's history while she is absent, and burn house and flee. Mother pursues. Misp' kills her by strategy. Boys come upon an aunt who is killing children by swinging them. Misp' has match with his aunt, overcomes and kills her. Restores some of the children to life. Boys go on and come upon another aunt doing the same as [129] before. Misp' overcomes her in same way. They proceed, and find third aunt killing children in a game, xwo'tel. Misp' overcomes and kills her. Discover another aunt killing children by tattooing. Misp' beats her by strategy and kills her. Brothers travel through country and reach Neah Bay. Call people, who come out as dogs. Misp' changes them to men, and makes them whalers. Come to Quilleutes. People come out as wolves. Misp' transforms them into men, and gives them whaling and fishing outfits. Proceed along coast to Hoh River. People come out weak and miserable. Misp' helps them. Arrive at Queets. No people appear. Misp' makes people from dirt on his arm, and gives them fishing outfits. Reach Raft River, where younger brother loses his life and is changed into a duck. Misp' goes on alone, and comes to Quinault, where he finds people as they are to-day. Comes to mountain below Quinault, where he finds a man grinding shell knives to kill him. Fastens shells on man as ears and tail, so transforming him into a deer, and sends him into the woods to live. Reaches Copalis, and finds

Quinault texts

man being dragged into sea by lice in his hair. Gives him comb, and teaches him to use it. Finds other people upside down, and turns them right side up. Comes to Oyhut and finds people upside down, and using heads as hammers. Turns them right side up, and gives them stone hammers. Goes south benefiting the people until he reaches mouth of Columbia River, where he is turned into stone.

II. — THE ADVENTURES OF BLUEJAY

Bluejay and his wife Jui visit Magpie, who provides food by magical means. Bluejay invites Magpie to return visit following day, when he attempts to use the same means, and fails. Soon after, has a similar experience with Sawbill Duck; then, in turn, with Bear, Land Otter, Beaver, *Kwēt*, Kingfisher, Shadow, and Hair-seal. In imitating Hair-seal, he kills one of his own children. Squirrel and Black Diver mock him. Bluejay captures them, but they escape by strategy. Bluejay moves with his family to the beach, *xwōnē' xwōnē'* and Snail have a contest in eyesight. Snail wins, and they exchange eyes, but afterward trade back again. Snail marries Crow, who induces him to give her his eyes. As a consequence, Snail is blind. Crow's white dress is burnt by accident, and since then she has been black. Bluejay leaves his wife and goes to live with his master at Oyhut. Master has two daughters. Wonderful shining duck appears in bay. People fail to kill it. The two girls finally succeed, and give feathers to all the people, which is origin of birds' colors to-day. People move to Damon's Point. Certain young man and his sister are best duck-hunters. Girl becomes pregnant by licking moisture from nose-ring. Parents suspect her brother of being father of the child, and people desert them. Crow hides fire in clam-shell. Girl gives birth to male child. Brother is very successful in hunting whales, etc. Father of child appears and lives with them. Crow discovers them and their prosperity. Takes whale-meat back to her children. One of the children chokes, and Bluejay discovers the whale-meat. People decide to go hack. Arrive after much difficulty. Girl, with husband and child, are carried off to westward by a whale. Brother gathers people together to search for her. Start in many canoes. Bluejay hides in brush in bottom of canoe to avoid work. Is discovered and put to work. Finally they reach a village. People give them presents. They go ashore, and find girl and her husband living there. Bluejay has various adventures. They are given pieces of pearl-shells when they leave. Bluejay finds out where the pearl comes from, and after they reach home persuades his master to go with him to gather more shells. They do so, but Bluejay only gets the broken shells for his share. They go again and the same thing happens. A third and a fourth time, the same. On the fifth trip, Bluejay deserts his master on the pearl island, and, returning in the canoe, takes his master's wives and assumes his place. Master is brought back to land by a whale. Punishes Bluejay, and drives him out. Bluejay takes his wife Jui and sends her to the Underworld. Later he follows her. Has various experiences in lower world. Finally returns to earth and lives quietly.

III. — ANOTHER STORY OF BLUEJAY

Bluejay and four other men hunt seals together. Grouse lives in same house with them. They give h im poor parts of the seals. Bluejay scolds at him constantly. Grouse makes wooden seal and [130] sends it to sea. Hunters spear it, and are carried out to westward, beyond sight of land. Finally are freed and start to paddle homeward. Come to strange coast. Reach a village. Bluejay has climbing-match with Squirrel, and wins. Reach another village. Bluejay has diving-match with Hair-seal, and wins by trickery. Come to another village, and are challenged to stay in hot sweat-house with some of the village people. They accept, and win by strategy. At the next village are challenged to sit up five days and five nights without sleeping. They accept and win by a trick, and escape in canoe. People pursue, but are drowned in a great storm. Eluejay and his friends reach home and are careful to treat Grouse with respect.

IV. — HOW BLUEJAY BROUGHT THE DEAD GIRL TO LIFE

Chief refuses to give his daughter to Bluejay. Bluejay threatens the girl, who defies him. Girl sickens and dies. Body is placed on scaffolding. Bluejay steals body, and brings it to life. Parents discover their daughter living with Bluejay. Persuade her to return with them. Bluejay warns her not to go. She goes in spite of him, but soon falls ill and dies. Parents send for Bluejay to treat her, but he refuses to come. Reason why medicine-men cannot bring dead to life now.

V. — THE ASCENT TO THE SKY

Raven's two daughters sleep out at night. Wish for two stars. When they wake, find themselves in sky country, with stars for husbands. Young girl runs away and comes to Spider. Spider lets her down on rope. Rope not long enough to reach earth, and girl dies suspended in the air. People organize attack on sky to rescue other sister. People gather. Make large bow. No one can bend it. Finally Wren shoots arrow at sky. Snail alone can see it. Snail aims while Wren pulls, and second arrow sticks in notch of first. Fish Hawk gets Snail's eyes by trick. Raven and Skate have contest, and Skate wins. Chain of arrows reaches to ground. People climb arrow-chain and arrive in sky country. Are cold, and send Robin for fire. Robin fails to return. Other messengers also fail. Finally Beaver succeeds. Fight in which many are killed on both sides. Earth people retreat down arrow-chain. Chain breaks, and some are left hanging in sky. Are constellations.

VI. — RAVEN'S VISIT TO THE UNDERWORLD

Raven goes to Underworld. Fishes, and catches knots of wood. They are really salmon. Raven marries wife. Whale drifts upon beach. Appears to Raven like a log of wood. He astonishes the people by his feats of strength in cutting it up. Fishes for salmon, and catches many knots of wood, which are salmon in the Underworld. At last learns to see them as salmon. Decides to return to earth. Takes scales from salmon, and, hiding them about his person, starts by night. People pursue and overtake him, and recover all the scales but one. Raven reaches earth, and throws scale into Quinault River, It turns into a salmon, and from it sprung all the Quinault salmon of to-day.

Quinault texts

VII. — How Eagle and Raven Arranged Things in the Early Days

Eagle proposes that Quinault Lake shall be a prairie. Raven objects, because it would be too easy for the people. Eagle proposes that one side of the river shall run up, and one down stream. Raven objects for same reason as before. Eagle proposes that the milt of the male salmon shall be fat. Raven objects, because it would be too pleasant for the people. Eagle's child dies, and Eagle proposes that the dead shall come to life again. Raven objects. Raven attempts to imitate Eagle's method of fishing, and drowns his daughter. Raven then proposes to Eagle that they reconsider, and allow dead to come to life. Eagle objects. For this reason, dead never come to life now.

VIII. —The Origin Of The Quinault Salmon

Two brothers out spearing porpoises spear a large one and it tows them out to sea. Reach a wall of rock, which opens and admits them. Come to a village. Porpoise emerges as a young girl, [131] and leads them up to a house. Proves to be the home of the salmon. They kill two of the village boys for food, but save the bones, and the boys come to life again. One of the brothers marries the girl. She becomes pregnant. They start for home. Child is born as they reach the shore at the Quinault River. The mother declares that there shall always be plenty of salmon in Quinault River.

IX. — How Sisemo Won Thunder's Daughter

Thunder's daughter marries man named Sisemo. Thunder is displeased, and sets Sisemo various tasks. Tells him to get snow from mountains. Sisemo returns with single handful. Thunder thinks it too little, but cannot eat it up; and when he throws it outside it covers the whole region. Begs Sisemo to return it to mountains, which he does. Tells Sisemo to get him two mountain lions for pets. Sisemo brings them tied together, but they nearly tear Thunder in pieces when he tries to play with them. Sends Sisemo for two bears, and has same experience as with mountain lions. Takes Sisemo out to cut wood, and leaves him caught in cleft of a log. Sisemo later appears carrying the log. Sends Sisemo to Underworld to get ball of light. Sisemo succeeds. From this ball came the red colors of birds and animals, as well as the lightning. Thunder then allows Sisemo to keep his daughter in peace.

X — The Magic Flight

Of five brothers the four older were elk-hunters, while the youngest, Wildcat, usually staid at home to watch the fire. One day he lets it go out, and crosses the bay to an old monster woman's house and by strategy steals a log of fire-wood. Old woman pursues him. When she reaches the water, she throws down a belt and it becomes a sand-bar. Uses five belts in the same way, and gets across the bay; but Wildcat is still ahead and gets into the house, which he turns to stone. Wildcat induces the woman to put her head in the doorway, and a great stone falls on her and kills her. The brothers flee. They camp. Woman comes to life and pursues. Catches and swallows the four older brothers one after another. Wildcat escapes. Woman nearly overtakes him. Wildcat turns his dog into a mountain and gets ahead again. Does this five times. Woman finally catches dog and swallows him. Wildcat takes refuge in a cedar-tree. Heats stones, and wraps them in elk-fat. Woman comes near and opens her mouth. He throws the stones down her throat. She drinks, and the water boils in her stomach and kills her.

XI. — THE ADVENTURES OF SPEARMAN AND HIS FRIENDS

Three seal-hunters are lost in a storm at sea. Reach a strange shore. Meet White Owl, who warns them of dangerous people living there. One of the three investigates, and is killed and eaten, The other two flee. Come to giant's house. Giant is East Wind. He sets a dish of reptiles before them. They pretend lo eat, but drop the reptiles through hollow tubes. East Wind tries to kill them at night, but they escape by a trick. Reach West Wind's house. Have similar experience as before, but one of the men is killed. Spearman escapes. Comes to South Wind's house. Has same experience, but gets away. South Wind pursues. Spearman crosses river on man's leg. South Wind tries the same, but is thrown off and drowned. Man is Thunder. Spearman marries his daughter. Finally returns home. People doubt his identity. Spearman proves it by White Owl. Starts to travel with his wife. Five wolves attack and kill the man. Eldest Wolf takes woman for his wife. Spearman comes to life, pursues and finds the Wolves. Kills them by strategy, and recovers his wife.

XII. — THE YOUNG WIFE WHO WAS ABANDONED IN A TREE-TOP

Young girl marries an old man and treats him badly. He is angry. Takes her to the woods to get cedar-bark. They climb a tree and he ties her in a crotch of the tree by her hair. Deserts her after stripping bark from tree, leaving it too slippery to climb. Girl's brothers miss her and are [132] suspicious. One day while fishing, they hear sister calling for help. Follow the sound, and find her. Try to rescue her, but cannot climb tree. People gather, but no one can reach the top. Finally youngest brother, Woodpecker, succeeds, and rescues his sister. Brothers take old roan out- to a rock to gather shellfish at low tide. Desert him, and tide rises and drowns him.

XIII. — THE GIRL WHO MARRIED OWL'S SON

Girl agrees to marry Owl's son, and her father describes the trail to her. Misses the trail and comes to Screech Owl's house by mistake. Screech Owl tries to persuade her to marry him, but she refuses and next day runs away. Screech Owl pursues. Girl hides in tree by a river. He sees her reflection in water. Jumps in after her, and is nearly drowned. Girl comes to the other Owl's house. Marries his oldest son. Screech Owl finds her and claims her, but is killed by the girl and her husband.

XIV. — THE STORY OF Sə'p'āk'ā'

Girl dreams of a strong man, Sə'p'ak'a', who finally appears and takes her to his house. He spits on her abdomen, and she becomes pregnant and gives birth to a boy with two heads.

Later gives birth to a girl baby. Woman's oldest brother finds her. She warns him, and he starts for home. SE'p'ak'a' comes in. Two-headed boy tells his father. SE'p'ak'a' follows him, but returns and says he could not find him. Same thing happens with four other brothers. Woman mourns. Finds piece of flint. Throws it into fire, and it flies into body of little girl, who immediately gives birth to a boy. Woman tells SE'p'ak'a' it is her own. Boy grows up very fast. Woman tells him her story. He follows the trail of her brothers, and find their bodies. Pretends to be one of them, and returns to house. Two-headed boy is deceived, and tells his father. SE'p'ak'a' follows, and is killed by the young man. Two-headed boy appears, and is killed. Young man takes his baby mother in his arms, and they all return to the woman's home.

XV. — Tsa'alo the Giant

Five brothers and a sister fish in certain stream. Eldest brother meets giant, who kills him. Same thing befalls three more of the brothers. Giant hides bodies under bed in his house. Sister seeks brothers, finds giant's house and discovers bodies. Giant enters and discovers young woman. She escapes during night. Returns home and tells youngest brother. Youngest brother makes ready his weapons and seeks giant. Meets and kills him by strategy. Takes away his belt as trophy. Giant's sister comes to recover belt. People are frightened, and give it up.

XVI. — Wren and Elk

Wren, while fishing, meets Elk. Elk takes away his salmon-spear. Same thing happens second time. Third time Wren fights Elk. Flies into Elk's nose. Elk cannot get him out. Wren scratches Elk's nose so that Elk bleeds to death.

XVII. — Story of the Dog Children

Young girl has dog who sleeps with her at night in human form. Girl becomes pregnant. Parents guess the cause, and are angry. People put out fires, and desert the girl. Crow hides fire in clam-shell, and tells girl. Girl gives birth to five pups. Discovers them playing in human form, and destroys their dog blankets. Teaches the children to hunt. They are very successful, and lay up much meat. Crow comes to get news of them. Takes home whale-meat for her children. One of them chokes; and people discover what has happened and return to the old village. The dog children become chiefs of the place.

Quinault notes

American Philosophical Society, Philadelphia
Livingston Farrand Quinault 15 Notebooks 1897 [3 Chilcotin]

   #1 orange Composition no #s
1 "wolf wanted?? means of packing meat, w. packer of cedar bark"
"Mat made of long reeds or grass wh. grows at Grays Harbor = grass = sx̱wēt-shE"
5-6 basket pattern names
7 strap, mat, Quilleute basket pencil
8 ink
9 blank
10 list of prices for artifacts pencil
11 same ink
12 ink
13 ink $101.80
14 expenses > by outfit $178.94 by cab to Dixon 175.   June 15, 16,
15 17, 18, 19, 20, 21, 22, 23
16 24 25 [hotel Seattle 1.50] 26 27
17 27 28 29 30 July 1 2 3 4
18 5 6 7 8 9 10 11 12 13 14 15 16 17 18 19
19 19-30 27 phonograph songs Liza Quilleute
20 Aug 1-26
21 26-31
22 Sept 1-10 O ? HH 10 HH 1.00 board 5.00 total = 342.95
23 12-18
24 19-24
25 25-27
26- blank

   #2 unbound, tan folder
1 sentences
2 phrases
3 phrases
4 Quinault by Harry Shale
5 words
6 words
7 words on back
8 words sentences
9 #s
10 #s on back
11 words
12 words
13 words
14 sentences on back

Quinault notes

15 directions planets
16 sentences
17 sentences afraid
18 sentences go
19 sentences
20 women anatomy birds on back
21 words sentences
22 fish
23 sentences on back
24 words on back – horse
25 words sentences
26 sentences words
27 sentences walk hungry on back Pluperfect same as perfect according to Harry
28 sentences on back we inc / ex
29 words sentences on back
30 where
31 sky words
32 ocean words sentences laughing
33 sentences shout this / that
34 these / those
35 sentences my
36 sentences rain on back

  #3

Quileute
1 sentences hit run
2 sentences bitten struck 2 columns English / Quinault
3 1 of , 2 of horses
4 words animals 2 columns
5 words clothes 2 columns
6 words jewelry tools 2 columns
7 words tools birds fish 2 columns
8 words fish trees berry 2 columns
9 words day times 2 columns
10 words kin 2 columns on back a prefix
11 words my / your / thy on back seems to be no difference in sing. When noun is absent or present
12 words my where brother dog
13 words list in English 1 column
14 words list in English 2 columns
15 words my her older younger B Z 2 columns
16 words kin great / grand 2 columns
17 words kin descending 6 lines on back a few plurals apparently change form, most however add ālewāh

Quinault notes

18 words dog house canoe 1-5
19 blank to end

#4

1 text pencil word breaks 1 girl & 5 brothers
2 continued
3 continued
4 continued
5 continued
6 continued
7 continued
8 continued end
9 blank to end

#5

1 Granville, Wash captain numerals 3 columns = country days canoes
2 words body house
3 words sky man woman
4 words body parts
5 words colors animals directions
6 blank
7 blank
8 blank
9 blank
10 blank
11 blank
12 song 5. Grandmother's song (1) on back
13 songs I love – promised to come & didn't   II refers to discharge of judges on this reservation – set to old tune III not tell truth IV turn around judges V same tune, same words on back VI med man in love charm VII refers to love charms VIII scoffing song to one of the men who won a jumper ? and was in love w. a woman
14 text song VI VII   VIII   IX what kind of tamanwus have you got X m/l makes me crazy
15 text XI blank XII   XIII tell a lie XIV let me alone for I am very poor XV
16 XV I am crazy XVI XVII poor XVIII no words XIX in Quilleyute
17 XX shamed   XXI she names a place far away Steilacoom XXII he is making up his mind, not very prepossing XXIII big lake dried up caused by western tamanawus
18 XXIV heart a little afraid of someone that reached the prairies XXV I will not go with that dirty old horse XXVI you cannot cure that with your tamanwus XXVII won't live another year
19 XXVIII as if your tamanawus   XXIX woman sings to another jealous woman XXX girl sings to a hesitating lover on back explanations line 51>57
20 text 51>57 twice high hills strong man
21 text on back exp
22 text on back exp

175

Quinault notes

23 continued   on back exp
24 continued   on back blank
25 continued 77>82
26 blank
27 blank
28 Texts   on back exp
29 a long time ago Raven & Eagle
30 continued
31 II continued   on back note
32 III continued
33 continued
34 continued
35 continued   pencil word breaks
36 continued
37 continued
38 continued end
39 blank to end

#6
1 blank pencil in English
2 26 Once this Crow was looking for something on beach & carrying a pack on back
3 continued
4 27 Once Queeteh was walking around and saw Duskea come w. lakaman on his back
5 continued
6 28 Once woman went fishing in this creek when the salmon were running.
7 continued
8 29 Once Raven wanted to go to underground world
9 continued
10 continued
11 continued
12 continued end   on back note tsehak kind of thing like fruit found in clay, short, dark colored
13 30 once Raven said to Goose to go to get some tsehad & Goose said there is no one to look after my children.
14 31 Once there was a doctor man – this Bluejay
15 continued
16 continued
17 continued
18 continued
19 continued
20 continued end
21 blank to end

Quinault notes

#7 Chilcotin

Chilcotin Mike Krause 4/11/64 Old Charles S? July 29 97 page #s on both sides front odd, back even

1 text
2 continued
3 continued end
4 text
5 text end notes
6 kin terms
7 blank on back pronouns
8 words dog horse tree
9 sentences
10 words camp water
11 text
12 continued
13 continued
14 continued
15 continued
16 continued
17 continued
18 continued
19 continued
20 continued
21 continued
22 continued
23 continued
24 continued
25 continued March 1 99
26 continued
27 continued
28 continued end
29 blank
30 text dictated in Eng Once there was an old woman catching salmon
31 continued
32 continued
33 continued
34 continued
35 continued
36 continued
37 continued
38 continued
39 continued
40 continued
41 continued end

Quinault notes

42 I Once the raven used to sing all? to him
43 continued   end
44 4 long time ago no daylight in this country. Raven wanted to get it.
45 continued
46 continued
47 continued end
48 notes canoes
49 >65 blank
66 chinaman captain Gladstone
67 blank
68-69 expenses July 15>30 1897 105.75
70-73 expenses board aug 23-29 7.00

   #8 orange composition
  No #s
1 XX Bluejay #8 pencil English
2 continued
3 continued
4 continued
5 continued
6 continued
7 continued
8 continued
9 continued
10 continued
11 continued
12 continued   end   Finally they got safely home & after that when they went sealing they would give this
13 XXI People used to live on Quinault River from mountains clear down to the mouth.
14 continued
15 continued   on back
16 continued kāmātsl = sawbill duck
17 continued
18 continued
19 continued
20 continued
21 continued
22 continued
23 continued
24 continued
25 continued
26 continued
27 continued
28 continued

Quinault notes

29 continued
30 continued
31 continued
32 continued
33 continued
34 continued
35 continued
36 continued
37 continued
38 continued
39 continued
40 continued
41 continued
42 continued
43 continued
44 continued Then they came to Oyhut to a village
45 continued
46 continued
47 continued
48 continued
49 continued

#9 Chilcotin
Tan folder
No #s both sides
1 1 Instrument of caribou horn
2 Anahem July 16 1897 Little Johnny pencil in English
3 continued
4 continued
5 continued
6 continued
7 continued
8 continued
9 continued
10 continued
11 continued
12 continued
13 continued
14 continued
15 continued
16 continued forgot the ? so the bear kills the man. Daseko =
17 youngest / oldest
18 blank
19 2 woman out alone picking roots. Man comes w. bear blanket

Quinault notes

20 continued
21 continued
22 continued
23 continued
24 continued
25 3 lots of boys playing close to a big river – only one boy not playing
26 continued
27 continued
28 continued
29 continued
30 continued   end "lost his woman because he did not call in the old woman."
31 blank
32 4 typewritten Long ago all dark – no daylight. A woman was picking berries. A man had light but would give none to the other people.
33 continued   end 5 typewritten Once 2 girls were playing w their brother and pulled his arm off. Women afraid of their mother and ran away
34 continued
35 continued
36 continued   end 6 typewritten Raven made lots of dried salmon – brought lots of big roots to his house.
37 continued
38 blank
39 7 typewritten Long ago no fire in country – a certain man had fire – the day Raven tried to steal fire –
40 continued
41 continued
42 continued
43 continued   end 9 Waiwaitoos   Long ago a man had a gun (Hudson bay gun – shotgun) half was poison and half good . trusted people with gun.
44 continued
45 continued   Sun is magic. One side can bring people to life – the other side kills them Bob Straus sentences says big animal was whale.
46 10 Then the Raven came to a village to tell them the Salmon had come.
47 11 typewritten   once a man & his wife and baby go to snow mts to hunt ground hogs. Started to trap g.h. in a big gulch in mts. Make lots of traps.
48 continued
49 continued
50 continued   end typewritten to here
51 12 the night a little boy cried all the time – everybody in bed – some one tried to call to him – come out I give you some (Salmon fat)
52 continued   Owl = neo'ston
53 continued
54 continued
55 continued

Quinault notes

56 continued
57 blank
58 13 long time ago a man die and was buried. Somebody takes him away and no one knows who did it and couldn't find out.
59 name of man = Esstēnīq'ot' continued
60 continued
61 continued 2 lines he grew big and now he kills babies by rubbing his tongue (known as little Stēnēīq'ot')
62 blank
63 14 long ago big river w. stone island and a big man sit there cry all the time – canoes come down the river & people are afraid the man will kill them.
64 continued end
65 15 once a man went out with his 2 dogs to hunt little snow on ground in Anaheim.
66 continued end
67 16 only this #
68 blank
69 blank
70 blank
71 blank hunk torn out
72 blank
73 blank
74 Bear's skulls on poles long ago a man killed a bear but didn't put skull on pole. Bear came & found head on ground and went around and put bear's heads he found on poles but the man who didn't put it up he killed. End
75 blank
76 Little Johnny says never had totems or clams among Chilcotin – had them about Skeena River & Clussins Lake. man may not marry his first cousin or any known relations.

#10
tan folder
one sided
1 #10 A long time ago a young girl had a dog – she had the dog a long time – and there was quite a village there where she went she took the dog with her.
2 continued
3 continued on back note: The crow used always to be thinking about new?this girl. He loved her greatly.
4 continued on back note: people had been living on whale meat.
5 continued on back note: Quinaults claim that this story came from the North.
6 continued end
7 II Story of Misp' [and his brother KwemoleLen]
8 continued drying platform
9 continued
10 continued
11 continued

Quinault notes

12 continued
13 continued
14 continued
15 continued   on back note: In the case of 1st dead sister he found dead children in her belly.
16 continued
17 continued   on back there is an interval in the story here which the narrators do not know.
18 continued
19 continued
20 continued   on back the man was … deer
21 continued
22 continued
23 continued
24 continued   end he came to the Chinook people and there he turned into a rock and is there yet.
25 III once 2 sisters went out to dig roots and had to spend the night thee and as they lay there they were talking and came to speak of the stars and the youngest one said, "I wish I were up there in the bright star" and the older one I wish I were on that smaller star.
26 continued
27 continued   on back: She came down just over her father's house.
28 continued
29 continued
30 continued
31 continued
32 continued
33 continued end
34 blank
35 blank
36 blank

#11
Orange composition
1 blank
2 1 qwn sentence
3 Misp told by Mason pencil in English A young man had a wife & the man was Bluejay's master & Bluejay said, "I don't see why that woman don't laugh." (This was before the child Misp was born)
4 continued
5 continued
6 continued
7 continued end
8 told by Mason the man who first made this people came from the North and went South.
9 continued
10 continued end top 3 lines came to Chinook & other people came out
11 Kwēēteh 6 lines

182

Quinault notes

12   blank to end

#12

1   #12 Sally XX combined "3rd brother came & asked his sister & she told him & told him to go right back & he did & same thing happened." 4th brother
2   continued
3   continued
4   continued   they all went back to her old home. 2 headed boy
5   XVI Txēēhs-ōmish : a chief who lived in the water & he had a daughter & she went nearly every day to get salal berries. on back under boards or sticks they put in bottom of canoe to keep ictas dry.
6   continued
7   continued   on back large beaver like animal lives in sea
8   continued
9   continued end
10 XVII told by Tōshin (Bob Pope) A young man has a shack near by a salmon river and he went to clean his fish himself & he had lots of salmon sometimes when he would come back from fishing he would find that someone had cleaned his salmon ..
11 continued
12 continued
13 continued
14 continued
15 continued   on back 2 posts with faces
16 continued
17 continued
18 continued
19 continued
20 continued
21 continued
22 continued   At Quinault people were upside down   song
23 continued
24 continued
25 continued
26 continued
27 continued   end that was the end of Msp
28 XVIII xwonehxwoneh had a house by a river and he had no grub and was poor.
29 continued
30 continued
31 continued
32 continued
33 continued
34 continued
35 continued
36 continued

Quinault notes

37 continued
38 continued
39 continued
40 continued
41 continued
42 continued   end She took water along to stop the eclipse which is caused by the big fisher swallowing the moon. Fisher was left up in the sky after the eclipse to ?? the two girls.
43 XIX xwonehxwoneh was living at LaPush 1 morning he would go out to hunt on the beach but the wolves would always have been ahead of him & he could not find anything to eat.
44 continued
45 continued on back lot of combs with him to throw. other side of Columbia rubbed coal on his face
46 continued on back end 2 lines

#13
Pencil in English
1 IV Thunder had a daughter
2 continued
3 continued
4 continued
5 continued end thunder is a big bird
6 V xwonehxwoneh was a trickster
7 continued
8 continued
9 continued end
10 VI Once Quinault Lake was going to be a prairie. The eagle had said it.
11 continued
12 continued
13 continued end if it had not been for Raven people would come to life again now.
14 vii bluejay had a sister named Jū'ī & told his sister to go and marry a man from down below in the underworld.
15 continued
16 continued
17 continued
18 continued end Then he was dead for good. on back youngest brother of North wind lives and blows, other 4 killed (hurricanes, tornados)
19 xiii there were four brothers who made the West Wind & five who made the South Wind.
20 ix Raven had a wife, had from the underworld, she was mole = *pōkwŏlōmīūx̱*
21 continued
22 continued end the river would be solid w. blueback
23 x   five brothers used to live up a small stream near mouth of Quinault River. Silver side salmon used to go up there.
24 continued
25 continued

Quinault notes

26 continued   end
27 xi once a young girl went & lived w. an old man against her will.
28 continued
29 continued
30 continued
31 continued
32 xii continued 2 brothers went out to spear porpoises (*skāāLEnōx̱*) and soon saw one without a dorsal fin & though he came close they were afraid to spear him.
33 continued on back reason for lots of bluebacks in Quinault River
34 continued
35 xiii there were once 5 brothers who were good elk hunters. Sons of Ucitsomanail̲x
36 continued
37 continued
38 continued
39 continued she explained to *Hohohus* that she had only come by mistake to this house.
40 continued they tore him to pieces
41 xiv told by Sally There were 5 brothers on the N. side of Grays Harbor just below James Rock.
42 continued
43 continued
44 continued
45 continued
46 continued
47 continued
48 xx young girl dreamt about strong man sᴇpa'k'a 5 times. Was gone after roots of ferns brakes & dreamt of him 5 times
49 continued
50 continued & brought his whale stuff back

 #14 Chilcotin
 both sides
1 Chinaman's stories continued 4 long time ago, everybody used to fool all the time, dance, play lehal – all the time – everything bad they used to do an old man named Lui made a big canoe on back not typewritten
2 5 the Raven once fished for salmon all alone on back not typewritten
3 6 Once the mt goat got a woman & started for home. on back 7 Raven used to go to the village & go to every house & call the man a bird (a small black bird) Datsea say he go call on in his house
4 not typewritten
5 8 these 3 brothers hunted together – youngest
6 continued on back continued end that's all
7 9 once 4 men went hunting a long way off in mts. An old man & his 3 boys
8 continued
9 continued

Quinault notes

10   10 once his men played slehal together & one man lost everything, dead broke
11   continued
12   continued   on back 11 once upon a time big villages in winter time chief had a daughter & the man had touched her and a man slipped into her bed at night
13   continued   on back
14   continued   on back
15   continued   on back
16   continued   on back
17   continued   on back
18   continued   on back
19   continued   on back   1st time women learned to use poles in childbirth
20   continued   on back
21   blank
22   35 Narwilus great hunter had a gun
23   continued   on back
24   continued   on back
25   continued   on back
26   continued   on back
27   blank   on back blank
28   36 once a small boy wanted meat to eat very badly Mother tells him to go to another man's camp nearby and get it. Boy comes to camp and 2 women say You sit down between us. So he got the 2 women.   on back continued
29   37 once these were 3 or 4 brothers & the oldest was a doctor   on back   continued
30   continued   on back top 3 lines
31   38 once a young man used to decorate himself w. raven wings w. wings & feathers of other birds   on back   continued
32   continued   on back crossed out 5 lines
33   to become a doctor it was necessary for a man to dream some remarkable dream or have something remarkable happen to him.   on back   continued
34   dr = dī-yĭn   on back old seat of Chilcotin was Anaham Lake as a centre and including Tttah Lake, Pautzin, and Chzailut Lakes Life much less stationary than now.
35   cooking done by roasting or boiling   Chinaman has never seen picture writing among Chilcotin   on back story by Little Johnny Long time ago used to be robbed and nobody knew who did it.
36   continued   on back continued
37   continued   end   on back   2nd stenegut story by little Johnny
38   continued   on back   continued
39   typewritten to here   continued   on back   continued
40   continued
41   continued   on back   tattooing   formerly pretty universal
42   blank to end 46

Quinault notes

#15 Quinault
One-sided
1 xxi continued 4 long time ago everybody
2 continued
3 continued xxi/23
4 continued
5 continued
6 continued
7 continued xxi/26
8 continued xxi/26
9 continued
10 continued
11 continued
12 continued
13 continued
14 continued
15 continued
16 continued
17 continued
18 continued
19 continued Quinault xxi/34
20 continued
21 continued
22 continued
23 continued
24 continued
25 continued
26 continued
27 continued
28 continued
29 continued
30 continued
31 continued & took out wedge (see other story)
32 continued end this ends Tōshin's story of Bluejay
33 xxii told by Bob Pope (Tōshin) In the old days 3 men used to go out sealing went?? often & always had good weather
34 continued
35 continued
36 continued on back plant has barbs?? about ½ -2 inches diameter
37 continued
38 continued
39 continued
40 continued
41 continued

Quinault notes

42 continued
43 continued   on back Man who made bridge with his leg was *Hanesāh* Thunder. Only went out then to get a whale – only goes certain times of year
44 continued
45 continued
46 Quinault xxii / 9
47 continued
48 continued
49 continued end
50 blank to end

  #17 APS
1 census   = 300

APS/Livingston Farrand

Misp[h]

Missing Misp[h]:
Restor(y)ing the Transformer of Tsamosans of coastal Washington

Jay Miller

Abstract

Virtually unknown among Northwest Changer ~ Transformers is Misp[h] of the Tsamosans in southwest Washington. As twins born miraculously to a murderous mother, they destroy her ogress sisters, save nebulously-formed children, and decree skills, foods, and customs at specific places and times. Their living embodiment is a duck – once call old squaw (old swawk), now longtail – with appropriately complex changes in bright plumage by season and gender.

Introduction

The major loss, academically, from the life-long institutionalization of Thelma Adamson after her fieldwork among Tsamosan Salishan speakers of Southwestern Washington has been the continuing failure to recognize Misp[h] as a major transformer in the oral literature of the Tsamosan Coast Salish of Southwestern Washington. As a graduate student, Adamson spent 1926 collecting folklore among the Upper Chehalis at Oakville, followed by a concern with ethnography in 1927, when her mentor Franz Boas joined her to conduct linguistic research at the same community. Her dissertation, completed, approved, but never filed in May of 1929, was a study of transformers and tricksters among Coast Salish. Her supporting folklore collection was published, through the efforts of Ruth Benedict, in 1934 and reissued in 2009.

Salish oral literature is particularly well known because of the sustained efforts of linguists and storytellers concerned with recording in these natives languages, as well as the interest of internationally known scholars and folklorists (Walls 1987), such as Franz Boas, Melville Jacobs (1959, 1960), Del Hymes, Dale Kinkade, Arthur Ballard (see all), June Collins (1952b), and Vi Hilbert (Miller and Hilbert 1993, 1996, 2004), as well as popular collections (Matson 1968, 1972), culminating in a recent Salish compendium (Thompson and Egesdal 2008) and the Adamson reprinting.

This reissue makes more available the epic of Misp[h] and his brother Kumol told by Lucy Heck (pp. 329-432), a noblewoman from the Lower Chehalis of Grays Harbor. Earlier, among Quinault, Livingston Farrand heard versions of Misp[h] from Bob Pope in 1902. Ronald Olson learned it from Billy Mason, Bob Pope, John Dixon, and Jonah Cole in 1926.

The earliest reference found so far appears in a letter, dated 20 July 1855, from James Swan at Shoalwater to George Gibbs, who asked for word lists of various native languages of the Northwest. Swan's source seems to have been Old Toke, a Chinook leader living at Tokeland on Willapa Bay, now the location of the tiny Shoalwater Bay reservation. The six page letter includes stories of Thunderbird, the Smisspee (duck), the winds, and customs and religious beliefs of Indians from Columbia River to Nisqually. Smisspee is obviously Misp[h], as explained in this extracted quote from page 2:

The Smisspee is a small duck of the Sheldrake species and the only tradition about it that I have heard is that it was formerly a man or as the Indians express it they were "ankartz Tillikums" [*ahnkutty tilakums*, past people]. This bird came to the ?ema? [Nemah] River in this bay when a great many Indians lived and seeing the river full of salmon asked why they did not catch them. The Indians replied they did not know what salmon were, and were afraid of them. The Smisspee then showed them how to make nets and spears and they took immense quantities of fish. And from this bird all Indians learned to catch fish.

Edmond Meany (1905: 6) of the University of Washington visited local reservations to make notes and write a series of newspaper articles, that for the Chehalis includes a version by the famous Secena, who worked with Franz Boas in 1927:

After some persuasion, See-see-nah told legends and stories of the old life, which I was very glad to write down with the aid of the two interpreters.

Long ago, before the whites came, his people owned all the prairies and land around the Chehalis river. Misp and his older brother, *Kom-mol-owish*, taught the Indians how to make fire by spinning one dry piece of wood on another. They also taught the people how to use fish and roots for food. Then they used flint and bluestone for arrowheads and axes.

Quinault creation, according to a cultural and economic overview by Justine James and Leilani Chubby (2002: 99), involved three distinct epochs, each with its own reformer. At the beginning was Xwani Xwani [X^{w}ani X^{w}ani], then came the protean Animal People, and third, setting the stage for the time of human people, was Misp[h] – the culture hero ~ transformer ~ reformer.

Misp[h] and his twin, in particular, did much to form present Grays Harbor, and coastal Washington state. He was a key ancestral figure for Tsamosans. While other regional reformers are well known, such as *Kw'ati* of the Quileute and Makah, Misp[h] is not. In part this is a consequence of the fate of Thelma Adamson. Thus, Misp[h] has remained unheralded for seventy-five years.

Such great epics of Native American can easily be misunderstood by mainstream readers because they teach by negative examples, rather than extolling the rewards of virtue or financial success. Presenting these stories in English voids many of their nuances. The idioms used in the native language explicitly indicate what is real and what is not, what is worthwhile and what is greedy, or what is good for everyone and what is selfish. By the end of these epics morality, decency, and community values are instituted, not always in the easiest or safest manner.

Only at the end of each epic are Misp[h] and his brother identified with their duck avatar – the immature male in winter plumage most like a "long-tailed", once also known (among 20 local names) as "old squaw," though "old squawk" is more appropriate since its species Latin name *Clangula hyemalis* refers to its noisy clanging in winter. The attributed to the female, it is the male which is the most noisy. This species is remarkably apt for a transformer since it is so changeable, going through two complete annual bright plumage changes, unlike the bright and dull ones of most birds, as well as gestational ones. It can also dive to 200 feet deep. Its diet is also human like, relying on mollusks, crustaceans, insects, and aquatic plants.

To aid in following the epic versions, a generalized condensation of versions follows:

An industrious young man (Wildcat) camps alone, either drying fish or making a canoe. He soon becomes backlogged, while continuing to gain more materials. One day, while he is away, his work is done for him. After several days of this unknown help, he hides to see who is doing it. A young woman appears who then marries him. They live together until the fishing season or canoe is done and then go back to his home town. Before they get there, she lets down her hair to hide her face and, once inside, sits backward looking at the wall. She lives quietly in the house, tormented by Bluejay who wants to see her face and hear her laugh. When she can endure no more, she hides her husband, pulls back her hair to reveal a frightful face and laughs five times, killing more people each time until everyone is dead, even her disobedient husband. She eats all of them, but saves her husband's genitals in a basket above her bed. She becomes pregnant and has twins. The oldest one is Misp^h, the other Kəmol.

The twins grow quickly and precociously. When their mother leaves for the day, they do everything she had forbidden them to do, finding their father's parts in the basket and his former town littered with gnawed bones. Alarmed, they go home to burn down their own house and flee. The mother sees the smoke and ash, including a bit retaining the design on the side of her cherished basket. Angry, she rushes home, finds the smoldering ruins, and chases after her sons.

They trick and kill her, then move on. Along the way they meet and kill her four sisters, each of whom kills children (unformed souls/spirits) in a special way before eating them. Each aunt is gutted and the more recently dead children are revived and given professions that are thereafter passed down family lines. They go from town to town around the Olympic Peninsula, decreeing livelihoods and abilities specific to each community. Near the end, the brother is killed and revived as a duck, while Misp^h becomes a stone at the mouth of the Columbia River. Their spirits return as ducks in the late Summer.

Since the motivation of Misp^h and his twin is to make the world ready for today, the epic by Lucy Heyden Heck is summarized next because it is the most detailed one known and would have been the basis for Adamson to properly highlight the importance of Misp^h's role among the Coast Salish.

The Reformer Twins
paraphrase of Lucy Heck to
Thelma Adamson (1934: 329-342)

Chief Woodpecker lived in a town of twelve houses at present Humptulips City. He was a skilled carpenter who built all the houses and many of the canoes. His son worked with him, so as to master woodworking. When it came time, the son was sent alone into the forest to make his first canoe, and his father insisted that no one was to help the boy. He had to succeed on his own.

The boy selected a cedar tree, felled it, and began shaping it until dusk when he returned to his camp for the night. The next day he shaped the inside. When he came back on the third day, he found a big camas bulb inside the canoe form. It was tied with a long black hair. Surprised and suspicious, he hid the bulb in nearby brush. The fourth day, two bulbs were in the canoe, each tied with a long hair. On the fifth day, there were three bulbs, and on the sixth, four camas and elk marrow used for a protective greasing (sun block) of the face. When he returned the seventh day to rough out the canoe, nothing was there. Instead, he worked for a while until he became sleepy and took a nap inside the canoe.

Misp[h]

He dreamed a pretty girl with very long hair was sitting beside him, asking why he did not eat the camas she brought to him. She pledged her love to this boy of royal blood. When he awoke, she was actually sitting there and they agreed to marry. She said she lived upriver, but would move to his town as long as it was after dark because she was very bashful.

Just outside the town, the girl unbraided her hair so it hung over her face. Inside the house, she sat with her face to the wall. At bed time, she slept beside her husband in the chief's section. The next morning, she again sat facing the wall with her hair down, weaving a basket. She ate her meal of camas in the same position. Ever nosey, Bluejay began to mutter about this overly modest behavior. When he got no response, he kept insisting to see her face and hear her laughter. He kept this up for five long days.

The fifth morning, the wife asked her husband to go with her far beyond the prairie while she dug camas. Instead, when they got there, she dug a very deep hole and told her husband to hide inside it. She stuffed his ears and nose with fine cedar bark, covered him with a box, and left him in supposed safety. Too curious, the husband raised the edge of the box, waiting to hear her laugh.

Back at the house, the girl began to dress up, braid her hair, and grease and paint her face. Then she went to Bluejay and said they would now laugh. She clapped her hands together and shouted. Bluejay fell over dead. As she continued laughing out loud, everyone in the house died, their eyes bulging out and tongues lolling. She went house to house in the town, shouting and killing. Then she started at one end and ate everyone up.

When she went to find her husband, he was dead. She wept. Then she took his torso, put it in a basket, and hung it over their bed at home. During the night, the basket shook. The next morning, the girl was pregnant with twins, who were born five days later. The elder was Misp[h] and the younger was Kmol. Two days after birth, they were walking and using bows and arrows. She favored Misp[h] and always threatened to eat Kmol if he cried. After five days, they were men. Each day their mother left to dig camas, warning them not to look in her basket nor go downriver.

They became suspicious and looked in the basket, identifying their father's remains. They went downriver and found his village, littered with skeletons. They knew the worse and decided to flee from home. They burned their house and walked away, with Misp[h] behind his brother in front. Their mother sensed something was wrong, then saw ashes in the air. One cinder showed the design pattern of her basket, and then she realized her home had burned up. She raced after her sons, singing a song to weaken them. They prepared for her attack by climbing to the top of a tree covered in loose bark, praying to the tree to hold on tightly to its own bark. The tree gave them special words (dicta) to grip onto its trunk. When their mother saw them in the tree, she spoke softly and nicely to lure them down. Instead they suggested she climb up, telling her the special words. She did not always remember them so she only got up slowly. Near the top, Misp[h] pushed the bark with his foot and it fell off and crushed their mother.

They climbed down and went on, knowing they had four aunts who were cannibals like their mother. A prairie, named Seated Children, near Humptulip City had a stepped slope filled with children, who were known as "Always Tears" because they were crying, dirty, and fearful. At the bottom were two trees leaning together with a swing between them. Further out was a huge bloody rock. Those children warned the twins that the woman who lived on the prairie would eat them.

Misp[h]

They greeted their aunt, and she asked after their mother. They said she was slowed by a heavy pack and would be along soon. Their aunt tried to get Kmol to swing, but Misp[h] took his place, teaching the children instead to chorus "Go and Come Back". Misp[h] jumped off the swing beyond the rock and survived. He told his aunt it was her turn to swing, urging the children to sing "Go and Never Come Back". She hit the rock and died as her belly burst open. The twins revived the most recently dead children, but those longest dead stayed dead. The uneaten children were washed, dressed, and painted. They were told they would live there to become very old. Those who revived would live to middle age, while those (pre-souls) who stayed dead became stillborns.

The twins went on until they came to a prairie where they saw a pile of dirt covered in clam shells, shaped like a seated child. Five wide seats behind this figure were filled with children. The men greeted their aunt, and she asked after their mother. They said she would be along. The children explained that each was sent to fetch a stick standing near the figure without laughing, but he or she always failed, was dashed against the rock, and eaten. Misp[h] fetched the stick soberly, then said it was the aunt's turn. She laughed, so he grabbed her by the heels and dashed her against the rock so that she burst open and children's bodies tumbled out. The most recent victims revived fully after they were washed and cleaned, but those longer dead were slower to recover. Some never did. These children founded royal-blooded families.

At the next prairie, children were speared as each came to sit on a large fungus. Misp[h] sat but was not harmed, so it was the third aunt's turn. He speared her heart and threw her against a rock so her belly burst open. Again, the most recent meals were revived, but those longer dead were less lucky. These children became spirit helpers for hunting (Hunt power).

The twins went on to the prairie at Carlyle, where they met the fifth aunt, who killed children with a boy's game of see-saw that had a flat rock at either end. The aunt and Misp[h] got on the teeter-tauter. He jumped off when she was on the high end and she burst on the rock below. Victims were cleaned up and revived, founding a community of hunters, both men and skilled women.

At the mouth of the Humptulips, where they decreed the building of fish traps, the twins resolved to right the wrongs of the world. They went westward, coming to a house where people were shooting arrows inside. It was raining and no one there knew how to fix leaks in the roof. Instead, they shot arrows at the drips to try to stop them. Bluejay spoke for the household, explaining their tactic. The twins went up on the roof and saw that the shingles were placed the wrong way, so they set them right and the leaking stopped. All subsequent roofs were built this way.

They went toward the shore and came upon a house where Bluejay and his wife were cohabitating on the roof, so the Twins decreed modesty in the future. Further up the beach, clams were stuck on sticks to cook in the sunlight. Instead, the twins taught people there to cut out the clams from the shell and cook them on sticks over an open fire.

They went on and, at the surf, met a man walking upside-down carrying firewood between his legs. They set him upright and instructed everyone to carry firewood on the right shoulder. Farther up the coast they came to a house where they heard groaning, "Ouch, my head; Ouch, my hand." A man was splitting wood by driving the wedge into the log with his head. Instead, Misp[h] made him a stone mallet and gave instructions still followed to split wood. People there tried to cook their food by dancing on it. The brothers told them to get their nets to catch salmon, but the people instead got digging sticks for clamming.

At Corner Creek, they met a man sharpening the edges of three big clam shells and singing about how he would deal with the reformers. Instead, Misp[h] stuck the shells in his head and butt, turning him into a deer to be hunted to feed people. At Copalis, they met a man being dragged into the sea by his own head lice. The twins washed his hair in urine and rinsed it in fresh water, killing the lice. Then they carved him a comb that was made of wood, and taught him to comb, oil, and braid his hair. Finally, they called for people to bring out their salmon nets, but instead they got their clamming sticks. Ever after, they have clammed there.

At the Rocks, Wolves were eating raw crabs. Misp[h] tried to reform them into proper people who cooked their food, but they asked to remain as they were and so became five brothers consisting of four Wolves and a Dog. At Moclips, they taught proper sex technique to the people (especially modesty and respect by girls). At Rock Creek, they found a deeply sleeping man and attached clam shells to his front teeth. He became X^{w}ani X^{w}ani [active in a later age]. At Taholah, they called for people to bring out their fish gear and they did. As a reward, the twins taught them to make tight basket traps. Farther on they found empty houses, and following the stream [Raft Creek] there came to a suspicious whirlpool. They heated rocks in a fire and dropped them into the water until it began to boil. A huge black being with an enormous mouth floated up and they cut it open, finding whole families, canoes, and houses. Those most recently killed could be revived. Among them were Bluejay and *X^{w}ani X^{w}ani*, who decided to repopulate that locale using skin rubbed off Misp[h] and himself. They blew on the exfoliate pellets and they became people, gifted with a special fish trap.

They went on and shouted for people to build fish traps because they already had fire, good houses, and tools. But they were dirty, so the twins taught them to bathe and groom. At Quileute, they shouted for fish traps but instead people launched canoes and ran out trolling lines, as they still do. Feeling threatened, the twins ran away and decreed the Quileutes would be mean. At Ozette, they also called for fishtraps, but some went into the hills to hunt and others went out to troll. They did everything properly.

They went on, calling for fish traps at each town, but some just went out to sea, others embraced warfare, and some developed other skills. At one town, they cleared away rocks creating a whirlpool and so killed a monster.

When they got along the Columbia River, at Clatsop, they called for fish traps but instead people caught crabs. Clatsops were confirmed in their royal blood. At Astoria, people came out with their nets and received runs of huge Chinook salmon. Across the river, people were drying sturgeon heads on warm rocks, but the twins instead taught them to smoke sturgeon. Further on they met people who did not know how to eat, putting food into every body orifice but the mouth. They were taught to chew and swallow, as well as drink. They then had to teach them how to sleep and to use a net.

At the next town, people packed everything they had and then went to sleep, thinking that was how things could be moved. Instead, the twins taught them to pack things up and move them by canoe. At Fort Columbia, everyone had a huge snake as a pet. If they did not feed these serpents enough, they ate children. Misp[h], instead, arranged to kill all the snakes and burn them up on a high hill, where the place where he sat to rest is now marked by a rock shaped like a duck.

At Chinook City, the town was infested with woodrats, who ate people alive. The twins set fire to the area, killing all the rats and enabling people to set out their nets. At Ilwako, people had their nets and used them well. At Nasell, they called for nets, but instead people went out to hunt or to hook sturgeon. They had no fires and had to be taught to use firesticks and to cook. At Nemah, people went out to hunt or built small salmon traps. At Bay Center, people brought out herring traps. Then the twins went across the bay and met people spearing salmon.

At Westport, people got crabs and clams, and the twins decreed "A whale will always wash ashore here; you are good people [and deserve it]". Further on, people at Ts'e'tc hunted elk and were decreed to have royal blood to establish the chiefly families of the Harbor people. At Mulla, people hooked sturgeon. At Hoquiam, people hooked sturgeon and set out herring traps. At James Rock, people had herring traps and boxy canoes. Instead they were taught to make proper canoes. At Owl, people ate gophers and changed into these night birds. At Chinoose Creek, people kept their herring traps and sturgeon hooks. At Cold Water, people caught only silver salmon.

Finally, they returned to the Humptulips, where they started and decided that they would finish by becoming a kind of duck that arrived in the middle of the fishing season. Before they came, salmon had to be prepared in a very strict manner, using a sharpened clam shell to gut the fish and separate head and tails from the body. After these ducks arrived, people could prepare fish in whatever manner was convenient. These are river ducks that are always in pairs, like the twins, that go north in the spring and arrive back in the fall.

Conclusions

Restored to the scholarly record, Misp[h] and his twin transformed the Tsamosan world to be as it is today. Their living embodiment is the longtailed [old swawk] duck, which breeds in the high arctic, and visits coastal waters. Its very changeability makes it an apt representative of Transformers ~ Changers who prepared the world for the humans were "coming soon".

Appendix A: Roster of Old Squawk Duck Names (Terres 1980: 197)

Calloo	John Connelly	Old Wife	Scoldenore	Swallow-tailed duck
Cockawee	Long-tailed	Old Molly	Scolder	Uncle Huldy
Coween	Old Billy	Old Injun*	South Southerly	Winter Duck
Hound*	Old Granny	Quandy	Squeaking Duck	

*Hound references its baying cry
*Old Injun for its traveling in single file

Mispʰ

Works Cited

Adamson, Thelma
 1927 Unarranged Sources of Chehalis Ethnography. Seattle: Melville Jacobs Collection, University of Washington, Special Collections.
 1934 *Folktales of the Coast Salish*. Memoirs of the American Folklore Society 27.
 2009 *Folktales of the Coast Salish*. William Seaburg and Laurel Sercombe, eds. Lincoln: University of Nebraska Press.

Ballard, Arthur C.
 1927 Some Tales of the Southern Puget Sound Salish. University of Washington Publications in Anthropology 2 (3), 57-81.
 1929 Mythology of Southern Puget Sound. University of Washington Publications in Anthropology 3 (2), 31-150.
 1999 Mythology of Southern Puget Sound. Kenneth (Greg) Watson, ed. North Bend, WA: Snoqualmie Valley Historical Museum.

Barnett, Homer
 1957 *Indian Shakers, A Messianic Cult of the Pacific Northwest*. Carbondale: Southern Illinois University Press.

Bent, AC
 1919 Life Histories of Diving Birds. US Nat Mus 107
 1925 Life Histories of North American Wild Fowl. USNM 130, part 2.

Boas, Franz
 2002 Indian Myths and Legends of the North Pacific Coast. Victoria: Talonbooks. Randy Bouchard and Dorothy Kennedy, eds. Dietrich Bertz, translator. Originally Indianishe Sagen von der Nord-Padifischen Küste Amerikas. Sonder-Abdruck aus den Verlandlungen der Berliner Gesellschaft fur Anthropologie, Ethnologie und Urgeschichte. Berlin: Verlag von A Asher. 1895.

Bright, William, ed.
 2004 *Native American Placenames of the United States*. Norman: University of Oklahoma Press.

Collins, June
 1952 The Mythological Basis For Attitudes Toward Animals Among Salish-Speaking Indians. *Journal of American Folklore* 65 (258), 353-359.

Elmendorf, William
 1961a Skokomish and Other Coast Salish Tales. Washington State University Research Studies 29 (1), 1-37; (2), 84-117; (3), 119-150.
 1993 *Twana Narratives*. Native Historical Accounts of a Coast Salish People. Seattle: University of Washington Press.

Farrand, Livingston
 1902 Traditions of the Quinault Indians. With assistance by WS Kahnweiler. NY: Memoirs of the American Museum of Natural History IV, Publications of the Jesup North Pacific Expedition III, 77-132.

Gibbs, George
 1855 Report on the Indian Tribes of Washington Territory. Pacific Railroad Report 1, 402-36.

1877 Tribes of Western Washington and Northwestern Oregon. Washington: Department of the Interior, United States Geographical and Geological Survey of the Rocky Mountain Region, Part II: 157-241.

1970 Dictionary of the Niskwalli (Nisqually) Indian Language - Western Washington. Extract from 1877 Contributions to North American Ethnology 1: 285-361. Seattle: The Shorey Book Store Facsimile Reproduction.

Gunther, Erna

1925 Klallam Folk Tales. University of Washington Publications in Anthropology 1 (4), 113-170.

Haeberlin, Herman

1916-17 Puget Salish, 42 Notebooks. DC: National Anthropological Archives. # 2965.

1918 "SbɛtɛtdaꞋq: A Shamanic Performance of the Coast Salish." *American Anthropologist* 20 (3), 249-257.

1924 "Mythology of Puget Sound." *Journal of American Folklore* 37 (143-144), 371-438.

Haeberlin, Herman, and Erna Gunther

1930 The Indians of Puget Sound. University of Washington Publications in Anthropology 4 (1), 1-84.

Harrington, John Peabody

1981 The Papers of John Peabody Harrington in the Smithsonian Institution, 1907-1957. Elaine Mills, ed. 30 reels. Millwood, NY: Krause International Publications.

Hymes, Dell

1981 "In Vain I Tried to Tell You:" Essays in Native American Ethnopoetics. Philadelphia: University of Pennsylvania Press.

1987 Anthologies and Narrators: *Recovering the Word: Essays on Native American Literature.* Brian Swan and Arnold Krupat, eds. Berkeley: University of California Press.

Jacobs, Melville

1959 *The Content and Style of an Oral Literature.* NY: Viking Fund Publications in Anthropology 26.

1960 *The People Are Coming Soon.* Analysis of Clackamas Chinook Myths and Texts. Seattle: University of Washington Press.

James, Justine E., Jr., with Leilani Chubby

2002. Quinault, pp. 99-117. *Native Peoples of the Olympic Peninsula. Who We Are.* Jacilee Wray, ed. Norman: University of Oklahoma Press.

Kinkade, Dale

1983 'Daughters of Fire: Verse Analysis of an Upper Chehalis Folktale.' Pp. 267–278 of Thayer, ed.

1984 'Bear and Bee: Narrative Verse Analysis of an Upper Chehalis Folktale.' Pp. 246–261 of Rood (ed.) 1984.

1987 Bluejay and His Sister. In Brian Swann & Arnold Krupat. eds. *Recovering the Word: Essays on Native American Literature,* pp. 255-296. Berkeley: University of California Press.

1992 Translating Pentlatch. In Brian Swann, ed. *On the Translation of Native American Literatures*, pp. 163-175. Washington: Smithsonian Institution Press.

Misp^h

McAtee, WL
 1955 folk names of NE birds

Matson, Emerson
 1968 *Longhouse Legends*. Camden, NJ: Thomas Nelson and Sons.
 1972 *Legends of the Great Chiefs*. Tacoma: Storypole Press.

Meany, Edmond
 1905 Washington Redmen Who Helped Palefaces in War: Chehalis Tribe of Twenty-Five Braves Who Fought For Whites. 15 October: 6. *Seattle Post-Intelligencer.*

Miller, Jay, and Vi Hilbert
 1993 Caring for Control: A Pivot of Salishan Language and Culture. *American Indian Linguistics and Ethnography in Honor of Laurence C. Thompson.* University of Montana, Occasional Papers in Linguistics 10, 237-239.
 1996 Lushootseed Animal People: Mediation and Transformation from Myth to History. pp. 138-156 in *Monsters, Tricksters, and Sacred Cows*: Animal Tales and American Identities. A. James Arnold, ed. New World Studies. Charlottesville: University of Virginia Press.
 2004 "That Salish Feeling…" *Studies in Salish Linguistics in Honor of M. Dale Kinkade.* Donna B. Gerdts and Lisa Matthewson, eds. University of Montana, Occasional Papers In Linguistics No. 17, 197-210. (Vi Hilbert first author)

Olson, Ronald
 1936 The Quinault Indians. University of Washington Publications in Anthropology 6 (1), 1-190.

Seaburg, William
 1999 Whatever Happened to Thelma Adamson? A Footnote in the History of Northwest Anthropological Research. *Northwest Anthropological Research Notes* 33 (1), 73-83.

Swan, James
 20 July 1855 letter from James Swan at Shoalwater to George Gibbs at Steilacoom. NAA

Terres, John
 1980 The Audubon Society Encyclopedia of North American Birds. NY: Alfred Knopf.

Thompson, M. Terry, and Steven Egesdal
 2008 *Salish Myths and Legends. One People's Stories*. Lincoln: University of Nebraska Press.

Walls, Robert
 1987 *Bibliography Of Washington State Folklore And Folklife*. Seattle: University of Washington Press.

Wickersham, James
 1898 "Nisqually Mythology, Studies of the Washington Indians." *Overland Monthly* 32, 345-51.

Clangula hyemalis   Clangula clang, noise   Hyemalis of Winter

James Swan

James Gilcrist Swan
1818-1900

James Gilcrist Swan lived one of the most varied and colorful lives in the early history of Washington Territory. He was variously an oysterman, customs inspector, secretary to congressional delegate Isaac Stevens, journalist, reservation schoolteacher, lawyer, judge, school superintendent, railroad promoter, natural historian, and ethnographer. Above all, Swan was a chronicler. He wrote one of the earliest books describing life in Washington Territory, two Smithsonian monographs, many newspaper articles and technical publications, and more than 60 volumes of still-unpublished diaries. These works document not just pioneer society but also the Northwest Indian cultures that pre-dated white settlement and existed along-side it. Swan's appreciation of and efforts to record Indian art, technology, history, legends, and language made him a rarity among early Washington settlers.

Early Fascination with the Northwest Coast

James Gilchrist Swan was born on January 11, 1818, in Medford, Massachusetts. His father, Samuel, captain of a trading ship, was lost at sea when James was 5, and he and his siblings were raised by their mother, Margaret Tufts Swan. As a boy, James was fascinated by his uncle William Tufts' stories of his travels on the remote Northwest coast during an 1806-1810 trading expedition to the Columbia River and Vancouver Island.

Swan went into the ship-fitting business in Boston, married and had two children. However, the pull of the West Coast remained strong. The California gold rush gave him an opportunity to head west, and in 1850 Swan joined the thousands from New England sailing to San Francisco. Swan's family stayed in Massachusetts, and he never again lived with them.

Although he spent two years in San Francisco, mostly outfitting vessels, Swan's real goal was not the California gold fields, but the Northwest coast of his uncle's stories. His interest in the area was increased when Chetzemoka, a leader of the Clallam Indians on the Olympic Peninsula, visited San Francisco and Swan spent several weeks showing him around.

Three Years At Shoalwater Bay

In 1852, Swan settled for the first time in Washington, on the shore of Willapa Bay, then known as Shoalwater Bay. Swan's friend Charles J.W Russell had settled there in 1851 to harvest oysters from the Bay's rich tidelands for shipment to San Francisco, and in 1852 he invited Swan to join him. Swan lived on Shoalwater Bay until 1855. In 1857 he described the Bay and his experiences there in *The Northwest Coast, Or, Three Years' Residence in Washington Territory,* one of the earliest books about life in Washington.

When Swan arrived, there were only about 15 settlers on the Bay, virtually all engaged in the oyster trade. During the three years he lived there, pioneer settlement increased significantly, and by 1854, Swan wrote, "We had now grown into the dignity of a village" (Swan, *Northwest Coast,* 319). The settlers named the town Bruceville but soon changed it to Bruceport, the name it bears today.

James Swan

Besides the settlers, Swan met and got to know the Indians of the region. He became friends with Toke, a local chief, and his wife Suis, who lived with their family across the Bay from Bruceport, on a point still known as Toke Point. Swan found Toke and especially Suis to be excellent sources of information about the history of the Bay and its inhabitants. Another friend was Kape, a chief of the Quinault Indians who lived farther up the coast, from whom Swan purchased an impressive cedar canoe, 46 feet long by 6 feet wide and capable of carrying more than 30 people.

Swan learned the Chinook Jargon, a trade language that Northwest Coast Indians used to communicate between tribes and with non-Indians, as well as the Chehalis language the local Indians spoke among themselves. He spent long winter evenings conversing with the Indians and learning their history, legends, and way of life. *The Northwest Coast* includes detailed descriptions of Indian homes, crafts, hunting and fishing tools and techniques, religious ceremonies, songs, games, vocabularies of the Jargon and Chehalis languages, along with illustrations by Swan, who was an accomplished artist. The book also describes Swan's travels, often with Indian friends, around the Bay and its tributary rivers, to Chinook and Astoria on the Columbia River, and up the Pacific coast to Grays Harbor and the Quinault River.

A few months after arriving on Shoalwater Bay, Swan took advantage of the Donation Land Claim Act and filed a claim to almost 300 acres at the site of a former Indian village {longhouse} near the mouth of the Bone River, then called the Querquelin (Mouse) River. The site was suggested by Toke, who offered to find Swan a good place. It had oyster beds and rich soil for gardening, and was sheltered from the rough water of the bay. {Chinook say a native woman lived with Swan and kept house.}

Along with harvesting oysters from his claim, Swan worked at a variety of jobs. In 1854, he was appointed inspector of customs for the coast from the Columbia River to Cape Flattery. When the first court was established in Bruceport, Swan, who had studied admiralty law, served as one of the lawyers, although he had not yet taken the bar exam. "Squire" John Champ, the elected justice of the peace, was an old settler who had no legal experience at all. While neither the arguments nor decisions were "very learned," Swan wrote, they "gave the same results that all lawsuits do – satisfaction to the winner and indignation to the loser" (Swan, *Northwest Coast,* 320). Swan had even less training in medicine than in law, but occasionally acted as doctor, providing medicine to the Indians and caring for Indians and settlers during a smallpox outbreak soon after his arrival.

In February 1855, at the invitation of Territorial Governor Isaac Stevens (1818-1862), Swan traveled up the Chehalis River to the treaty ground near the present site of Cosmopolis, where Stevens presented a proposed treaty to the coast Indians. {Heavy drinking that included Stevens' aborted the meeting.} Although Swan admired Stevens and believed that he had the Indians' best interests at heart (a belief not necessarily shared by the Indians or by subsequent historians), his book expressed concerns about Stevens' proposal for the various coast tribes to be placed together on one reservation. Swan thought it wiser for each tribe to retain a portion of its traditional lands.

East Coast Interlude and Move to Port Townsend

Swan left Shoalwater Bay in the fall of 1855 and went east to write his book. He settled in Washington, D.C., where he also wrote articles for newspapers in Boston and Olympia. After *The Northwest Coast* was published in 1857, Swan worked as private secretary to Isaac Stevens,

James Swan

who had been elected Washington Territory's delegate to Congress. With his interest in natural history, Swan took advantage of living in the capital to visit the Smithsonian Institution. He met the director, Joseph Henry, and began a lifelong friendship with Spencer Baird, a Smithsonian naturalist. Baird was building up a network of collectors, whose ranks Swan soon joined.

Swan's stay in the East was temporary. In 1859 he moved to Washington Territory for good, choosing his destination based on Isaac Stevens' advice "that from its Geographical position, Port Townsend would become a place of commercial importance" (Swan, "Sketches," 4-5). While Port Townsend never achieved this importance, he remained fiercely loyal to the town, where he lived the rest of his life except for some years teaching Makahs at Neah Bay.

Swan Diaries

January 29, 1859, was a doubly significant date in Swan's life: he boarded the ship on which he would sail from San Francisco to begin his life in Port Townsend, and he made the first entry in the voluminous diaries that may be his greatest achievement. Swan undoubtedly kept journals previously – he mentions "having lost a valuable collection of notes" made at Shoalwater Bay (Swan, *Northwest Coast,* 6) – but none survive except a manuscript account of a trip to England and Scotland in 1841.

However, the 60-odd diaries, notebooks, and memorandum books of various sizes and shapes that Swan filled with over 2,500,000 words from 1859 until just before his death in 1900 remain today a comprehensive record of his travels, studies, and daily experiences. Except for the final two years (1900 is at the Beinecke Library at Yale; it is unclear whether a volume for 1899 survives), the diaries are housed in Special Collections at the University of Washington Libraries, where they have inspired subsequent writers. Journalist Lucile McDonald (1898-1992), who discovered the diaries in the 1950s, wrote a series of 32 articles about Swan for *The Seattle Times Sunday Magazine* and later published *Swan Among the Indians* (1972), the only Swan biography to date. Some years later, novelist Ivan Doig (1939-2015) spent a season exploring the diaries and the places in Washington where Swan lived and traveled. Doig's *Winter Brothers* (1980) is a unique and fascinating memoir that combines an account of Swan's life, including many quotations from the diaries, with Doig's meditations on Swan's life and times as well as his own.

Years earlier, Swan himself used the experiences recorded in his diaries as raw material, spending much of his first few years in Port Townsend contributing articles to newspapers in California and Washington. A century later the Washington State Historical Society reprinted some of the most interesting articles written between 1859 and 1862 in *Almost Out of the World* (1971). Soon after arriving in Port Townsend, Swan renewed his friendship with the Clallam leader Chetzemoka, who lived nearby. He wrote about fishing excursions with Chetzemoka and his family, and described religious ceremonies they invited him to attend.

Travels Around Sound, Strait, and Coast

Many articles recounted Swan's journeys around Puget Sound and the Strait of Juan de Fuca. He sailed to Bellingham Bay, Whidbey and Camano Islands, Clallam Bay and Dungeness with two prominent pioneers – Colonel Michael T. Simmons (first American settler on Puget

James Swan

Sound, having arrived in 1845) and Captain Robert Fay (commander of the vessel that brought the first Denny Party scouts to Alki Point in September 1851) – who, as Indian agents, were distributing "treaty goods" to the Lummi, Skagit, Snohomish, and Clallam Indians. Swan visited lighthouse keepers on Smith Island, and homesteaders on Protection Island and at Port Discovery, Sequim Prairie, and "False Dungeness" (now Port Angeles), describing the early settlers' farms and lifestyles.

He traveled to the Quileute Indian village of La Push, at the mouth of the Quillayute River on the Pacific Coast, where a Quinault chief he knew from Shoalwater Bay introduced him to the Quileute leaders. With the Indians, Swan canoed and hiked inland through thick forest to an extensive prairie near the present site of Forks, and climbed to the top of the large island just off the village, which the Quileutes had used as a refuge fort in wartime. Swan reported the Quileute name for the island as Alekistet, but proposed in his article that it be named for F.W James of Port Townsend, whom he asserted was the first white man to ascend it. The island is indeed called James Island today, though some sources state the name honors a Quileute chief.

Although he ranged widely, Swan's travels began to take him repeatedly to one destination: Neah Bay, near Cape Flattery at the entrance to the Strait of Juan de Fuca. The cape – the northwestern tip of the continental United States – and its inhabitants figured prominently in the stories of early European and American exploration of the Northwest coast that so fascinated Swan as a boy. The land around the cape was and is the home of the Makah Indians, with the largest village at Neah Bay.

Life with the Makah at Neah Bay

Swan first visited Neah Bay in March 1859, within weeks of arriving at Port Townsend. For the next three years he traveled repeatedly up and down the Strait between the two ports, often in Makah canoes, spending weeks or months at Neah Bay. Early on he met and was greatly impressed by a young and well-liked Makah chief called Swell, whose murder several years later was a personal blow and a dramatic subject for Swan's articles. He also met Henry Webster, who operated a trading post at Baada Point near Neah Bay and became a good friend and patron to Swan. By the fall of 1861, Swan was living in Neah Bay. He traveled on foot to all five Makah villages – Neah and Baada on the Strait, and Sooes, Waatch, and Ozette on the Pacific Coast – to conduct the first census of the Makah, counting a total of 654 tribal members.

The ambitious Webster was appointed Indian agent for the newly created Makah reservation, taking charge in 1862 and putting Swan on the payroll as schoolteacher. After conducting a survey of the reservation boundary, Swan supervised the construction of a schoolhouse and other Indian agency buildings. He spent the next four years living in the schoolhouse and teaching school when he could persuade children to attend. Since families had other priorities, Swan had difficulty keeping his pupils in school. Nevertheless, unlike those in charge of many Indian schools, Swan respected the Makah enough that he did not force school on them.

Swan's first and favorite pupil was Jimmy Claplanhoo, who went on to become a tribal leader and captain of a schooner. Claplanhoo and his family remained close to Swan, and helped care for him in his final years at Port Townsend. Swan was as much a friend as a schoolteacher to the Makah children and their families. He cooked for the children and gave them toys. In turn, they helped him find shells, fossils, birds, and animals for his Smithsonian collections.

James Swan

Swan had sent his first specimens to Professor Baird from Port Townsend, and continued to send shipments from Neah Bay. Swan also purchased examples of Makah baskets, blankets and other crafts for the museum.

As at Shoalwater Bay, Swan spent much of his time learning the Indians' language and way of life. He wrote and illustrated a detailed ethnography of Makah culture, published in 1870 as a Smithsonian monograph, *The Indians of Cape Flattery*. According to Swan, the Makah vocabulary in his monograph was later used on the reservation to teach English to Makah children and to teach Makah to the whites. Along with his natural history collecting and ethnographic studies, Swan kept and later published detailed meteorological records documenting the prodigious rainfall at the cape. In another similarity to life at Shoalwater, Swan again found himself in the role of doctor. He was in charge of the reservation's medical supplies and the schoolhouse often doubled as a clinic.

Much as he liked life at Neah Bay with the Makah, between inconsistent attendance and the constant interruptions of his other duties Swan found teaching frustrating. His irritation mounted when his superiors in the Indian department criticized his methods. In 1866 he resigned and left the reservation, gratified by a demonstrative send-off from the Makahs.

Return to Port Townsend

Back in Port Townsend, Swan continued his pattern of working in numerous fields without settling down to one position. He passed the bar exam, practiced admiralty law, and served as United States commissioner. He helped draft a pilot bill and a fisheries bill for the Washington Legislature, and subsequently served on the Pilot Commission. He was at different times probate judge and justice of the peace for Jefferson County, and also served as school superintendent.

For several years Swan devoted much of his energy to convincing the Northern Pacific Railroad to locate the western terminus of its transcontinental line in Port Townsend. Cities throughout the territory competed for this prize, and Swan firmly believed that his adopted town was the best choice. The railroad paid Swan to travel to various sites and prepare reports evaluating them, but it did not follow his advice. Swan was bitterly disappointed when Tacoma was chosen as the terminus, a decision he denounced as based on "the influence of the land monopoly of the Board of Directors ... for private motives of gain" (Swan, "Sketches," 8).

At Haida and Makah

Swan did not neglect his interest in ethnography. He continued to seek out Indian friends and many visited his Port Townsend office. Swan was particularly fascinated by the art of the Haida Indians from Canada's Queen Charlotte Islands, copying the tattoo designs of his visitors and purchasing their carvings. In 1874, he published another Smithsonian monograph, illustrating and explaining Haida designs and recounting the stories behind them. Swan continued collecting Indian artifacts for the Smithsonian and for display at several major exhibitions. In 1875, the Smithsonian provided funds for him to travel to Alaska and purchase items for the 1876 Centennial Exhibition in Philadelphia, including totem poles, a 60-foot canoe, and an entire lodge that Swan had built, as well as many smaller objects.

James Swan

Henry Webster, by then collector of customs for Puget Sound, enabled Swan to spend another three enjoyable years at Neah Bay when he appointed Swan customs inspector there in 1878. The duties were not demanding, and Swan had time to study, write, visit with old friends and former pupils, and cultivate a garden. Swan became close to the new Indian agent, Charles Willoughby, and his family. He interpreted for Willoughby and assisted him in arranging the first election conducted by the Makahs. Swan wrote in his diary (23 January 1879, long before women had received the right to vote in any state): "One feature in the election was that several women voted by permission of the Agent ... thus establishing a precedent in this tribe of womans suffrage which is right, as the women of the tribe always have a voice in the councils" (Doig, 165-66). When Webster lost his position, Swan lost his as well, and returned to Port Townsend in 1881.

Two years later, at the age of 65, Swan made his last major journey, fulfilling a longtime wish by traveling to the Queen Charlotte Islands homeland of the Haida Indians he so admired. After years of suggestions from Swan, the Smithsonian funded a four-month trip and Swan spent the summer of 1883 collecting artifacts and studying Haida culture. He was assisted by Johnny Kit Elswa, a Haida artist he had worked with in Port Townsend, some of whose drawings and explanations of Haida legends are included in Swan's notebooks. Besides collecting, they made a daring trip in Haida canoes to the wild west coast of the Queen Charlottes, virtually unpopulated since smallpox had ravaged the Haida two decades earlier.

Final Years

Swan lived to see Washington, which was not yet a territory when he arrived in 1852, achieve statehood in 1889. As vice-president of the Washington Pioneers, Swan marched near the head of the grand procession in Olympia. Two years later, he helped organize the Pioneer convention at Port Townsend, arranging with the Clallam Indians for a huge clambake on the beach.

Swan remained active, writing articles and collecting artifacts well into his 70s, and keeping up his correspondence and diaries until the end. James G Swan wrote his last diary entry on May 16, 1900, just two days before he died of a stroke at the age of 82.

by Kit Oldham posted 1/09/2003
https://www.historylink.org/File/5029

James Swan (1818-1900) and Haida Johnny Kit Elswa, Victoria B. C. , 1883
Courtesy UW Special Collections (NA1412)
James Swan (1818-1900) in front of his Port Townsend office, ca. 1895
Courtesy UW Special Collections (UW3840)
Salmon Fishing at Chenook, 1857
Sketch by James G. Swan *The Northwest Coast*

Bob Pope

Bob Pope ~ Tōshin
(1830?–1930?)

The place where I first came to myself[74] was at the village of *nokedja'kt*. There were three houses there at that time. In one lived the village chief *sa'utonux*; the second was owned by *tci'tamin*; and in the third lived my father. These men were heads of their houses, but there were several families in each.

In those days people wore only robes for clothes. It was customary to bathe each morning the year round. Almost every night there was singing and dancing in one of the houses. Usually the only food was salmon, salmon eggs, and potatoes.

From that village the people of all three houses moved downriver to *t'o'nans*. Soon afterward there came an epidemic (smallpox?) and most of the people of the village died, and only a few of their descendants are alive today. We used to come frequently to the village of kwi'naił to gamble at slaha'l. Here we would meet people from Queets and Grays harbor. Sometimes a game would last for several days. Gilbert Sodomic's {Sotomish} father once lost everything he owned – even his dried salmon, even to the last kettle of salmon that was cooking at the time, and the kettle as well. When the Queets and Chehalis had lost all they had, they would send back to their relatives for more. The women would also gamble with beaver teeth dice. Doc Hays Otuk's mother usually won at this.

The war between the Queets and Quinault was before my time; they were living in peace ever since I can remember.

When I first started to hunt I was just old enough to handle a gun. At first I hunted only ducks with a flintlock. Later on I killed a deer; then a bear. The first big game I killed was two elk. After that I often went to the mountains with other hunters and we killed all kinds of game. I also trapped for furs. At that time there was a trading post at Wynooche and we went there to trade furs and hides for whatever we needed. We would come down the river by canoe, then go by horse down the coast to Oyhut, then by canoe to Wynooche.

In those days the old people of my village were able to get a young man a wife when he was about fifteen. They bought me a wife and soon I moved downriver to *no'skałan*. There I lived for a long time, hunting and fishing for a living. When I had collected enough property I began to think, about giving a big potlatch. This was the beginning of my potlatching. But the idea was not from my own mind, but my "property guardian spirit" told me to give it. To my first potlatch I invited the Queets tribe.

About that time many of the Quinault were invited to a potlatch given by the *djołodjol* (a Nootka tribe). The Queets, Hoh, and Quilleute were also invited. On the way we passed one village where there were only women and children. All the men had been drowned while hunting seal. At the potlatch only blankets were given away. The white trader had a large store full of blankets. He had been there so long he could speak the Nootka language. Most of us were given nothing, even after coming so far. Chiefs were given two or three blankets each. We were fed only rice, with dried halibut and herring eggs. The next year eight of us went to the same place again to invite them to a potlatch that Chief *Tåxo'lå* was giving at *kwi'naił*. It took us two and a half days. The first day we got as far as Neah bay. There was a southwest wind and we used a sail. Near that village is a dangerous place. One can go between the island and the mainland only at high tide. Outside the island is a great monster that sinks all canoes and ships. I have heard that the whites have tried every means of killing it but never can. [This is Devil's pass?]

Across the strait from Neah bay we stopped at a village where a potlatch was being held. Ten tribes (villages) had been invited. When they danced they used two houses, for not everyone could get into the one. A middle-aged man was the host, but he did not give many presents. It was mainly a feast. He had a whole house filled with pilot bread. Chief *Tåxo'lå*'s younger brother (who was married to a Makah woman) was given nothing, and his wife received only a tin pan.

At Neah bay there was a canoe of *xosit* (another Nootka group) who had come from the north to invite the Makah to a potlatch. But as the Makah were at this other potlatch they were waiting for them. The *xosit* appeared to us to be real savages. They wore only fur robes and their [183] bodies were covered with grease. *Tåxo'lå*'s brother asked us if he should give them some food. Finally he gave each of them a blanket. We were wearing red shirts and we took these off and gave them as presents. They looked clean then, for the time being. Then they stood up and danced for us. Their spokesman made a speech, saying they had never before met such good people.

The potlatch which *Tåxo'lå* gave was the greatest ever given. They built a roof over the space between two big houses and thus made a single house so large one could hardly see from one end to the other (perhaps 200 feet). All the Hoh, Quilleute, Makah, and Queets were there. At that time I saw a Quilleute man with a strange guardian spirit. He came dancing into the house, a curious bird resting on his hand. When he extended his arm it would disappear. When he closed his hand it disappeared into his hand. It was the most real thing of its kind I have ever seen. He was a short man and was naked except for a belt of cedar bark. He led the Quilleute dancers into the house. It was one of the few times that I have seen a really great medicine man – most supposedly-good ones never did much.

At the same potlatch I saw two shamans challenge each other to a contest. One was a Queets, named *Xwåtå'm*, the other a man from Grays harbor. We liked to see such contests. They went down to the river and dove in. When they came up each had a piece of ice several feet long on his shoulder. They started ashore with it. But the Grays harbor shaman was beaten, for his ice melted before he got ashore. *Xwåtå'm* carried his ashore and up the bank. Then he threw it down and it turned to water and ran into the river. It was not hard ice but was soft and quivered like jelly. Then the Grays harbor man planned to kill *Xwåtå'm* with his power, in revenge for the beating. *Xwåtå'm* was lying across an ocean canoe in the river. The Grays harbor man shot his power at him but missed because *Xwåtå'm*'s power warded it off. But I heard it hit the canoe, and it was so strong it split the canoe from end to end. *Xwåtå'm* jumped up and said, "He missed me!" Later *Xwåtå'm* told his friends, "Now I will try to get even with him for that." Soon he got a chance and shot the other from behind with his power. The Grays harbor man told his friends that the other had "got" him. He no sooner reached home than he was taken ill and soon died. (When *Xwåtå'm* first got his power it was in him so strong that he could walk up to a green tree, seize a limb and tear it out, together with the knot to the heart of the tree.)

It was customary in those days to carry a nearly dead person out of the house and lay him near the grave. Once they had taken out a dying woman. I went over to her to test my spirit power. I saw that there was nothing really wrong with her except a "pain" (disease object). I told her she must not tell anyone if I cured her.

She said, "I am sure not to tell if you do me a favor and cure me." I told her she would not die if I took that "pain" out. Then I took it out and showed it to her and said, "This is the only thing wrong with you; now you will be all right." I asked her to give me a little camas root when she was well. She walked back to the village, bathed, and went into her house.

(That is the secret of some medicine men – they never tell that they have power until they have had a chance to test it. If they find that they can really cure people then they tell what spirit it is they have. But they do not talk about it except when they are curing. If a man talked frequently about his spirit power he would not live long.)

That was the beginning of my career as a medicine man. I knew then that I had power to cure people. It was one of the most real things in my life. Most shamanism is mere playing and contesting at potlatch time.

During my life I never traveled a great deal, only when I was invited to go somewhere to a potlatch.

When it was rumored that some new shaman had a powerful helper, then I used to like to see if he had the real thing. In my time not many men had great power. I know this because I went to see many. Perhaps long before my time there may have been many great shamans. That is all.

Please report typo gnomes and other needed corrections!

Sold @ Amazon.com

Index

A

Adamson, 189f
Ahchawat, 12
ahnkutty tilakums = past people, 189
Ron Allen, 3
Anaham Lake, 186
Anaheim, 181
anchor, 39
Astoria, 33, 194, 200

B

Bäada, 9, 12, 77
Babylon, 15
Babylonian cherubim, 14
Spencer Baird, 201f
baskets, 45
bastard cod, 27, 30, 114
battledore = *ko-ko-wi*, 19, 87
Bay Center, 195
Bear, 131f, 161, 168, 181[86]
bear, 162, 179
Bear blanket, 160
Bear skin, 20f, 67
Beavers, 98, 132f, 146f, 168f
Beaver teeth, 44
Beinecke Library, 201
bird lime, 20
Black Diver, 135, 168
blankets, 12, 20, 34, 119, 140; bark, 43; bear, 144, 160; down, 21; colored, 88; dog, 166, 172; pine bark, 21; red, 67; sea otter, 140f; surf duck, 140; wooly dog, 21, 43, 122; wool, 58
bleaching, 13, 41f
blubber, 25f, 33f, 80f
blue, 22, 30f, 66f, 88, 91, 138
bluebacks, 2, 153, 184f
blue face, 69
Bluejay, 124f, 130f, 147f, 167f, 176f, 191f
bluejay = *kwish-kwishee*, 60f
bluestone, 190
Franz Boas, 2, 117f, 189f
bone shark, 32
bracelets, 21, 46, 67, 76, 89, 123
Bruceville, 199
buoyance, 42
buoys, 20f, 32f, 40, 107, 115; bladder, 84; *dopt-ko-kuptl*, 25; sealskin, 17

C

calumet, 30
Cape People ~ Makah = qʷidičč'a•tx̱, 8
Carlyle, 193
John Champ JP, 200
chastity, 18
"Cha-tik" artist, 13, 114
Cha-tic = James Swan, 15
Chetzemoka = Prince of Wales, 199f
Chicken Hawks, 157f
Chehalis, 127, 189, 200, 205; Chihalis, 9f, 33; Lower, 189
Chimakuans, 2
Chimsyan, 15, 46, 54; See Tsimshian
Chinese dragon, 15
Chinooks, 9f, 13, 23, 33, 125, 130, 182
Chinook City, 194
Chinook salmon, 194
Chinoose Creek, 195
Chinuk wawa, 112, 117, 200
Clallams, 5f, 12, 18, 33f, 38, 48, 54, 64, 113, 117, 199f
Jimy Claplanhoo = Makah pupil, 202
Classets, 8, 54f
Clatsops, 194
club knot, 21
coal, 8, 45
coals, 27, 138, 150, 166, 184
Columbia River, 8, 13, 22f, 32f, 50, 54, 130, 168, 184f, 191f, 199f

---

[86] Throughout this list the names of mythic animal characters are capitalized, while the species is lower case, Raven is a spirit, raven is a black shiny bird. All native words are in *italics*.

index

Comcomly ~ Chinook chief, 33
Capt James Cook, 5, 54
Copalis Rock, 130
Cowitchin, 21; ~ Cowichan
cradle, 13, 23
Crow, 176; wife, 62, 135f, 166f, 172
crows, 60, 87

D

Damon's Point, 138, 147, 155, 168
dancing, 19, 66f, 83, 143f, 166, 193, 205f
dice, 44, 205
Ditidat, 2
diversity, 9, 28, 125
Doc Hays Otuk, 205
dogfish, 92
dogfish oil, 26, 31f
dogs' hair, 21
Ivan Doig (1939-2015), 201
dorsal fin, 25, 31f, 142, 153, 185
drums, 17, 48, 64, 67f, 71
duck avatar, 190
duels, 20, 52, 114
duk-wal-ly, 22 ~ Tlukwali
Dungeness, 3, 8, 201f

E

eagle, 38, 60, 87, 92, 124, 152, 170, 176; double headed, 15
Eagle, 152f, 170f, 176, 184
eagle feathers, 17, 24, 67
eagle quills, 69
eagle tails, 67, 77; lure, 129
East Wind, 158, 171
Equisetum = horsetails, 28

F

Livingston Farrand, 2, 173, 189
Captain Robert Fay, 202
feathers, 12f, 21, 42f, 60f, 93, 114, 129, 168, 186; bright, 138; capes, 37; white, 162
fire, 12f, 22f, 28, 31, 35f, 46f, 57, 66, 71f, 80f, 116, 122f, 130f, 142f, 150f, 161f, 170, 172, 180, 190f; aurora borealis, 80; firebrand, 150; firewood, 16, 79, 143, 170, 193; fireworks, 14; flowers, 144
fireworks, 14
Fish Hawk, 150, 169
flattening, 10, 23, 114
Flattery Rocks, 8f, 12, 50f, 70, 113; see Cape, 22f, 31
Fraser River, 2
fungi, 163, 193

G

George Gibbs, 2f, 117, 189
gimlet = borer, 36
Captain Gladstone, 178
gold rush, 199
Goose, 95, 176
goose, 87, 95
gooseberry, 84, 114
greenish-blue, 30
greenish-brown, 30
Grouse, 144f, 168
grouse, 88
Gulf of Georgia, 5
guns, 17f, 32, 34, 46, 49, 51f, 58, 63f, 76f, 83, 186f, 205; wadding, 44
Gwēlshā'lātōmĕn = further dead, 144

H

Haida, 2, 15, 46, 54, 203f
Hair-seal, 32, 134, 145f, 166f
halibut, 13, 23f, 31f, 41, 70f, 83, 94f, 115, 206; hook, 42
haliotis, 21, 46, 70f, 115; = abalone
Hanesāh = Thunder, 188
harpoons, 17, 24f, 32, 39f, 47, 115, 146, 166f; toy miniatures, 20; harpooner, 25
Harvard, 2
head flattening, 10, 23, 114
Lucy Heyden Hck, 190f
herald, 19
Hohohos = Screech Owl, 163f, 186
Hood Canal, 3, 118
Hosett, 9, 12, 56f, 71, 82
Hudson's Bay Company, 28, 33f

index

Humptulips, 129, 137, 157, 191f; city, 192f

I

ivory, 22

J

James Island, 203
James Rock, 156, 186, 196
Jamestown, 3
Johnny Kit Elswa ~ Haida artist, 205
Jū'ī, 185; Jui, 130f, 143f, 169

K

kāmātsl = sawbill duck, 179
kammas ~ camas, 28f
Kape ~ Quinault chief, 200
'Kāxā'lōmǐ'tcəmən, 156 place
kelp, 19f, 26f, 39f, 74
Kəmol, 191; Kmol, 192f
Kiddekubbut, 12, 114
Kingfisher = *Chesh-kully*, 62, 89, 133f, 168
Klallam, 2
knives, 20, 24, 25, 35, 37, 40, 52, 58, 64, 129, 150, 151, 167
Kom-mol-owish, 190
Komooks, 5
Kw'ati, 190f
Kwēt = warbler, 133f, 168
Kwilleyutes ~ Quileutes, 5, 22, 28, 31f, 44f, 50f, 70f
kwi'naił, 205
Kwinaiults, 10f, 33
Kwĭnō'ltcō'sīūx-nǐ'tL, 157
Kwǒtsxwō'ē, 127, 155, 168

L

labor, 9, 11, 16, 35f, 67, 75
Land Otter, 132, 144f, 168; hat, 132
livers, 31f
Louise ~ Chimakum speaker, 2, 117
Love matches, 18
Lucy Heck, 189, 191

M

Magpie, 130f, 168
maiden, 18
Maquinna, 33, 57
Billy Mason, 182, 189
Edmond Meany, 190
Misp^h, 3, 189f
Moclips, 194
mole = *pōkwǒlōmīūx*, 184; = *took-tooksh*, 98
monsters, 129, 156, 167, 170, 194, 206; sea 162 #81,
Mt Olympus, 2

N

Nantucket, 10
nasals, 2
Neeah Bay, 8f, 13, 27, 32f, 46f, 53f, 62f, 75f, 113f
Neshwats, 14, 116
Nootka Sound, 5
nose-ring, 134f, 168

O

Oakville, 189
oil, 22f, 31f, 43, 61, 73f, 140, 194
Ronald Olson, 3, 189
Owl, 103, 124, 157, 160f, 171; place, 195; those drowned, 81; White Owl, 157f
owls, 38, 60f, 77, 81, 180 = *neo'ston*
Oyhut, 130, 136, 168, 179, 205

P

painting, 13f, 22, 38, 47, 60
peg-tops, 19
pe-ko ~ small basket, 45
Pelican, 140
pelicans, 28
penis, 23
pillow, 12, 23, 142
pilot bread, 206
pitch, 28, 39, 41, 49, 62, 64, 73, 95, 146; = *kluk-ait-a-biss*, 62; pitch knot, 39; torch, 64; pitchwood, 28, 49, 155
polygamy, 18, 115

index

Bob Pope ~ Tōshin, 3, 125, 183f, 205*
Porpoises, 9, 32, 99, 142, 153, 170,
porpoises, 185 = *skāāLEnōx̱*
Port Gamble, 2, 117
Port Gamble Mill, 3
Port Townsend, 14, 39, 48, 55, 77, 117, 200f
potatoes, 9, 17, 26, 27f, 34f, 47, 58, 63, 102f, 115, 205
prairie, 9, 34, 55, 127f, 143f, 149, 152, 156, 160, 170, 175, 184, 190f, 202
prices, 14f, 34, 38, 173
Puget Sound, 13, 33, 54, 117, 201f
pups, 166, 172
purchase, 16f, 33f, 45, 50, 200f

Q

Queeteh, 176

R

Raft River, 129, 167
Raven, 125f, 149f, 169, 170f, 180f
ravens, 60, 88, 105
red ochre, 22, 38
reptiles, 158, 171
rice, 27f, 34, 63, 205
rings, 11, 46, 64, 67; nose ring, 138
ringworm, 73
Robin, 150, 169
Russians, 10

S

Saddle = *u-butsk*, 25
Salish, 2, 117f, 124, 189, 191, 196; Coast, 191; Straits,2; Tsamosan, 2, 189; see Selish
Sawbill duck, 131, 168, 178
scarphing, 24, 37f
scouring, 23
Screech-Owl, 143, 162, 171; see *Hohohos*
Secena, 190
Selish, 5, 59
SEpa'k'a, 171, 185; see Sə'p'āk'ā', 164f
Shadow, 134, 168
shadow, 107

Shaker, 125
Shakers, 124
shoal, 26, 31, 41, 80, 85
Shoalwater Bay, 33, 189, 198f; see Willapa
"shogh" = hoist, 11, 115
shuttlecock, 19, 107
Michael Simmons, 202
sinker, 26, 40
Sitka, 15 #2, 54
Skeena River, 181
Skokomish, 3
Sky People, 149f
slaves, 16f, 33f, 48f, 53f, 62, 79, 115
smallpox, 9, 84, 108, 200f
Smisspee, 189; see Misp[h]
Snail, 135f, 150, 168f
snails, 20; sea snail, 38
sockeye, 2; see blueback
song, 17f, 47f*, 60f, 70f, 115, 136, 142f, 156, 165, 173f, 183, 192, 200; *tamanowus*, 142
Sooke Harbour, 5
South Wind = *Kwartseedie*, 84, 112f, 159f, 171, 184
Southerner ~ ship, 36
Spaniards, 10, 53
Spider = *Kōkwā'nē*, 149, 169
Squid ~ cuttlefish, 26f, 115
Squirrel, 108, 135, 145, 161, 168f
Squirrels, 9, 28, 98, 108
stale urine, 23; see urine
Gov Isaac Stevens, 4, 8, 51, 199f
Straits Salish, 2
Suckley, 32
Suis ~ Toke's wife, 200
James Swan, 2f, 189, 199f*
Swell ~ Makah chief, 77, 202

T

ta-ma-na-was, 15f, 22, 36
tamanous, 13, 139 #43
tamanawas, 44, 51, 175
Tatooche Island, 8, 12, 27
Tatooche light, 26

index

Tatoosh, 50, 57, 79f, 113
Tatooshatticus ~ chief, 33, 57
tattooing, 22, 128, 167, 186, 203
tenses, 121
Thlu-kluts = Thunder, 13f, 59, 115; T'hlu-kloots, 14f, 55f, 67, 83
Thunder, 154f, 170f, 184; = *Hanesāh*, 188f
thunder-bird, 13f, 59, 63, 67, 69, 83
thwarts, 25, 37, 90
Tksē'lĭsōmĭsh ♂, 162
Toke ~ Chinook chief, 189; wife Suis, 200
Tokeland, 189
Tokwaksose River, 113
Tsā'ālō' = giant, 164
Tsamosan Salish branch, 2, 189f
Tsāxwō'nĕlx, 156
Ts'Ets'aut, 126 # 25
Tsuess, 9, 12, 34, 37, 49, 81, 116
Tu-tutsh, 14, 116
Twana, 2f
Twins, 75f, 116, 127, 167, 189f, 195
two-headed boy, 163f, 172

U

u-butsk = whale saddle, 25
Underworld, 126, 143f, 151f*, 168f, 184
urinals, 23
urine, 23, 194; warm, 23; stale, 23

V

Vancouver Island, 2f, 10f, 20f, 30f, 46, 49, 54, 57, 63, 199

W

Wäatch, 8f, 12, 34f, 113, 116
Henry Webster ~ trader, agent, 202f
West Wind, 112, 159, 171, 184
whalers, 167
whales = *chét-ā-puk*, 9f, 13f, 20f, 30f, 40f, 50f, 60f, 80, 98, 111, 129f, 138f, 151, 160f, 172, 180f, 195 (Westport)
whale blowing, 67
whale boat, 40
whale bone, 14
whale eyes, 25
whalemen, 24
whale meat, 139, 168, 181
whale oil, 23, 26f, 31f, 140
whale saddle = *u-butsk*, 25
whale sinews, 24, 39f, 46
whale skin, 151
whale taxi, 140, 168
whale traps, 160
white feathers, 62, 67, 69, 162
Wildcat, 150f, 170, 190
Willapa Bay, 189, 199
Charles Willoughby, 124 #21, 188, 204
Winds, 112; north, 139; southwest, 205; west, 112
Wolves, 160f, 171, 184, 194
wolves, 9, 50, 60f, 129
wreath, 21f; bark, 66; cedar, 22; evergreens, 21; seaweed, 67
Wreck Creek, 135f
Wren, 150, 165f, 172
wren, 166
wrestling, 20, 116
Wynooche, 205

X

xlĕō'lxtcū boy, 139
X^wani X^wani, 190f; *xwōnē' xwōnē'*, 135f, 168; *xwonehxwoneh*, 183f
xwŏ'tĕl = laughing game, 128

Y

yellow, 45, 68; bark, 69; belly, 30; dye, 45; ochre, 22
yew, 11, 24, 38, 42, 46, 62, 104 = *klá-hairk-tle-bupt*; 136

Sold @ Amazon.com